ARABS IN THE MIRROR

ARABS IN THE MIRROR

*Images and Self-Images
from Pre-Islamic to Modern Times*

NISSIM REJWAN

UNIVERSITY OF TEXAS PRESS

AUSTIN

A number of extracts and summaries quoted in this book appeared previously in articles and surveys contributed by the author to the *Jerusalem
Post*, *Jerusalem Quarterly*, *Jewish Observer and Middle East Review*, *Jewish
Chronicle* (London), *Hadassah Magazine*, and *Midstream* (New York),
among others. Thanks to the editors and publishers of these periodicals for permission to quote from this earlier work. Thanks also to the
director and staff of the Harry S. Truman Institute for the Advancement
of Peace, at the Hebrew University of Jerusalem, for their cooperation
and encouragement. Also, unless otherwise noted, all translations from
Arabic and Hebrew sources are the author's.

Requests for permission to reproduce material from this work
should be sent to:
Permissions
University of Texas Press
P.O. Box 7819
Austin, TX 78713-7819
www.utexas.edu/utpress/about/bpermission.html

∞ The paper used in this book meets the minimum requirements of
ANSI/NISO z39.48-1992 (R1997) (Permanence of Paper).

Library of Congress Cataloging-in-Publication Data
Rejwan, Nissim.
Arabs in the mirror : images and self-images from pre-Islamic to modern
times / Nissim Rejwan. — 1st ed.
    p. cm.
Includes bibliographical references and index.
ISBN 978-0-292-71727-5 (cloth : alk. paper) — ISBN 978-0-292-71728-2
(pbk. : alk. paper)
    1. Arabs.   2. National characteristics, Arab.   3. Arab countries—Intellectual life.
4. Intellectuals—Arab countries.   5. Democracy—Arab countries.   6. Egypt—Social
conditions.   I. Title.
DS36.7.R45 2008
305.892'7—dc22
                                                                            2007033592

CONTENTS

THE BEDOUIN, THE CAMEL, THE SAND, AND THE PALM TREE

The Arabian Peninsula is the cradle of the Semitic family of peoples, who later became known as the Babylonians, the Hebrews, the Assyrians, and the Phoenicians; it is one of the driest and hottest areas in the world. In the words of Philip Hitti, an Arab historian: "Though sandwiched between seas on the east and west, those bodies of water are too narrow to break the climatic continuity of the Afro-Asian rainless continental masses. The ocean on the south does bring rains, but the burning winds which seasonally lash the land leave very little moisture for the interior. The bracing and delightful east wind has always provided a favorite theme for Arabian poets" (*History of the Arabs,* 17).

Poetry was considered the highest manifestation of Arab culture in the century preceding Islam, so much so that the well-known Persian historian and geographer Ibn Wadhih al-Yaʿqubi, in his book *Kitab al-Buldan* (Book of Countries), wrote that poetry among the Arabs had taken the place of science, philosophy, history, and everything else. If an Arab had a bright idea, he would express it in a few verses.

The Arabs of the pre-Islamic era were people of a poetic bent, and Arabic nurtured many a great poet, although their land was not one of flowers and nightingales, but only thorns and sand. Since poetry was esteemed as the highest manifestation of culture, Arab poets were always on the lookout for a suitable spot to present their poems. The finest poems were inscribed on posters and hung on the walls of the Kaʿba during the poets' annual rendezvous. The Kaʿba (Arabic, "square building" or "cube") is Islam's most sacred sanctuary and pilgrimage site, located in the Great Mosque in Mecca. The Qurʾan states that the Kaʿba was built by Adam and rebuilt by Abraham and Ishmael; it houses the Black Stone (*al-Hajar al-Aswad*), the most venerated place for Muslims. These posters hung on the walls of the Kaʿba were called *muʿallaqat* (hanging verses), and the poets rewarded with such display became famous. Imrʾul-Qais and other poets of early Islam were among those thus honored. They were the authors of "the seven hanging pieces" (*al-muʿallaqat el-Sabʿ*), which eventually found a place of honor on the walls of the Kaʾba and in history.

It is important to add here, however, that there are still serious doubts about the authenticity of the *muʿallaqat*. In 1926, Dr. Taha Hussein, who in his life was known as "the doyen of Arabic literature," published a book titled *Fil Shiʿr al-Jahili* (On Pre-Islamic Poetry). In his introduction and in the course of the book, the author tries to prove that all this poetry—which, he says, was so abundant that one could imagine that all the ancients were poets—had been fabricated. He reaches the conclusion, in fact, that this poetry "proves nothing and tells nothing and should not be used, as it has been, as an instrument in the study of the Koran and the *Hadith*. "There is no doubt," Taha Hussein asserts, "that this poetry was tailored and invented all of a piece so that the ʿ*ulema* (religious savants) might prove by it what they had set out to prove" (quoted in Nissim Rejwan, *Arabs Face the Modern World*, 47, 48).

Few non-Arab ancient historians wrote about Arabia, and the traces in Herodotus's *Histories* (430 BC), Dio Cassius's *History of Rome* (AD 220), and Ammianus Marcellinus's *Roman History* (AD 380) are, with the possible exception of the last, hardly worth mentioning. Following are a few passages from Ammianus.

At this time also the Saracens, a race whom it is never desirable to have either for friends or enemies, ranging up and down the country, if ever they found anything, plundered it in a moment, like rapacious hawks who, if from on high they behold any prey, carry it off with a rapid swoop, or, if they fail in their attempt, do not tarry. And although, in recounting the career of the Prince Marcus, and once or twice subsequently, I remember having discussed the manners of this people, nevertheless I will now briefly enumerate a few more particulars concerning them.

Among these tribes, whose primary origin is derived from the cataracts of the Nile and the borders of the Blemmyae [a nomadic Nubian tribe], all the men are warriors of equal rank; half naked, clad in colored cloaks down to the waist, overrunning different countries, with the aid of swift and active horses and speedy camels, alike in times of peace and war. Nor does any member of their tribe ever take plow in hand or cultivate a tree, or seek food by the tillage of the land; but they are perpetually wandering over various and extensive districts, having no home, no fixed abode or laws; nor can they endure to remain long in the same climate, no one district or country pleasing them for a continuance.

Their life is one of continued wandering; their wives are hired, on special covenant, for a fixed time; and that there may be some appearance of marriage in the business, the intended wife, under the name of a dowry, offers a spear and a tent to her husband, with a right to quit him after a fixed day, if she should choose to do so. And it is inconceivable with what eagerness the individuals of both sexes give themselves up to matrimonial pleasures.

But as long as they live they wander about with such extensive and perpetual migrations, that the woman is married in one place, brings forth her children in another, and rears them at a distance from either place, no opportunity of remaining quiet being ever granted to her. They all live on venison, and are further supported on a great abundance of milk, and on many kinds of herbs, and on whatever birds they can catch by fowling. And we have seen a great many of them wholly ignorant of the use of either corn or wine. (*The Roman History of Ammianus Marcellinus*, translated by C. D. Yonge, 11–12)

Similarly superficial depictions of pre-Islamic Arabians and their way of life are to be found. The relatively few accounts in later works of history are equally brief, Arabic sources not excluded, except perhaps by their lengthy and typically ornamental prose. Of the more recent Arab historians, however, the one who has produced the most comprehensive though briefest summary has been Philip Hitti, the Lebanese American author of the monumental *History of the Arabs,* first published in 1937, updated throughout nine later editions, and still the standard one-volume history of its kind.

About the population of central and northern Arabia in the pre-Islamic era, Bernard Lewis writes that the dominant feature of this population was Bedouin tribalism: "In Bedouin society, the social unit is the group, not the individual. The latter has rights and duties only as a member of his group. The group is held together externally by the need for self-defence against the hardships and dangers of desert life, internally by the blood-tie of descent in the male line which is the basic social bond. . . . The tribe does not usually admit of private landed property, but exercises collective rights over pastures, water sources, etc." (Lewis, *The Arabs in History,* 29).

In his book *Muhammad and the Conquests of Islam,* Francesco Gabrieli rightly says that it is impossible to deal with Muhammad and his achievement without knowing something about the environment in which he was born, which "he partly revolutionized or altered profoundly and partly retained and consolidated." Following a brief description of this environment,

Gabrieli asserts that "beside this poor nomadic Arab way of life, biblical and classical tradition knew of more advanced and civilized Arab states in the south of the peninsula"—the kingdom of the Queen of Sheba and the Himyarite kings of Arabia Felix, "the owners of fabled wealth." According to Gabrieli, these two contrasting pictures—the prevalent nomadism and rudimentary conditions of the north and the sedentary and advanced agricultural states of the south—"reflect exactly the dual historical, geographic, economic and sociological aspects of ancient Arabia" (25).

As for the economic situation, the Arabs' economy at that time centered on animal husbandry and agriculture, where the latter was possible. Trade and exchange were carried on mainly with foreign lands; the Arabs of both Yemen and Hijaz engaged in this activity. The Arabs also arranged fairs in the form of seasonal bazaars. But the true basis of society was agriculture; according to Lewis, ancient inscriptions,

> with their frequent references to dams, canals, boundary problems and landed property, suggest a high degree of development. Besides cereals the southern Arabians produced myrrh, incense and other spices and aromatics. These last were their main export, and in the Mediterranean lands the spices of southern Arabia . . . led to its almost legendary reputation as a land of wealth and prosperity—the Arabia Eudaemon or Arabia Felix of the classical world. The spices of Arabia have many echoes in the literature of the West, from the "thesauris arabicis" of Horace to the "perfumes of Arabia" of Shakespeare and Milton's "spicy shores of Araby the blest." (*The Arabs in History,* 25)

In Arabia, the horse is a luxury animal whose feeding and care constitute a problem for the man of the desert. For the nomad, according to Hitti, the camel is certainly the most useful. "Without it the desert could not be conceived of as a habitable place. The camel is the nomad's nourisher, his vehicle of transportation and his medium of exchange. The dowry of the bride, the price of blood, the profit of gambling, the wealth of a sheikh, are all computed in terms of camels. To him the camel is more than 'the ship of the desert'; it is the special gift of Allah—so much so that some students of the scene called the Bedouin 'the parasite of the camel'" (24).

"Over all the living things of the desert," Hitti concludes,

> the Bedouin, the camel and the palm are the triumvirate that rules supreme; and together with the sand they constitute the four great actors

in the drama of its existence. To its denizen the desert is more than a habitat: it is the custodian of his sacred tradition, the preserver of the purity of his speech and blood and his first and foremost line of defence against encroachment from the outside world. Its scarcity of water, scorching heat, trackless roads, lack of food-supply—all enemies in normal times—prove staunch allies in time of danger. Little wonder then that the Arabian has rarely bent his neck to a foreign yoke. (24)

On the subject of religion, Gabrieli, summarizing the work of Muslim antiquarians and the fragmentary evidence of pagan poetry, writes that the religion of the greater part of the peninsula Arabs was "an elementary polydaemonism with elements of fetishism." The Arabs, he explains, "worshipped a varied pantheon of divinities none of which had ever assumed any human form, and not one of whom had ever been able to rise above the others to produce monotheism" (*Muhammad and Islam,* 39).

Hitti puts it slightly differently. The rudiments of Semitic religion, he writes, developed in the oases, rather than in the sandy land, and centered upon stones and springs, forerunners of the Black Stone (in the Ka'ba) and the Zamzam (a sacred well) in Islam and of Bethel in the Old Testament. Religion sits very lightly indeed on the Bedouin's heart. In the judgment of the Qur'an (9:98), "the desert Arabians are most confirmed in unbelief and hypocrisy." Up to the present day, they have never paid much more than lip service in homage to the Prophet (*History of the Arabs,* 26).

The clan is the basis of Bedouin society. As Gabrieli puts it, the tribal bond was

the essence, the only solid and accepted social structure of these primitive living conditions of Arabia in the centuries immediately preceding Muhammad . . . The tribe is the self-sufficient cell of the embryonic political and social life; it is the only structure to which the individualistic and anarchically inclined mentality of the Bedouin will in the nature of things submit; it guarantees support for him; thanks to the collective security in property disputes and blood feuds, it offers him personal protection; it also satisfies his vanity and desire for glory in its genealogical and marital traditions. (*Muhammad and Islam,* 30)

On clan organization, Hitti has this to say: "Every tent represents a family; an encampment of tents forms a *hayy;* members of one *hayy* constitute a clan (*qawm*). A number of kindred clans grouped together make a tribe (*qabilah*). All members of the same clan consider each other as of one blood, submit to the authority of but one chief—the senior member of the clan—and use one battle-cry."

In his comprehensive historical survey *The Middle East,* Bernard Lewis observes that "the ancient Arabs, like the ancient Israelites depicted in the books of Judges and Samuel, mistrusted kings and the institution of kingship." In Arabia, the tribal chief was the one who ruled. The choice of a tribal chief, however, was not bound by any rule of succession: "The chief of the tribe was usually chosen from members of a single family seen as noble. Often this family was holy as well as noble, and the descendants of a sheikhly family might enjoy the hereditary custodianship of a local shrine or sacred object. The choice was personal and was made for personal qualities—the ability to evoke and retain loyalty" (140, 142).

ARABS IN THE MIRROR

ONE

IDENTITY AND SELF-DEFINITION

IBN KHALDUN'S APPRAISAL

On the personal, individual level, identity can be defined as the understanding of oneself in relation to others. On the national, corporate level, identities are formed partly in relation to other nations, collectivities, and states. In both cases, identity is essentially a matter of self-definition—of how individuals, nations, states, or any other corporate groups choose to observe and define themselves.

In their attempts at self-definition, the Arabs have generally been soft-spoken, and their writings about themselves have been scant and inexplicably unwieldy. True, the Arabs, renowned as they justly are for the richness of their language and the beauty of their writings, have not been in any sense sparing in their self-praise and self-glorification, as was made evident in the prologue. Self-praise, however, scarcely amounts to self-definition or self-analysis. Indeed, strange as it may sound, virtually the only writer in Arabic who attempted a serious sociocultural study of the Arabs up through the Middle Ages was the fourteenth-century Tunisian historian and philosopher Abdul Rahman Ibn Khaldun—and even his observations are thought to refer not to the urbanized Arabs of his day but to the nomadic Arab, the Bedouin. And indeed, whereas in certain parts of his analysis he gives the impression of speaking of Arabs generally, as a race or ethnic group, some students of Arabic have maintained that the appellation "Arab" is always synonymous with "nomad" and "Bedouin" in the writings of Ibn Khaldun, regardless of any racial, national, or linguistic distinctions.

The headings that Ibn Khaldun chooses for those sections of his work devoted to the Arabs and their traits give an idea of the great historian's evaluations: "Arabs Can Gain Control over Only Flat Territory"; "Places That Succumb to the Arabs Are Quickly Ruined"; "Arabs Can Obtain Royal Authority Only by Making Use of Some Religious Coloring, Such as

Prophecy or Sainthood, or Some Religious Event in General"; and "Arabs Are of All the Nations the One Most Remote from Royal Authority." A careful reading of his pronouncements on the Arabs shows that, in his judgment, after a brief spell of lawful government and "royal leadership" that lasted for some two hundred years following the Arab conquests of the seventh century, the Arabs neglected their religion, forgot political leadership, returned to the desert, and became once more as savage as they had been before. Concerning the urbanized Arabs of his day, Ibn Khaldun considered them to be "descendents of the Arabs who were in possession of these cities and persisted in their luxury."

Ibn Khaldun's pronouncements on the Arabs are surveyed below, but first a few words about this unique historian and his work are in order. The main difficulty posed by Ibn Khaldun's work for the present-day student of Arab history and thought is that this thinker and man of action had no intellectual predecessors. In the history of man's intellectual endeavors, indeed, Ibn Khaldun stands so much alone that no attempt has been made to relate his work to any previous tradition or system of thought.

This may well be sheerly due to accident. Owing to well-known historical circumstances, the amount of extant Arabic literature from Spain and northwest Africa is so small that determining Ibn Khaldun's sources is currently impossible. Also, very little of the Western writings of Ibn Khaldun's times or from the period immediately preceding them is known. Under these circumstances, it may not be entirely unjust to assume that much that is found in Ibn Khaldun's work is probably not original, and that many of his seemingly original ideas may have been inspired by sources yet to be discovered.

However, even should this be the case, students of Ibn Khaldun generally agree that he was justified in claiming that the *Muqaddimah* (The Introduction), which he wrote as the first volume of his world history, was original and constituted a real departure in the methods of scholarly research. As Franz Rosenthal, the English translator of the work, has put it, the *Muqaddimah* "re-evaluates, in an altogether unprecedented way, practically every single individual manifestation of a great and highly developed civilization. It accomplishes this both comprehensively and in detail in the light of one fundamental and sound insight—namely, by considering everything as a function of man and human social organization" (*The Muqaddimah: An Introduction to History*, 1:xxxiv).

Ibn Khaldun's uniqueness is that he was the first historian to proclaim history a branch of philosophy, thus establishing himself as the father of all philosophers of history: "On the surface, history is no more than information about political events, dynasties, and occurrences of the remote past, elegantly presented and spiced with proverbs. It serves to entertain large, crowded gatherings and brings us an understanding of human affairs. . . . The inner meaning of history, on the other hand, involves speculation and an attempt to get at the truth, subtle explanation of the causes and origins of existing things, and deep knowledge of the how and why of events. History, therefore, is firmly rooted in philosophy. It deserves to be accounted a branch of philosophy" (1:xxxv).

In Chapter Two of the *Muqaddimah* (1:247–310), Ibn Khaldun introduces the principles governing the growth of human society, with these words: "It should be known that differences of conditions among people are the result of the different ways in which they make their living. Social organization enables them to cooperate toward that end and to start with the simple necessities of life, before they get to conveniences and luxuries" (1:249).

The two fundamentally different environments in which these societies develop are "desert, nomad life" (*badawa*) and "town, sedentary environment." According to him, the world is disputed between pastoral nomads and townsmen, and this war between nomad and townsman, desert and city, brute vigor and sedentary culture, has arrested progress. But the fact remains that "urbanization is found to be the goal of the Bedouin"; as their social organization develops, their needs increase accordingly and "they cooperate for things beyond the bare necessities." They use more food and clothes, build large houses, lay out towns and cities, build castles and mansions. In short, they become sedentary people—which means the inhabitants of cities and countries, some of whom adopt crafts as their way of making a living, while others adopt commerce (1:249–250).

The Bedouin's way of life makes them brave and hardy and gives them group feeling, *ʿasabiyya*, because they must rely upon the other members of their clan. The preponderance of *ʿasabiyya* renders one human group superior to others and determines leadership within a given group. For he who can make the strongest and most natural claim to control of the available group feeling will become the ruling and leading element in such a group. The leader who controls group feeling of sufficient strength and importance may succeed in founding a ruling dynasty and winning "royal authority"—*mulk*—for himself and his family (1:299).

Since the founding of a dynasty or state—*dawla*—involves large numbers of people, it is of necessity linked to "sedentary culture." A dynasty requires large cities and towns, which in their turn permit the development of luxuries and the cultivation of crafts that serve no actual need but are concerned with the production of things and the provision of services that Ibn Khaldun calls "conveniences" and "luxuries." Once this stage is reached, people are able to develop the sciences, which fulfill their higher aspirations in the domains of the spirit and the intellect. Rosenthal quotes in this connection Vico's six steps of human development and says that they correspond to Ibn Khaldun's three stages of necessities, conveniences, and luxuries: "Men first feel necessity, then look for utility, next attend to comfort, still later amuse themselves with pleasure, then grow dissolute in luxury, and finally go mad and waste their substance" (1:302).

But this development toward luxury carries its own penalty in that it is conducive to degeneration and dissolution. The pristine simplicity and rudeness of manners that flourish in small human organizations become corroded. Here again, Vico agrees with Ibn Khaldun: "The nature of peoples is first crude, then severe, then benign, then delicate, finally dissolute" (1:302). Here some commentators have detected in Ibn Khaldun a lingering and rather sentimental attachment to the simplicity of earlier Arab civilization, although he fully recognized the superiority of sedentary culture as the goal of all man's efforts to become civilized. In fact, Ibn Khaldun takes a balanced view. He admits, on the one hand, that city people have many defects: they use improper language, and their souls are "colored with all kinds of blameworthy and evil qualities"; they are also sinful and degenerate (1:302). Savage groups, on the other hand, are braver and therefore superior.

There is no consensus among scholars about the exact import of Ibn Khaldun's writings on the Arabs, which are incorporated in Chapter Two of his *Muqaddimah.* The ambiguity arises from his sometimes using "Arab" as a synonym for "Bedouin" or "nomad," and at other times giving the impression of speaking of the Arabs as a race and as a nation. Rosenthal maintains that "Arab" is always synonymous with "Bedouin" when used sociologically in Ibn Khaldun, "regardless of racial, national or linguistic distinctions" (1:302). But what happens when the term is used in other than sociological contexts? And when, precisely, is it used in these latter contexts? Contemporary Arab scholars such as Satiᶜ al-Husri and Muhammad Jamil Bayham maintain that Ibn Khaldun directed his "criticism" at the Aᶜaraab (Bedouin), not the Arabs, and mobilize impressive evidence to back up their claim; other students, including Syrians and Egyptians who do not quite acknowledge their Arabness, cite him in support of their often derogatory views of the Arabs.

In fact, it is very difficult to decide this issue without an exhaustive study of its various facets. In four sections of Chapter Two, Ibn Khaldun makes some rather sweeping assertions about "the Arabs." But it is obvious that in all these sections, which come under the general heading of "Bedouin Civilization, Savage Nations and Tribes," Ibn Khaldun is referring to the Bedouin, or nomad Arabs. The following is the gist of what he has to say about them. The Arabs, he writes, are people who plunder and cause damage: "They plunder whatever they are able to lay their hands on without having to fight or to expose themselves to danger. They then retreat to their pastures in the desert. They do not attack or fight except in self-defense" (1:302).

The Arabs are a savage nation, fully accustomed to savagery and the things that cause it:

> Savagery has become their character and nature. They enjoy it, because it means freedom from authority and no subservience to leadership. Such a natural disposition is the negation and antithesis of civilization. All the customary activities of the Arabs lead to travel and movement. This is the antithesis and negation of stationariness, which produces civilization. For instance, the Arabs need stones to set them up as supports for their cooking pots. So, they take them from buildings which they tear down to get the stones, and use them for the purpose. Wood, too, is needed by them for props for their tents and for use as tent poles for their dwellings. So, they tear down roofs to get the wood for that purpose. The very nature of their existence is the negation of building, which is the basis of civilization. (1:250–252)

Furthermore, the Arabs are not concerned with laws: "They care only for the property that they might take away from people through looting and imposts. When they have obtained that, they have no interest in anything further, such as taking care of people, looking after their interests, or forcing them not to commit misdeeds. . . . Under the rule of the Arabs, the subjects live as in a state of anarchy, without law" (1:303–304).

Finally, every Arab is eager to be the leader.

> Scarcely a one of them would cede his power to another, even to his father, his brother, or the eldest member of his family. . . . It is noteworthy how civilization always collapsed in places the Arabs took over and conquered, and how such settlements were depopulated and the very earth there turned into something that was no longer earth. The Yemen where the Arabs live is in ruins, except for a few cities. Persian civilization in Arab Iraq is likewise completely ruined. The same applies to contemporary Syria. When the Banu Hilal and the Banu Sulaym pushed through

from their homeland to Africa and the Maghreb in the beginning of the 5th century and struggled there for 350 years, they attached themselves to the country, and the flat territory in the Maghreb was completely ruined. Formerly, the whole region between the Sudan and the Mediterranean had been settled. This fact is attested by the relics of civilization there . . .

The reason for this is that because of their savagery, the Arabs are the least willing of nations to subordinate themselves to each other, as they are rude, proud, ambitious and eager to be the leader. . . . But when there is religion among them, through prophecy or sainthood, then they have some restraining influence in themselves. . . . When there is a prophet or saint among them . . . they become fully united (as a social organization) and obtain superiority and royal authority. Besides, no people are as quick as the Arabs to accept religious truth and right guidance, because their natures have been preserved free from distorted habits and uncontaminated by base character qualities. (1:302–304)

The Arabs are by nature remote from royal leadership: "They attain it only once their nature has undergone a complete transformation under the influence of some religious coloring. This is illustrated by the Arab dynasty in Islam. Religion cemented their leadership with the religious law and its ordinances, which, explicitly and implicitly, are concerned with what is good for civilization. The caliphs followed one after another. As a result the royal authority and Government of the Arabs became great and strong. . . . Later on, however, the Arabs were cut off from the dynasty for generations. They neglected the religion. Thus, they forgot political leadership and returned to the desert" (1:307–308).

It is to be kept in mind that in all these appraisals Ibn Khaldun refers to the Bedouin, or nomad Arabs. To appreciate the full implications of his strictures, one must be quite clear as to the date on which Arab rule "disappeared and was wiped out." In the introduction to the *Muqaddimah,* Ibn Khaldun speaks of a "hidden pitfall in historiography," which he defines as "disregard for the fact that conditions within the nations and races change with the change of periods and the passing of days." In explaining his point, Ibn Khaldun points out that the old Persian nations, the Syrians, the Nabataeans, the Tubbaʿs (kings of a pre-Islamic Yemeni kingdom), the Israelites, and the Copts "all once existed . . . their historical relics testify to that." When they were succeeded by the later Persians, the Byzantines, and the Arabs, however, the old institutions changed and former customs were transformed: "Then, there came Islam with the Mudhar dynasty, and all institutions underwent another change."

But then, Ibn Khaldun adds, "the days of Arab rule were over. The early generations who had cemented Arab might and founded the realm of the Arabs were gone. The power was seized by others, by non-Arabs like the Turks in the east, the Berbers in the west, and the European Christians (the Franks) in the north. With their passing, entire nations ceased to exist, and institutions and customs changed. Their glory was forgotten, and their power no longer heeded" (1:304). Elsewhere, he speaks of the end of Arab rule as having occurred "during the generation of Harun al-Rashid's grandsons"—which would seem to show that the date Ibn Khaldun was thinking of was not 1258, when the Mongols conquered Baghdad, but two generations after Harun al-Rashid, i.e., about two hundred years after the great Arab conquests of the seventh century. (For a discussion of this topic, see Shlomo Dov Goitein, "ʿArabi ʿal ʿArabim: Birrur Hadash ʿal De ʿotav shel Ibn Khaldun ʿal ha-ʿAm ha-ʿArabi" [An Arab on Arabs: Fresh Light on Ibn Khaldun's Views on the Arab People]).

Is Ibn Khaldun saying here that the Arabs had, since circa AD 950, lapsed into barbarism and became as savage as they had been before Islam? And does he mean all the Arabs? It is true that Ibn Khaldun believes that the urbanized "Arabs" of his day were merely "descendants of the Arabs who were in possession of these cities and perished in their luxury." This shows, if anything, that he did not consider the city-dwelling Arabs of his time to be "Arab" in his own sense of the term. Such Arabs existed, to be sure, but they were the nomads of Hijaz. Be that as it may, Ibn Khaldun's use of the epithet "Arab" has thrown many modern students of his work into utter confusion. For while it is clear in some places that he is speaking of the nomads and of the nomads alone, there is considerable ambiguity in other places. For instance, on the first page of his book, Ibn Khaldun speaks of Muhammad as "the Arab Prophet," an appellation that does not seem to fit his "sociological" use of the term.

PROFIT AND SUSTENANCE

Ibn Khaldun returns to the subject—though somewhat indirectly—in the conclusion of Chapter Five, which he devotes to urban civilization, in which he parts with his favorite cycles and starts a discourse on all branches of human activity. The title of the chapter gives an idea of its scope: "Of the various aspects of making a living, such as profits and the crafts. The conditions that occur in this connection, including a number of related problems." After a short introduction explaining the meaning of profit and sustenance (profit is "the value realized from human labor," Ibn Khaldun explains, while sustenance is "that part of the profit that is utilized"), he lists "the various ways, means and methods" of earning a living. Profit is obtained in a number of ways: "through having the power to take them [goods] away from others"—i.e., by imposts and taxation; from hunting (including fishing); from agriculture; from human labor, which, when applied to specific materials, is called a craft "such as writing, carpentry, tailoring, weaving, horsemanship"; or from commerce: "Commerce is a natural way of making profits. However, most of its practices and methods are tricky and designed to obtain the profit margin between purchase prices and sales prices. Therefore the law permits cunning in commerce, since it contains an element of gambling" (2:383).

Some scholars, Ibn Khaldun adds, submit that a living can be made by exercising political power (*imarah*), but this "is not a natural way of making a living." Other ways of making a living that Ibn Khaldun considers unnatural include being a servant and digging for buried treasure. On the general problem of servants, he has interesting things to say. There are four kinds of servants: capable and trustworthy, capable but untrustworthy, trustworthy but incapable, and incapable and untrustworthy. The first category is "almost non-existent": a capable and trustworthy person can be more than just a servant. The fourth kind of servant, he who is neither capable nor trustworthy, "should not be employed by any intelligent person." The choice therefore is between the second and third categories—capable but untrustworthy, or trustworthy but incapable: "There are two opinions among people as to which of the two kinds is preferable. Each has something in its favor. However, the capable servant, even when he is not trustworthy, is preferable" (2:384).

Treasure hunting, also objectionable, is pursued by "weak-minded persons" who believe that the European Christians who lived in Africa before Islam buried their property and entrusted its hiding place to written lists so that they could dig it up again when they found a way to do so. In the Maghreb of Ibn Khaldun's time there were many "students" who used to approach well-to-do people with ragged sheets of paper containing what they claimed were such lists: "These swindlers create remarkable situations and employ astounding techniques" (2:391).

Rank is useful in securing property, Ibn Khaldun rules, since a person of rank receives much free labor from others, and is made rich "in a very short time." We therefore find "that the person of rank who is highly esteemed is in every material aspect more fortunate and wealthier than a person who has no rank." The person who has no rank whatsoever, on the other hand, "acquires a fortune only in proportion to the property he owns and in accordance with the efforts which he himself makes." Such a person, however, may still seek and desire rank. If he does so, he "must be obsequious and use flattery, as powerful rulers require"; otherwise, "it will be impossible for him to obtain any rank." Since obsequiousness and flattery are ways through which a person may be able to obtain rank, it follows that "most wealthy and happy people have the quality of obsequiousness and use flattery." Thus, too, "many people who are proud and supercilious have no use for rank. Their earnings, consequently, are restricted to the results of their own labor, and they are reduced to poverty and indigence." Always the wise realist, Ibn Khaldun adds here: "It should be known that such haughtiness and pride are blameworthy qualities; they result from the assumption that one is perfect" (2:391).

TWO

IBN KHALDUN'S APPRAISAL
APPRAISED

In their attempts to explain Ibn Khaldun's derogatory though somewhat ambiguous remarks on the Arabs, some modern Arab scholars have tried to attribute his "vagueness" and "inconsistency" to the fact that he was an opportunist, a self-seeker, and an arriviste who was willing to serve any master in order to attain self-promotion.

Two renowned Egyptian scholars and historians, Dr. Taha Hussein (1889–1973) and Muhammad Abdullah ʿAnan, his contemporary, tried to trace Ibn Khaldun's ancestry, asking whether the famous historian was an Arab himself. In his book *Falsafat Ibn Khaldun al-Ijtimaʿiyya* (Ibn Khaldun's Social Philosophy), Taha Hussein—at one point quoting Ibn Khaldun himself—reaches the conclusion that Ibn Khaldun was not an Arab (31). At the other extreme, in his book *Ibn Khaldun: His Life and Intellectual Legacy*, ʿAnan concludes emphatically that Ibn Khaldun came from one of the oldest of Yemen's Arab tribes (113–114).

Trying to explain Ibn Khaldun's often disparaging remarks about the Arabs, another Arab scholar, Muhammad Jamil Bayham, maintains that the Berber rulers of Ibn Khaldun's time "were pleased to listen to criticism of the Arabs." Citing Ibn Khaldun's biography to show that he was deliberately vague and ambiguous in his writing on the Arabs, this writer explains that the great Tunisian historian was brought up on the love of exalted position and obsequiousness to rulers. Since it was then the fashion to denigrate the Arabs, he wrote what he wrote in the *Muqaddimah* only to please those who at the time wielded power and distributed positions and ranks (Bayham, *Al-ʿUruba wal-Shuʿubiyyat al-Haditha* [Arabism and the New *Shuʿubiyyas*], 58, 64, 65).

This argument can hardly be maintained as far as the early stages of Ibn Khaldun's life are concerned. True, he managed to fill a number of high positions in Fez before he wrote his history, but he subsequently fell into disfavor with the authorities. What is more, in his analysis of civilization in its various aspects, he did not spare the Berbers themselves.

Writings in Arabic on Ibn Khaldun and his comments and conclusions thus vary widely, especially regarding his statements on the Arabs and their history. One Arab scholar, Muhammad Jabir al-Ansari, writes at some length to show that for Ibn Khaldun "there is no Islam without Arabness and no Arabness without Islam" (al-Ansari's remarks are quoted in Nissim Rejwan, "Was Ibn Khaldun an Arab Nationalist?"). It is difficult to see just how the writer reaches that conclusion, especially since he goes on to make Ibn Khaldun out as virtually an Arab nationalist. "Nationalism," he writes, "is something ordained by a universal and divine order in the life of mankind, although it is not a religion or a religious doctrine. Since it cannot turn itself into a religion, nationalism has to find a suitable religious doctrine and a number of spiritual values that go hand in hand with its essence and with its historical mission."

Arab nationalism, adds al-Ansari, "after it asserts itself as a natural and social reality, will have only the Islamic essence from which to draw its beliefs, its principles, and its solid and durable content." Wondering whether "this Khaldunian message" has reached and been absorbed by the Arabs in both its facets, al-Ansari concludes by asserting that "nationalism is essential for religion" and that nationalism in both its facets is "a divine order"—exactly like religion "within its limits."

GUSTAVE VON GRUNEBAUM
AND ABDALLAH LAROUI

Ibn Khaldun's analysis was written in the fourteenth century. Between his time and the last few decades of the nineteenth century, the Arabs passed through what must be described as the darkest and culturally least productive period in their history. Yet even in most recent times—say, since the middle of the nineteenth century, when Arab nationalist sentiments started to be cultivated in countries of the Levant—there have been no serious attempts at self-interpretation or self-appraisal in Arabic Islam. Nearly half a century ago, the British Orientalist Hamilton Alexander Rosskeen Gibb (1895–1971) remarked on this phenomenon: "I have not yet seen a single book written by an Arab of any branch in any Western language that has made it possible for the Western student to understand the roots of Arab culture. More than that, I have not seen any book written in Arabic for

Arabs themselves which has clearly analyzed what Arabic culture means for the Arabs" ("Social Change in the Near East," 60).

Al-Ansari's emphatic assertions are generally shared by all Arab nationalists. To take one example, Sati⁣ᶜ al-Husri (1880–1967), one of the founders of the ideology, maintains that Ibn Khaldun in the *Muqaddimah* uses "Arab" to denote the desert Bedouin, i.e., the nomads, and not the Arabs as a whole or "the Arab nation" (quoted in William F. Cleveland, *The Making of an Arab Nationalist*, 126; see also al-Husri, *AlᶜUruba Awwalan* [Arabism First and Foremost], 99–114).

Gustave von Grunebaum (1909–1972), another Western authority on modern Islam, asserts that Gibb's observation could be extended to include non-Arabic Islam as well. He gives three reasons for this failure on the part of Muslims to attempt an analysis of the fundamentals of their civilization. To start with, he writes, the old-school Muslim considers Islam the final religion, the ultimate truth, the one road to salvation. He also is likely to be conscious of an Islamic way of life, "but he will not think of Islamic civilization as one among several civilizations, whose differences in structure result in differences of possibilities and values" (this quotation and those in the next several paragraphs are taken from von Grunebaum, *Islam: Essays in the Nature and Growth of a Cultural Tradition*, 185–186). To him, the finality of the Qur'anic revelation entails an approach to history that rates the several religions according to their proximity to, or remoteness from, the absolute truth as embodied in Islam. For Muslims themselves, as von Grunebaum explains, the Muslim scene "needs scrutiny with respect to its harmony with the unalterable divine ordinance, but not with respect to its cultural elements and the forces responsible for its birth and growth."

The second reason that von Grunebaum gives for the phenomenon is that modern Muslim society as a whole is lamentably ignorant of the origin, development, and achievements of its civilization: "This ignorance is due partly to a defective educational system and partly to absorption by the adjustment problems of the moment. Moreover, scientific research methods have not yet found universal acceptance."

The third and last reason for the Muslims' failure to furnish an analysis of their civilization, according to von Grunebaum, is that the present situation of the Muslim East tends to stimulate such discussion of religion or civilization as falls easily into any one or more of the following categories: apologetics of one sort or another; reformist—or "reactionary"—theology; appeals for Westernization; and political discussion or propaganda.

Thus, according to von Grunebaum, religious, political, and cultural aims and factors tend to prevent, or at least interfere with, any attempt on the part of Muslims to study and interpret their civilization. This "culturist" reading of Islam, its history, and its present status is, however, understandably rejected in its entirety by an increasing number of Muslim Arab intellectuals and scholars, who perceive it as negative and "reductive." In *The Crisis of the Arab Intellectual* (1974), for instance, the Moroccan historian Abdallah Laroui (b. 1933) includes a lengthy critique of von Grunebaum's Islamic studies, pointing out that the adjectives this Orientalist affixes to the word "Islam" (medieval, classical, modern) are neutral and even superfluous. For von Grunebaum, he explains, "there is no difference between classical and medieval Islam or simply Islam" (59).

A quick perusal of von Grunebaum's work, Laroui maintains, will convince the reader of the truth of this assertion. For von Grunebaum, he repeats, there is only one Islam, which mutates within itself when tradition takes shape on the basis of a reconstructed "classical" period: "From that time onward the actual succession of facts become illusory; examples can be drawn from any period or source whatever; the logic of the matrix, taken as the given, is our only guide in the selection of illustrative events."

For Laroui, the search for the fundamental aspiration, or "matrix," of Islam is "necessarily the description of a classicism and a tradition: the three notions amount to the same thing." However, because decadence is implicit in the very definition of tradition, von Grunebaum's approach is seen by Laroui as leading to the following equation: Islam = unitary principle = classicism = tradition = decadence. "One can," he adds, "certainly speak of attenuating or aggravating circumstances that precipitate or delay decadence; but the real cause is the matrix, the principle of exclusion that is also the principle of identity. Every culture, being a closed system structured by a choice, is eventually doomed to stagnation and sterile repetition. Once tradition has been formulated, it is condemned to reformulate itself again and again, with ever narrower limits and increasing sterility . . . Therefore, properly speaking, there is neither a decadent Islam nor a modern Islam" (60–61). According to Laroui, the question one ought to ask about modern Islam—in von Grunebaum's view—is this: Is there maintenance or abandonment of the fundamental principle? Is there cultural continuity or a winding up, which in turn marks the beginning of another culture?

Laroui's summing up of von Grunebaum's approach to Islam is scathing:

Modern Islam is a geographical denotation; it is the world that used to be the domain of Islam, a world whose experience today is, and has been for the past century, one of utter intellectual disorder. The numerous

studies that von Grunebaum has devoted to nationalism, to acculturation, to Westernization, and to Muslim self-interpretation, all boil down
to this: Islam today denies the West because it remains faithful to its
fundamental aspiration but cannot undergo modernization unless it re-
interprets itself from the Western point of view and accepts the Western
idea of man and the Western definition of truth. (60–61)

It is interesting to note here that Laroui, despite the manifestly critical
view he takes of von Grunebaum's methodology and conclusions, disclaims
having taken "a critical attitude"—since, in his words, "self-indulgence in
this direction can too easily lead to the dismissal of every scientific undertaking." "These days," he explains, "we are sufficiently aware of the epis-
temological presuppositions of the social sciences, and even the natural
sciences, to know that formal criticisms of this kind are completely inadequate. In the same way, a pragmatic critique that asks, Can these analyses
provide us with the blueprint for a workable polity in the Muslim countries?
would also be inadmissible, for von Grunebaum explicitly states that his
works aim in the main at an introspection of Western culture" (62).

Has Laroui anything "constructive" to offer, some alternative approach
to that of von Grunebaum? The truth is that Laroui is too subtle a thinker,
and his study is too involved, to make it easy for the reader to glean such
conclusions. Nevertheless, toward the end of his critique Laroui hints at an
alternative approach. The history of Islam, he admits, is both seductive and
dangerous: "Seductive because it calls for system and structure; everything
comes to us in a framework of culture and ideology: We have a theory of
religion and a few evidences of the actual lived religion, a political theory
and few political documents, a theory of history and a few specific dates,
a theory of social structure and few series of economic data, etc. We are in
constant danger of confusing theory with fact; the one is readily available
while the other demands research and elaboration." It is this state of affairs,
he adds, that lends an appearance of truth to the analyses of cultural anthropologists, since the temporality of tradition they postulate, as well as
the "culturist" analysis "conforms with the temporality that the Islamic tradition has itself imposed."

Thus, while "we ourselves sometimes have to be—or appear to be—
'culturist' . . . it is our part never to forget that this temporality is no more
than a formulation and is not the naked reality. The formal agreement between several facts and their reduction to a common meaning may well
provide the 'culturist' with a heuristic construct, but it is not an explanation of these facts; the factor determining the agreement does not belong

to the culture itself. We must demonstrate this where we can; where we are not yet able to, we must draw attention to the assumptions that have been made" (72).

Laroui, then, refuses to reduce history to its theory. This refusal, he says, results in a conceptual differentiation: "structure is not a priori an isomorphic reflection; culture is not the primordial choice between possible developments; rather, it is the ensemble of cultural artifacts, whether or not all of these can be presently systematized." Taking his point of departure from these premises, Laroui finally suggests "a division of labor" among those who study Islamic countries. He distinguishes between four separate "domains"— Islam as history, on which level it has a geohistorical meaning only; Islam as culture; Islam as behavior or morality; and Islam as faith (72–73).

EDWARD SAID'S RESERVATIONS

More severe—and far more "political"—are the strictures made by Edward W. Said (1935–2003) in his book, *Orientalism* (1978), in which von Grunebaum serves as only one of the targets. Said—who is not himself a student of Islam, professionally speaking—provides what can best be considered a follow-up to Laroui's critique. He escalates the debate by attributing to von Grunebaum the view that while Islam can modernize itself only by a self-interpretation from the Western point of view, such a development is manifestly impossible since Islam as a culture is incapable of innovation. He further supplements Laroui's thesis by pointing out that "the need for Islam to use Western methods to improve itself has, as an idea, perhaps because of von Grunebaum's wide influence, become almost a truism in Middle Eastern studies"—citing the work of one American author who urges "maturity" on Arabs, Africans, and Asians, arguing that such maturity can be gained only by learning from Western objectivity (Said, *Orientalism*, 298).

The net result of von Grunebaum's scholarly endeavors, Said asserts, "is a historical vision of Islam entirely hobbled by a theory of a culture incapable of doing justice to, or even examining, its existential reality in the experience of its adherents" (298–299). Von Grunebaum, he argues, fell prey both to the Orientalist dogmas he inherited and to a particular feature of Islam that he has chosen to interpret as a shortcoming. His Islam is "the Islam of the earlier European Orientalists—monolithic, scornful of ordinary human experience, gross, reductive, unchanging" (299). At bottom, Said says, such a view of Islam is political, "not even euphemistically impartial." The strength of the hold that this view of Islam continues to have on the new

Orientalist, the Western student of the modern and contemporary Middle East, "is due in part to its traditional authority, and in part to its use-value as a handle for grasping a vast region of the world and proclaiming it an entirely coherent phenomenon" (299).

Since Islam, Said goes on to argue, "has never easily been encompassed by the West politically—and certainly since World War II Arab nationalism has been a movement openly declaring its hostility to Western imperialism—the desire to assert intellectually satisfying things about Islam in retaliation increases" (299). As proof, he cites one authority, Professor Manfred Halpern, as saying of Islam—"without specifying which Islam or aspect of Islam he means"—that it is "one prototype of closed traditional societies." Said invites the reader to note "the edifying use of the word Islam to signify all at once a society, a religion, a prototype, and an actuality." He then quotes a passage from Halpern that Said says constitutes an "invidiously ideological portrait of 'us' and 'them,'" and that cites certain Islamic practices—marrying four wives, fasting or eating, etc.—as evidence of Islam's all-inclusiveness and of its tyranny. "As to where this is supposed to be happening," Said complains, "we are not told. But we are reminded of the doubtless nonpolitical fact that Orientalists 'are largely responsible for having given Middle Easterners themselves an accurate appreciation of their past,' just in case we might forget that Orientalists know things by definition that Orientals cannot know on their own" (299).

Said returns to these themes in a long afterword to a new edition of *Orientalism* published in 1995, in which he also speaks more openly of his personal predilections and the reasons for writing a book that was, strictly speaking, outside his fields of interest as a scholar and teacher.

The discourses of Orientalism, he writes, "its internal consistency and rigorous procedures, were all designed for readers and consumers in the metropolitan West" (336). This applied as much to people he genuinely admires, like Edward Lane and Gustave Flaubert, who were fascinated by Egypt, as it did to "haughty colonial administrators like Lord Cromer, brilliant scholars like Ernest Renan, and baronial aristocrats like Arthur Balfour, all of whom condescended to and disliked the Orientals they either ruled or studied" (366). Said concludes:

I must confess to a certain pleasure in listening in, uninvited, to their various pronouncements and inter-Orientalist discussions, and an equal pleasure in making known my feelings both to Europeans and non-Europeans. I have no doubt that this was made possible by being someone who traversed the imperial East-West divide, entered into the life of the West, and retained some organic connection with the place I originally came from. . . . This is very much a procedure of crossing, rather than maintaining barriers; I believe *Orientalism* as a book demonstrates this, especially at moments when I speak of humanistic study as ideally seeking to go beyond coercive limitations on thought towards a nondominative and nonessentialist type of learning. These considerations did in fact add to the pressures on my book to represent a sort of testament of wounds and a record of sufferings the recital of which was felt as a long overdue striking back at the West. I deplore so simple a characterization of a work that is . . . quite nuanced and discriminating in what it says about different people, different periods, and different styles of Orientalism. To read my analyses of Chateaubriand and Flaubert, or of Burton and Lane, with exactly the same emphasis, deriving the same reductive message from the banal formula "an attack on Western civilization" is, I believe, to be both simplistic and wrong. (336)

He describes *Orientalism* as "a study based on the rethinking of what had for centuries been believed to be an unbridgeable chasm separating East from West." His aim, he asserts, "was not so much to dissipate difference itself but the notion that difference implied hostility, a frozen reified set of opposed essences" (338).

Said refers to the subject of self-image and self-view only indirectly, in the context of Arab Muslim reactions to his work and the ways in which the works of the Orientalists affect the self-view of Western-educated Arab scholars and thinkers. He starts with a personal statement in which he outlines his general attitudes. In all his works, he writes,

I remained fundamentally critical of a gloating and uncritical nationalism. The picture of Islam that I represented was not one of assertive discourse and dogmatic orthodoxy, but was based instead on the idea that communities of interpretation exist within and outside the Islamic world, communicating with each other in a dialogue of equals. My view of Palestine, formulated originally in *The Question of Palestine*, remains the same today: I expressed all sorts of reservations about the insouciant nativism and militant militarism of the nationalist consensus; I suggested instead a critical look at the Arab environment, Palestinian history, and the Israeli realities, with the explicit conclusion that only a negotiated settlement between the two communities of suffering, Arab and Jewish, would provide respite from the unending war. I should mention in passing that although my book on Palestine was in the early 1980s given a fine Hebrew translation by Mifras, a small Israeli publishing house, it remains untranslated in Arabic to this day. Every Arabic publisher who was interested in the book wanted me to change or delete those sections that were openly critical of one or another Arab regime (including the PLO), a request that I have always refused to comply with. I regret to say therefore that the Arabic reception of *Orientalism* . . . still managed to ignore that aspect of my book which diminished the nationalist fervor that some inferred from my critique of Orientalism. (337)

Said goes on to express his regrets that "the sense of fraught confrontation between an often emotionally defined Arab and an even more emotionally experienced Western world drowned out, whittled down, finally brushed aside the fact that *Orientalism* was meant to be a study in critique, not an affirmation of warring and hopelessly antithetical identities" (337). In some Arab circles, he reports, *Orientalism* was criticized for not appreciating the great achievements of Orientalism, the West, etc.

Concluding this part of his account, Said writes:

The difference between Arab and other responses to *Orientalism* is, I think, an accurate definition of how decades of loss, frustration, and the absence of democracy have affected intellectual and cultural life in the Arab region. I saw my book as part of a preexisting current of thought whose purpose was to liberate intellectuals from the shackles of systems like Orientalism: I wanted readers to make use of what I did so that they might produce new studies of their own that would illuminate the historical experience of Arabs and others in a generous, enabling mode. That certainly happened in Europe, the United States, Australia, the Indian subcontinent, the Caribbean, Ireland, Latin America, and parts of Africa. The invigorated study of Africanist and Indological discourses; the analyses of subaltern history; the reconfiguration of postcolonial anthropology, political science, art history, literary criticism, musicology, in addition to the vast new developments in feminist and minority discourses—to all these, I am pleased and flattered that *Orientalism* often made a difference. That does not seem to have been the case (insofar as I can judge it) in the Arab world, where partly because my work is correctly perceived as Eurocentric in its texts, partly because . . . the battle for cultural survival is too engrossing, books like mine are interpreted less usefully, productively speaking, as defensive gestures either for or against the "West." (337–338)

The reception of Said's book in the Arab world was on the whole en-thusiastic, and his assault on Western Orientalists was applauded. One notable exception is worth mentioning here. It came from Sadiq Jalal al-ʿAzm (b. 1934), one of the most outspoken and perceptive observers of the cultural scene in the Arab world and the author of two noted works of self-criticism—*Naqd al-Fikr al-Dini* (The Critique of Religious Thought) and *Al-Naqd al-Thati baʿd al-Hazima* (Self-Criticism after the Defeat). In an es-say entitled "Orientalism and Orientalism-in-Reverse," an Iranian Islamist named Jalal Ali Ahmad argues that if there is a condition such as *ghar-bazadegi* (from a Persian word literally meaning "West-struck-ness," here referring to a Westerner who makes his living producing myths about the Orient—an Orientalist), there is also one which can be called *sharqzadegi,* an Oriental uncritically reproducing myths about the region in the name of anti-imperialism, solidarity, understanding, and so on (cited in Nissim Rejwan, "A Wild Goose Chase: To Cope, Must Islam 'Westernize'?" 165).

Fred Halliday (b. 1946), a noted British student of the Middle East, quotes Said's strictures, adding that here, of course, "the myth-makers of the region see their chance, since they can impose their own stereotypes by taking advantage of confusion within their own countries and without" ("'Orientalism' and Its Critics," 160–161). Halliday is also critical of Said's failure in *Orientalism* to deal with what he calls "the myths of the Middle East and of its politicians"—a failure that, he says, "allows for a more incau-tious silence, since it prevents us from addressing how the issues discussed by the Orientalists and the relations between East and West are presented in the region itself."

Here, he adds,

> it is not a question of making any moral equivalence between the myths of the dominators and the dominated, but of recognising two other things: first, that when it comes to hypostasis, stereotyping, the projec-tion of timeless and antagonistic myths, this is in no sense a preroga-tive of the dominator, but also of the dominated; and, secondly, that if we analyse the state of the discourse on the contemporary Middle East, then the contribution of these ideologies of the dominated has been, and remains, enormous, not least because those outside the region who try to overcome the myths of the Orient rather too quickly end up collud-ing with, or accepting, the myths of the dominated within the region. (160–161)

THREE

"ARABIZING THE ARABS"

Abdallah Laroui and Edward Said, some of whose views were discussed in the last chapter, represent a new generation of Arab intellectuals whose knowledge of and familiarity with Western culture and Western ways have evidently given them new insights into their own society and culture, as well as the tools to cope with what they consider a challenge posed by traditional Orientalists to their culture and self-image. Members of the older generation of Arab thinkers, however, were less suitably equipped. Those who were forward-looking and reform-oriented seem to have accepted, almost as given, the findings and conclusions of traditional Orientalism; in some cases, indeed, they responded to the calls for self-interpretation and self-appraisal by contributing to it themselves and by implicitly accepting the selfsame Western view of such an undertaking to which Laroui and Said so eloquently object.

A relatively early example of this reaction was the one provided by a number of Arab writers for whom the very term "Arab" and the nature of Arabism were far from clear. The late Ishaq Musa al-Husaini (1904–1990), a Palestinian Muslim of considerable scholarly standing, wonders about "the content of the Arabs' Arabness—or their Arabism, as they are now prone to call it." Before political leaders start to put the ideology of Pan-Arabism into practice, al-Husaini argues, a thorough study must be conducted of the Arab peoples, "so as to find out to what extent Arabism is ingrained in the soul of the Arab individual" (*Azmat al-ʿAql al-ʿArabi* [The Crisis of the Arab Mind], 112–113).

Such an investigation, he explains, would help us know the foundations on which Arab unity and inter-Arab relations in general can be erected. Enthusiasm there is in plenty, to be sure—enthusiasm that led politicians to think that there was enough ground for establishing contacts and strengthening ties between Arab countries. The truth, however, is that "enthusiasm should not be taken as a measure of the peoples' actual readiness for unity, or for understanding, or even for the conclusion of treaties of friendship amongst themselves" (113–114). For al-Husaini, the main obstacle to Arab unity is that the Arabs' very "Arabness" is a mere facade, that it is not rooted in their souls, and that its degree varies as Arab environments vary. This, he says, is what leads him to come out frankly with the call for "Arabizing the Arabs."

"ARABS ONLY BY NAME"

But what does "Arabizing the Arabs" mean, precisely? Who, in other words, is an Arab? According to Juan Cole, a professor of Middle Eastern and South Asian history at the University of Michigan, "Arab" is actually "a linguistic category, like 'Romance' or 'Latin'" ("Is Iraq an Arab Country?" February 22, 2004; available at http://hnn.us/articles/3746.html). Most of the people in the zone from Morocco to Iraq speak Arabic, he explains: "The 2,000 spoken dialects of Arabic are quite diverse and until recently not always mutually comprehensible." It is true that modern standard Arabic has been adopted for the purposes of writing and public discourse, yet the region remains linguistically diverse.

Turning again to the question as to who an Arab is, Cole writes: "'Arab' is not a racial category; the Arabs are just a people who speak a language." Nor is "Arab" a religious category: "About a third of Israelis are Arab Jews, i.e., Jews from Arabic-speaking countries who traditionally spoke Arabic as their mother tongue. While the term [Arab Jew] is rejected by many, it is certainly the case that in 1945 Moroccan and Yemeni Jews were 'Arab.' All Arabs are not Muslim. And only a minority of Muslims is [sic] Arab."

To answer the question of what "Arabizing the Arabs" means, al-Husaini goes a little further; he draws a distinction between what we call the "Arab nation" and what we term "Arab culture." In his view, the Arab nation consists of elements "that have not yet fully grown," whereas Arab culture consists of "concrete realities that have grown out of centuries and that time has served only to entrench and reinforce." The trouble is that the Arab peoples of today "have not assimilated Arab culture and the Arab spirit, or the immortal elements of Arab civilization." Indeed, al-Husaini adds, "the Arabs have not comprehended these elements sufficiently well to make the Arab nation a well-cemented entity with its own laws, culture, literature, and ideals" (*Azmat al-ʿAql al-ʿArabi;* quotations in this paragraph and the next several are drawn from pages 116–117). Arabizing the Arabs entails bringing them nearer to these elements.

This is all very well as far as it goes. Yet al-Husaini, not untypically, fails to make the nature of these elements of Arab civilization quite clear. Those who have studied Arab culture thoroughly, he asserts, "do not hide their deep admiration for it: they praise its vitality and laud its cohesiveness and its ability to withstand the various setbacks it suffered through the centuries." But a huge gap yawns between Arab culture and its bearers today, and admirers of this culture fail to see in the Arab peoples what they see in Arab culture.

Al-Husaini at this point recalls an anecdote that he offers as an illustration of this gap. Though the anecdote has to do with Islam and Muslims, he believes that its moral applies specifically to Arabs and Arab culture. A Frenchman of standing in North Africa, he relates, had studied Islam as a faith and was awed with admiration for it—so much so that he decided to embrace Islam. When his conversion became known to the Muslim inhabitants of the land, they were so overwhelmed with enthusiasm and joy that they assembled in song and music and marched toward the Frenchman's residence to congratulate him on his action. However, as soon as the procession reached his residence, and upon seeing the people's ecstasy, their large turbans and wide robes, the banners they bore, and the long necklaces around their necks, the Frenchman came out on his balcony and addressed the crowd in a clear voice: "Gentlemen, go back to where you came from, and know that what I have come to admire is Islam, not the Muslims!" Upon which the celebrants turned round and went back, deeply disappointed.

Like the Muslims, who have strayed from the spirit of Islam and from its lofty ideals, the Arabs have similarly deserted Arab culture, its ideals and its legacy, al-Husaini writes. "Let us have a look at the present state of the Arab peoples," he explains. "The Arab peoples of the Arab East—let us temporarily leave aside the Arab West—consist of many elements that have not been merged into a whole, into a single entity with similar leanings and aspirations. There are groups of Turkish origin and others of Circassian origin, and still others of Kurdish, Armenian, Assyrian, Aramaic, and Bedouin descent; these groups trace their origins to [races] with different languages, literatures, and temperaments. . . . It cannot be denied that political circumstances in recent times tended to exaggerate the differences between these groups and to prevent their assimilation into one single whole."

Other obstacles enumerated by al-Husaini include the fact that the overwhelming majority of Arabs are illiterate, and are thus deprived of the strongest tie on which the politicians rely in promoting the cause of Arab unity. Even the literate portion, which he believes may not exceed 10 percent of the total, is not sufficiently imbued with Arab culture to be fit to lead this multitude. "Cultural trends," he explains, "tended to take divergent roads in guiding this minority and determining its inclinations and ways of thinking, and so it became unfit to assume healthy leadership and offer guidance. All that was left were some enlightened and dedicated individuals who spread the word, bore the banner, and lighted the fire in immense and desolate spaces, and all their efforts came to naught" (116–117).

But this is not all. Even what is called the unity of language, which al-Husaini concedes is the heart and essence of culture, is not a sufficient indication of meaningful Arabness. In its present state, the Arabic language "cannot be considered a true manifestation of Arabism" (the quotations in this paragraph and the next several are drawn from pages 124–125). In his view, Arabic is in reality "a historical phenomenon, a crossroads rather than a meeting place." Arabic dialects indicate historical ties between the Arab peoples, whereas the actual manifestation of these ties ought to be classical Arabic, around which assemble the minds and hearts of these peoples as well as their sentiments and aspirations. "Where does this language in fact stand today in the various Arab societies?" al-Husaini asks. "Do these elements and groups to which we have just referred gather together in educational institutions over this classical language—and do this in spite of their environmental disparities? Does the Kurdish, Assyrian, or Turkish citizen draw on one linguistic spring? Is the school available that brings him together with his compatriots from all the other groups and makes him speak a correct Arabic tongue?"

So much for the two principal factors that make up "Arabness"—culture and language. Of religion, which he describes as "a third significant tie," al-Husaini writes that in the Arab edifice it is one of the foundations of Arab nationalism. "Our religion," he adds, "is monotheism." Islam and Christianity together, in their original manifestations and their pure essence, have to be considered one of the pillars of Arab nationalism. To what extent, he asks, have these two faiths "penetrated the souls of the faithful among the population of the Arab East, brought people together, confirmed nationalist doctrines, and upheld nationalist leanings and trends?"

The sad truth, al-Husaini writes by way of an answer to this question, is that in the Arab East religion is one of the factors of discord, and "constitutes a mark of degeneration and disintegration—not in its capacity as true religion but insofar as it is an assortment of views and beliefs added later out of fanaticism or ignorance or lack of understanding." Religion, he explains, is in essence a longing for justice and cooperation; it is the opposite of what we see nowadays, "when even the same religion has acquired several contradictory forms among various communities within the same land." The means that God has granted for bringing the population of the Arab East together, purifying their souls, and unifying their ranks "has thus been turned into the very opposite of this."

What makes al-Husaini wonder is that Islam in its early stages brought the multicommunal society nothing but well-being and cooperation. Even the controversies provoked by certain Muslim factions failed to affect the cohesion of society, he asserts. In his opinion, based on his travels in Arab lands, "the true believers are nearer to a consciousness of Arabism and are more faithful adherents" of the Arab-nationalist cause than those who are weak in their faith and their religious beliefs. He does not specify the religious identity of those true believers, but adds: "This alone constitutes conclusive proof that religion is a means of love and understanding, and ultimately one of the pillars of Arabism."

After thus surveying the present state of the "Arabness" of the Arabs, and after finding it so wanting, al-Husaini enumerates the criteria for measuring the extent of this Arabness. In his view there are five such criteria:

1. The extent to which a people clings to its language and the ability of that people to appreciate its literature—not as individuals but as a collectivity.

2. A people's pride in its history and its understanding of that history's turns and ramifications—as well as depictions of its history that are attractive to everybody.

3. A people's adherence to its national traditions and its inherited characteristics, free from whatever may distort them.

4. A people's jealousy of its national heritage, including laws, politics, religion, and everything that a nation tends to treasure.

5. Readiness to defend the culture, its homeland, and its bearers.

Using these five criteria, al-Husaini arrives at the grim conclusion that the Arab peoples "are Arabs only in name," though he concedes that conditions vary within the various Arab societies. To be sure, he adds, national consciousness and nationalist movements have emerged in all the Arab countries, "but these were purely political movements, not based on correct scientific foundations, and have no relation to the criteria which we have enumerated." In other words, "consciousness came in the form of eruptions, some caused by outside pressures and no more." Events have had a strong influence on these eruptions—now weakening them, now lending them strength, now again directing them to the right and now to the left. Al-Husaini concludes,

> Until this day, we cannot credit the nationalist movements with the attributes of firmness and cohesion, since they never managed to stand on the foundations that we have expounded above. The prevalent state of affairs in the Arab countries fully supports what we say, but we are in no position to reveal more than we have done already. It is obvious, however, that these nationalist movements have, both in their emergence and in their eclipse, relied upon what their advocates and leaders possessed in terms of power, of influence, and of fanaticism, rather than upon valid nationalist principles. (124–125)

LACK OF "CONSCIOUSNESS OF THE FUTURE"

If, according to one Arab thinker, the Arabs lack the real characteristics of Arabness and "are Arabs only in name," other Arab intellectuals of the older generation found their fellow Arabs wanting in other ways. In the growing body of Arabic literature of self-appraisal and self-criticism, the work of Qadri Hafiz Touqan occupies a secure and honorable place. Dead at sixty-one, in 1971, Touqan was a native of the ancient city of Nablus and came from one of the city's oldest and most prestigious families.

But it is mainly as an author, a thinker, and an educator that Touqan was known in the Arab world. In this capacity he was probably matched by only a few contemporary writers in Arabic—and certainly by no fellow Palestinian of his generation. His appointment as foreign minister and minister of education in the Jordanian cabinet in the early 1960s was in acknowledgment of his intellectual standing rather than his political skill.

Along with many Arab thinkers of his generation, Touqan shared a constant preoccupation with the problems and processes of modernization and the ways in which the Arab East could attain the scientific, educational, and technological standards of the West. The titles of most of his works evolve around the themes of science and reason. One of his books, published in Beirut in 1964, is entitled *The Place of Reason in the Arab World*—and his previous works include *The Scientific Legacy of the Arabs* (1941), *The Arabs and the Scientific Method* (1946), and *After the Catastrophe*, a book on the Palestine question, published in Beirut in 1950. Of his other works, however, the only one devoted wholly to social and cultural criticism is his *Waᶜy al-Mustaqbal* (Consciousness of the Future), published in 1953.

In this book, written under the pressures and strains of the Arabs' defeat in the 1948 war with Israel, Touqan is at his most outspoken. In chapter after chapter he enumerates, analyzes, and diagnoses the ills of contemporary Arab society—and then lays out his proposed remedies. Chief among the ailments, according to Touqan, is the Arabs' lack of what he termed "a consciousness of the future." The Arabs, he writes, are notorious for having no awareness of the future: "they think only of the present, and leave the future to luck and nature, not heeding it at all." The Arabs are "ever in the present in which they live, not troubling themselves with thinking about the future or preparing for it" (5–6).

Touqan, who, like so many contemporary Arab writers, displays a marked fondness for rhetoric and repetitiveness, goes on to ask with bitter irony: "And why should they [worry about the future]? They have mastered the art of improvisation and got used to it, and a consciousness of the future has become quite alien to them and far from their thoughts. Their actions furnish ample proof of this—and as a natural outcome of all this, failure has overtaken them in all walks of life" (8).

It would hardly be an exaggeration to say, Touqan adds, that this absence of a sense of the future in the Arabs is one of the causes of the series of disasters that befell them in their own lands and of their failures in the international arena: "There is no doubt that consciousness of the future—or awareness of it—is a factor in the success of the West and in its mastery of nature. Westerners think about the future, get themselves ready for it, and make efforts to be prepared for its happenings and surprises" (8).

Touqan then dwells briefly on the reason for this difference in temperament between Easterners and Westerners.

> Psychologists maintain that the sense of the future, or awareness of it, is a special faculty given to certain races of mankind, a trait which grows and becomes more pronounced in some nations, while stopping short in others. Psychologists maintain further that weather factors and a cold climate have a great influence on the strength of this sense of the future. Both of these theories may contain a certain amount of truth; in fact, this sense of the future is enhanced and becomes sharper as a result of the methods that nations adopt in teaching and education, and it is greatly affected by the spirit that informs school curricula and methods of instruction. (11)

However that may be, the absence in Arabs of this consciousness of the future does not spring from climate, weather, or the natural features of their lands. As Touqan sees it, it is rather attributable to the methods they follow in their lives and in solving their problems—methods that have resulted in the improvisation and anarchy noticeable in their actions and in various aspects of their work.

There is, thus, a deeper cause for this Arab disability. The Arabs, Touqan asserts, will not free themselves from the old ways and liberate their minds, nor will they succeed in cultivating a sense of the future or preparing for its eventualities and surprises, "unless they embrace science and the scientific method and apply it in education." Properly mastered and adequately assimilated, "the scientific method will help the present generation [of Arabs] comprehend life and master nature, so that it can look to the future instead of the past, and free itself from old and erroneous concepts" (11).

Referring to the Arabs' debacle in Palestine in 1948, Touqan writes that the catastrophe befell all Arabs; it was an inevitable consequence of the methods that Arabs pursued in their endeavors and of the conditions that governed their lives: "These methods and these conditions are alien to science and totally lacking in any basis in reality; they are dictated by the standards of the past and its aspirations, a state of affairs that has resulted in confused action and in improvisation in politics and intellectual trends" (12).

The Arabs' failure to solve their social and political problems scientifically led, in turn, to the weakening of their sense of the future, which resulted in the brand of improvisation that has so deeply pervaded their actions: "What is indisputable is that the Arabs' ignorance of the scientific method, and their remoteness from science, have helped their enemies and made them win the first round against them. How could these enemies fail to win when they were equipped with science and resorted to its methods and used them on a large scale, while the Arabs pursued old standards and acted in a way that was chaotic and devoid of organization and accurate calculation?" (12).

Touqan then enumerates the specific advantages that will accrue to the Arabs if and when they adopt the scientific method. The Arabs, he writes,

are facing abnormal conditions and grave problems that make it incumbent on each of them to realize his duty and feel his responsibility vis-à-vis the community; they require him to march to the arena equipped with the spirit of the age and armed with science on the one hand and determination and courage on the other—and to work for reform and reconstruction. This may lead to problems and difficulties, but these will be borne willingly for the general good and the welfare of the community and for the sake of one's beliefs . . .

The advantages of the scientific method do not end here, however.

This method helps eliminate the remnants of traditions and old habits and paves the way to continuous growth and nonstop progress. Those imbued with the spirit of science can avoid a good deal of mental confusion in politics and economics, and this clarity in turn will help them solve problems in a healthy way based on education, accurate knowledge, experiment, and example. In addition to this, the scientific method in essence is also a school for a higher morality, since it is based on absolute objectivity, patience, fair-mindedness, studiousness, diligence, and self-denial in the search for truth. These characteristics, which have to prevail in the researcher, all conform to high morals. Man must be guided by them in his life and in his striving (12–13).

THE ISLAM FACTOR

Despite this sincere display of enthusiasm for science and the scientific method, however, it can hardly be said that Touqan's own writing is quite free from the traditionalism and mental confusion he so eloquently deplores. This is especially the case when he deals with Islam as a religious faith and tries to apply to its study the premises of science and reason to which he so passionately adheres. It must be pointed out here, however, that this is a shortcoming common to all works written by Muslims on Islam. The question why the modern Muslim finds it so difficult to furnish an objective analysis and interpretation of his own religion and culture has to do with the very nature of Islam and how its followers are supposed to view it.

Apart from the general, lamentable ignorance within modern Muslim society of the roots, development, and attainments of its own civilization, Islam—as the final revealed religion, the ultimate truth, and the one road to salvation—is very much its own yardstick: if it has to be studied, scrutinized, or reexamined, such scrutiny must be conducted according to its own unalterable terms. The result has been that much of what passes for Islamic scholarship today falls easily in the category of apologetics of one sort or another. Touqan's book *Maqam al-ʿAql ʿind al-ʿArab* (The Place of Reason in the Arab World) is a case in point.

Though it purports to be a treatise on the place of reason in Arab thought and culture, the book in fact deals with the place of reason in Islamic thought. The distinction is important and, in this particular case, necessary. For Touqan here confines his inquiry exclusively to the Islamic period, refraining from mentioning anything about the role that reason played in either pre-Islamic Arab culture or what may legitimately be called the post-Islamic modern period, covering the past one hundred years or so. Besides, the overwhelming majority of the philosophers and theologians whose works are examined in this book were, strictly speaking, non-Arab Muslims.

Touqan refrains from involvement in any serious discussion of the relation between reason and revelation. His first chapter, entitled "The Meaning of Reason in Islam," deals with the place of reason in the Qur'an and the traditions, as well as in the works of the Prophet's companions, theologians, and Muslim savants (ʿulema). Reason, he establishes without much difficulty, occupies the highest place in Islamic thought. In addition to the suras cited from the Qur'an to reinforce his argument, Touqan cites some of Muhammad's own dicta on the subject: "Reason is the origin and the foundation of religion"; and "There is no religion for him who has not reason" (5).

Touqan deals with another specifically Islamic aspect of the subject—namely, *ijtihad* in Islam. He tries to show that in *ijtihad* (effort, study, exercise), the *mujtahid* (scholar) searches his reason and judgment when interpreting religious texts or assessing the authenticity of the traditions. *Qiyas* (analogical reasoning) is one form of *ijtihad*—a method by which the principles established by the Qur'an and other sources of Islamic law are extended and applied to the solution of problems not expressly regulated therein. Here, however, the author does not make it clear that although all this was formally quite the case, the role of juristic reasoning in Islam remained completely subordinate to the dictates of divine revelation. As any serious student of the *shariʿa* (Islamic law) knows, analogical reasoning and deduction in Islam must always have their starting point in a principle from the Qur'an, the *sunna* (customary practice), or *ijmʿa* (consensus), and cannot be used to achieve a result that contradicts a rule established by any of these three primary sources.

Touqan then turns to the place of reason in the works of the Muʿtazila, the great tenth-century theological school that gave rise to the speculative dogmatics of Islam as well as to a number of Islamic philosophers, such as al-Kindi, al-Farabi, Ibn Sina (Avicenna), al-Razi, Ibn Khaldun, and Ibn Rushd. He quotes profusely from all the sources and the thinkers with whom he deals, and these quotations serve to prove the book's thesis—namely, that reason occupied the highest place in Arab culture and in Islam. This, however, is plainly not the ideal method of objective, neutral inquiry, but as some Arab critics of Touqan's book pointed out at the time, it probably sprang from a desire to inspire and guide the Arab reader (166–174).

This tendency is even more pronounced in the concluding parts of the book, in which Touqan seeks to show that the Arabs knew of the modern scientific method, which is considered one of the discoveries of the present age, before the West did.

In the epilogue, Touqan deals briefly with the current state of Arab culture. In the past, he says, the Arabs managed to preserve the intellectual and scientific heritage of the Greeks, expand on it, and teach Europe its essence. In their present condition, the picture is widely different. Contemporary Arabs are in dire need of reviving the spirit of their heritage: "They will never be able to make their abilities productive . . . or their society flourish and reach fruition unless they liberate themselves completely from all kinds and forms of imperialism" (221), Touqan concludes, adding—as a last counsel—that the only way for the Arabs to achieve their aims and realize their potentialities is to believe in and practice freedom of thought and discard their fatalism and archaic beliefs.

FOUR

SELF-IMAGES OLD AND NEW

THE EGYPTIANS

One of the more striking results of the Yom Kippur War (October 1973) was how Egyptians, Arabs, and the world as a whole tended to change their images of the Egyptian as a person. Not only the Egyptians and their leaders, but many foreign observers also went on record, a few days after the outbreak of hostilities, as being greatly impressed by the discipline, daring, and resourcefulness the Egyptian soldier displayed in the course of the fighting. One foreign correspondent—Eric Silver of the *Guardian* of London—asserted that whatever the outcome of the war, the Egyptians had already shattered the myth that the Arab soldier was a coward, quick to flee when faced with an Israeli.

Outside observers' appraisals of Egyptian society and the Egyptian individual have never been too flattering. In that remarkable nineteenth-century compendium of anthropological information titled *An Account of the Manners and Customs of the Modern Egyptians,* the English traveler Edward William Lane asserts that

> influenced by their belief in predestination, [Egyptian] men display, in times of distressing uncertainty, an exemplary patience, and, after any afflicting event, a remarkable degree of resignation and rectitude, approaching nearly to apathy—generally exhibiting their sorrow only by a sigh, and the exclamation of "Allah kereem!" (God is bountiful!). . . . While the Christian justly blames himself for every untoward event which he thinks he has brought upon himself, or might have avoided, the Muslim enjoys a remarkable serenity of mind in all the vicissitudes of life. . . .
>
> The same belief in predestination renders the Muslim utterly devoid of presumption with regard to his future actions, or to any future events.

In another passage, Lane speaks of "indolence," which he says "pervades all classes of Egyptians, except those who are obliged to earn their livelihood by severe manual labor" (see especially Chapters 3 ["Religion and Laws"] and 13 ["Character"] of Lane's work; his descriptions are summarized in Nissim Rejwan, "Egypt's Search for a New Self-Image," 58–62).

Lane's observations were written in 1836. A century later, Ibrahim Abdul Kader el-Mazni, one of modern Egypt's most inventive and prickly writers, accused his fellow countrymen of being "given to luxurious living and indolence more than to power, courage and fighting—and have no knack for adventure" (the quotations in this paragraph and the next come from Rejwan, "Egypt's Search for a New Self-Image," 61–62). From 1936 to 1973—as an Egyptian writer put it once—Egypt "underwent important, radical changes, and today she faces a battle of destiny which she cannot wage from such a point of departure as those personality traits which el-Mazni had attributed to the Egyptian individual."

This discrepancy between what the Egyptian individual is and what he is called upon by circumstances to be drove Egyptian president Anwar el-Sadat to implement his Program for National Action, which set for himself and the Arab Socialist Union the goal of building a "modern State based on faith." There was hardly an aspect of society with which Sadat's program did not deal—combating illiteracy, accelerating the process of industrialization, modernizing agriculture, organizing Egyptian women for social and political action, instituting family planning, modernizing the state apparatus, and intensifying scientific research. In effect, the program called for nothing short of a revolution in the personality of the Egyptian individual, since, to quote Sadat again, "the construction of the new State cannot be accomplished without building the new man."

This, obviously, was an enormous task. In his well-known and widely quoted book *Al-Naqd al-Thati ba'd al-Hazima* (Self-Criticism after the Defeat; 1968), Sadiq Jalal al-ʿAzm detects a marked tendency in the Arab communications media to disavow responsibility and to blame others—a tendency that, he claims, became most pronounced following the debacle of June 1967. This tendency, al-ʿAzm argues, was closely related to a basic element in the structure of traditional Arab society and had a great deal to do with the kind of "social personality" that Arab society tends to cultivate in the individual. To support his thesis, the author cites studies conducted some years previously by a leading Egyptian social anthropologist, Hamdi ʿAmmar. On the strength of these studies, ʿAmmar discerned a certain personality type among the Egyptians, which he chose to call "the *fahlawi* personality." Not altogether unlike Spanish machismo, the fahlawi personality tends to substitute masculine bravado for the true essentials of fortitude (ʿAmmar's remarks are quoted in al-ʿAzm, *Al-Naqd al-Thati baʿd al-Hazima,* and in Rejwan, "Egypt's Search for a New Self-Image," 61–62).

The first characteristic of the fahlawi personality is "quick adaptability"; the fahlawi not only is capable of quickly adapting himself to new conditions and contingencies, but also can grasp quickly the kind of response expected of him and behave accordingly. This has two sides to it, as ʿAmmar points out. On the positive side are the flexibility, presence of mind, and ability to assimilate to the new; on the negative side is the tendency to respond superficially and with passing courtesy, the purpose of which is to evade facing real issues and to hide one's real feelings.

Another distinguishing feature of the fahlawi individual is his marked egocentrism and persistent tendency to show off in an effort to prove an unsurpassable ability to do things and dominate situations. This, ʿAmmar warns, is definitely not to be confused with self-confidence, a quality that springs from a person's genuine assurance of his worth and abilities. Unlike self-confidence, the fahlawi's attributes of egocentrism and ego inflation signify a lack of security and the refusal to evaluate situations objectively— as well as a very real sense of inferiority and an inability to face new situations. The kind of behavior to which this egocentric assertiveness leads, ʿAmmar says, sometimes takes the form of flippancy and a lack of caution, sometimes that of belittling others and making fun of them, and always expresses itself in an eagerness to prove that one is somehow capable of solving the insoluble and doing the impossible by mere gestures.

Disclaiming responsibility and attempting to blame others—a trait that ʿAmmar labels "disavowal and transfer"—is another characteristic of the fahlawi personality. "Perhaps the most significant aspect of this disavowal," ʿAmmar writes, "is the widespread habit of complaining about 'the times,' expressing impatience with those who disapprove of you, and invariably putting the blame on 'the government' and on the town which has no mayor." Another trait of the fahlawi personality is the preference given to individual over collective action. This, ʿAmmar points out, is not just egotism for its own sake; it is ineffectual self-assertiveness on the one hand and an unhealthy avoidance of others on the other. The fahlawi fears excess social contact because it can expose him to delicate situations in which he might feel overly insecure or else simply melt before the personalities of others.

The last characteristic of the fahlawi personality described by ʿAmmar is what he calls the tendency toward taking "the shortest path." This, again, has two sides to it. On the one hand, it can lead the fahlawi to commit spontaneous acts of daring and enthusiasm in the face of adversity; on the other hand, when effective action requires patience and diligence, the daring and enthusiasm soon peter out. This is one reason why Egyptian craftsmen, for instance, are often criticized for the lack of finish apparent in their work. It is easy enough to rouse people like this and fire their imagination for a time about a certain cause or goal, but it is often highly difficult for them to carry on with the care or perseverance to match their initial display of passion.

Unlike most social anthropologists, Hamdi ʿAmmar seems to be a believer in cultural selectivity—in distinguishing between the "good" and "bad" components of the same culture. In his section entitled "Positive and Negative Elements in Our Changing Culture," he urges Egyptians to try to make such distinctions so as to cultivate the former and try to weed out the latter. As examples of the latter, ʿAmmar describes a number of "complexes" from which he says Egyptian culture and society suffer. The first of these he calls "the authority complex," which he perceives in all of Egyptian history. In Egypt, where authority has always been strongly assertive, people have tried constantly either to avoid it or to appease and remonstrate with it, sometimes even to beg for mercy and humiliate themselves before it.

These are the qualities of what ʿAmmar terms "the authority-as-bogey complex." The result is that work is done in the required manner "only when subordinates feel that the boss possesses total control, and an element of intimidation is indispensable as an incentive to work: authority must be able to do harm and spring surprises." The other side of the coin in this complex is the desire to avoid all contact with authority and to lavish praise on everything it does—"just for the sake of appeasing it and avoiding its wrath."

Despite his scathing criticisms of many aspects of Egyptian culture and society, however, ʿAmmar is anything but pessimistic. The personality of the contemporary Egyptian, he explains, is the product of certain political, social, and economic circumstances through which Egypt has passed in its long history. The characteristics of this personality, therefore, are not immutable; on the contrary, they can be changed, readjusted, and reformed. ʿAmmar counterposes against the fahlawi personality what he terms the "productive personality"; this is what must be the predominant social type in the new Egypt.

Another ambitious study of the cultural traits of Egyptian society, written by Sayyid ʿAwis, one of Egypt's best-known social scientists, is entitled *Remarks about Culture: Some Facts concerning Egypt's Culture* (1970). The author describes it as springing from the setback of June 1967 and as a contribution "toward a modern society living in accordance with the values and concepts of the age" ('Awis's observations are quoted in Rejwan, "Egypt's Search for a New Self-Image," 61–62).

'Awis's thesis is that for Egyptians to plan and effect social change, they first have to understand the prevalent sociocultural reality: "We have to study our society, its structure and functioning, its values and ideals, and the factors making for stagnation and backwardness." He argues that, materially, Egyptian society is indeed in the process of active change. However, this change is accompanied by a persistent "cultural backwardness" that is apparent more in the nonmaterial components of social life—and most of these stand in direct opposition to the country's will to build a new, socialist society. Among them he enumerates attitudes toward death and the dead, relations between husband and wife, the spectacle of young scientists still believing in ghosts and witch doctors, pervasive fear of the evil eye, and the belief in an afterlife.

Yet despite this "cultural backwardness," 'Awis's conclusions are not as bleak as ʿAmmar's, for he also points to a number of "positive social values" capable of aiding modernization. Among these values, which 'Awis asserts are deep-rooted in Egyptian culture, are "patience, perseverance in collective efforts, faith in ultimate victory, readiness to volunteer for war, a satisfactory discharge of duty, spontaneous observance of laws and regulations, and a sense of responsibility." All these values, obviously, stand in distinct contradiction to the traits of the so-called fahlawi personality expounded by ʿAmmar.

"ROOTS OF THE TROUBLE"

Another sociological study written after the Six-Day War is worth mentioning here. *Hawla el-Masʾala al-Ijtimaʿiyya* (On the Social Question; 1970) by Muhammad Khalifa, a noted Egyptian social scientist and a former minister for social affairs, is concerned less with the components of Egyptian culture or the traits of the Egyptian personality than with Egypt's experiment in social change during the twenty-odd years after the Free Officers–led revolution of July 23, 1952. It consists of four parts—"Roots," which deals with the revolutionary social and intellectual process started in 1798 by the arrival of Napoleon's armies in Egypt; "Horizon," which deals with a number of possible vistas of sociopolitical development, such as democracy, socialism, revolution, and social organization; "Ploughing," whose central theme is growth in all its dimensions—human, social, and economic; and "Harvest," in which Khalifa subjects a variety of ideological misconceptions to severe scrutiny and criticism and gives his own prescriptions (Khalifa's observations are summarized in Rejwan, "Egypt's Search for a New Self-Image," 61–62).

ʿAwis and Khalifa wrote their books at a time when the War of Attrition on the Suez front was at its height. The cease-fire agreement that was concluded with Israel on August 8, 1970; Nasser's death, which came soon afterward; and Sadat, after making a great deal of warlike noise, apparently becoming resigned to the no-peace, no-war stalemate all combined to create a most somber Egyptian national mood. Apathy, remorse, and intellectual self-flagellation became rampant, and a number of leading Egyptian intellectuals and men of letters, such as Tawfiq el-Hakim and Naguib Mahfouz, started to agitate publicly for a quick end to the deadlock, even at the price of accepting Israel's terms for a settlement. But the Yom Kippur War changed everything. Egyptian opinion is indeed unanimous that the Ramadan War, as the conflict is called by Arabs, marked a turning point in the fortunes of the Arabs in general and the Egyptian people in particular. Many Egyptian writers and intellectuals—among them el-Hakim and Mahfouz—asserted that October 6, 1973, signified "a rebirth of the Arab nation." One Egyptian writer, Abdul ʿAzim Anis, on hearing of the Egyptian army's successful crossing of the Suez Canal, expressed his elation by sending the following telegram: "Had I not been an Arab I would have longed to be one!" (quoted in Rejwan, "Egypt's Search for a New Self-Image," 61–62).

As far as the Egyptians themselves were concerned, the war radically changed their self-image. The phrase "the October ethic" gained currency in Cairo's literary circles. Early in January 1974, Musa Sabri, editor of the Cairo daily *Al-Gumhouriya,* wrote a long article entitled "The New Revolution," which begins: "The truth is that our New Year started at 2 o'clock in the afternoon of October 6, 1973. Zero hour marks the birth of our new dawn." That historic hour brought the Egyptians "days of light," and the pressing question now was "how to preserve the purity of that light." An even larger and more meaningful question, according to Sabri, was "how are we to preserve the ethic of October 6, how to cultivate it and how to make it give more fruit?" (quoted in Nissim Rejwan, "The Arab Psyche," *Jerusalem Post,* June 13, 1975).

Delving a little deeper into this reappraisal, another Arab writer and university professor, the Egyptian ʿAlieddine Hilal, asked a number of piercing questions to which he proposed to give satisfactory answers. Writing in the London-based Lebanese daily *Al-Hayat,* Hilal begins "A Glance at the Arab Mentality" with well-defined, concrete matters and then goes on to tackle the more general subject of the state of "the Arab mind" today

(Hilal's article is quoted in Rejwan, "The Arab Psyche"). The questions he asks himself are given in the following order:

- What is the Arabs' contribution to agriculture today?

- What is their contribution to industry—apart from drilling for oil and other minerals?

- What have the Arabs achieved in the spheres of science and technology?

- What is the Arabs' record in the spheres of democracy and respect for human rights?

The answers to all of these questions, Hilal admits, are "a source of sorrow and remorse for us as a nation and as peoples, in that they make us realize how marginal a place we have in twentieth-century civilization." "For the fact," he adds, "is that we interact with this civilization as sellers and buyers, not as partners or contributors, and our dependence on the outside world, its industry, agriculture and science is on the increase rather than the decrease."

Turning from the particular to the general, Hilal points to a number of features of what he calls the Arab mentality that he considers negative and harmful. One of these is the tendency among Arabs and Muslims to perceive themselves as victims of a conspiracy—"an ongoing conspiracy that continues from generation to generation. States, regimes and rulers may change, but the conspiracy continues." What Hilal finds wanting in this kind of thinking is that it rules out any consideration of the real facts of a situation and excludes the possibility of reasoned historical inquiry.

Another shortcoming of the Arab mentality that Hilal enumerates is what he calls "the absence of priorities," a tendency to ignore the need for gradation and to try to realize all goals at the same time: "We want to attain democracy, social justice, economic development, technological progress, our distinctive national and spiritual values—all at once and in the same stage; the result is that in the end none of these objectives is achieved."

Other negative features of the Arab mentality pinpointed by Hilal include an absence of the concepts of give-and-take and compromise, which are the essence of the democratic process, and a related predilection for revolutionary change and military coups as means of, and alternatives to, a generally agreed-upon political process.

Another aspect of the Arabs' self-view subjected to critical scrutiny by Egyptian scholars and intellectuals is what these have termed "cultural chauvinism." One manifestation of this has to do with the school of thought known as *shuʿubiyya*. Shuʿubiyya, a historical concept rooted in the eighth century, originated in a fierce controversy in the Arab world concerning the cultural orientation of the newly established and expanding Islamic culture and society. Briefly, the issue at stake then was whether this culture and society were to embody a non-Arab culture into which Arabic and Islamic elements would be absorbed, or a culture in which foreign cultural contributions would be subordinated to Arab traditions and Islamic values. Those who advocated the ascendancy of non-Arab cultures were termed shuʾubiyya, a word deriving from *shuʿub* (the plural of *shaʿb* [people]).

Since those days, the term "shuʾubiyya" has been used to describe anti-Arab sentiments of all descriptions, and is still used as a polemical, emotionally loaded, and condemnatory adjective to discredit opponents of pan-Arab aspirations and ideology. In Iraq, especially, it was used freely as a term of abuse against communists and the left in general; the Baʿth Party and Arab nationalists generally used it to condemn General Abdel Karim Qassim of Iraq; Sunni Arab extremists use it against their Shiʿi compatriots for their general lack of pan-Arab fervor. In recent years, a spate of books and pamphlets have been written, mostly in Iraq but also in Lebanon, Syria, and Egypt, against alleged contemporary manifestations of shuʿubiyya. One of these, written by a well-known Iraqi historian and then dean of Baghdad University, ʿAbdel ʿAziz al-Douri, is called *Al-Judhur al-Taarikhiyya lil-Shuʿubiyya* (The Historical Roots of Shuʾubiyya; 1962), which, despite its academic title, remains a thinly veiled attack on contemporary opponents of Pan-Arabism.

Douri explains in his introduction how he came to write the book: "Voices have been heard advocating that the Arab heritage be discarded, disparaging Arab culture, attacking Arab and Islamic values, and considering it reactionary to turn to these values. These voices have begun to derogate the concept of an Arab Nation and are trying to spread dissension and revolt in the name of regionalism or racialism. . . . It is because of all this that the writer has sought to present a critical, scientific view of the roots of shuʾubiyya in Arab society" (1). It is made quite plain throughout the book that Douri's discourse amounts to little more than a historical parable from which clear and highly relevant conclusions must be drawn by contemporary pan-Arabs concerning the nature of their opponents.

It is therefore somewhat striking that this brand of Arab "cultural chauvinism" failed to impress Egyptian writers and intellectuals, fervent believers in Arab unity and Arab culture though they themselves were in the heyday of Nasser's Arab socialism. Ahmad ʿAbbas Salih, editor of Cairo's leading cultural monthly, *Al-Katib,* described the use of the shu'ubiyya bogey as dangerous and harmful: "Although they have used it to dispel anti-Arab nationalist trends, the weapon has proved to be two-edged—one edge, and the more dangerous of the two, leads to a despicable racialism and hysterical suspiciousness that attacks before it reflects or converses; the other edge is like an old weapon used to fight a new battle" (*Al-Katib,* February 1964).

In a later issue of the same review, another contributor, Abdel Jalil Hasan, took Douri to task for manifestations of prejudice and for "using a vague, generalized and misleading intellectual framework that makes him ignore the social significance of these [shu'ubiyya] movements." To Douri's contention that shu'ubiyya remained a danger, despite its failure to subvert Arab unity and undermine Arab culture, the Egyptian writer replied that "viewing all anti-Arab trends and events, both internal and external, in this unverified and uncritical way . . . leads to a failure to overcome the dangers which confront us today."

Another prominent Egyptian writer, Alfred Faraj, took up another aspect of Arab self-views. In an article titled "How Many Arabs Read?" Faraj writes: "We read recently that six million—or ten million—people visited the International Book Fair in Cairo; that publishers and distributors there sold eight—or twelve—million books or more; and that the cultural conferences and literary evenings held there . . . were attended by tens—or hundreds—of thousands of people" (in *Al-Wasat* [London], July 31, 1992).

"All these," adds Faraj, "are correct figures—touch wood." It is also possible, he continues, that there is in these statistics something to be proud of—something to make the Arab reader rest on his laurels or even go into a deep slumber. "But I have before me now an antidote to this," writes Faraj. "It is a report published by UNESCO a few years ago consisting of statistics about such matters as the paper consumed and the number of periodicals and book titles published in various parts of the world." He then goes on to quote some of the figures:

North and Central America, inhabited by 7.5 percent of the world's population, produce 16 percent of the newspapers and 15 percent of the books published overall, and their inhabitants purchase 270 issues of newspapers each annually, while the consumption of paper for books and periodicals amounts to 67 tons per year per thousand. Europe, with 4.5 percent of the world's population, produces 28 percent of all newspapers and 45 percent of all book titles published the world over, and the consumption of paper amounts to 23 tons per thousand annually.

After listing the statistics relating to Asia and Africa, Faraj turns to the Arab world, finding that the Arabs fall somewhere between the two. "We

Arabs," he explains, "who comprise 4.5 percent of the world's population, publish less than 1 percent of the newspapers published overall, and much less than 1 percent of the world's book titles. We consume only one-and-one-half tons of paper per thousand, and each 1,000 Arabs read 20 issues of newspapers per year."

Faraj follows with a number of complaints—the lack of bookshops and newsstands in large areas of Arab cities; the absence of schools and schoolchildren from cultural affairs like the Cairo book fair; the restrictions placed by Arab governments on the importation of Arabic books. He rejects the claim that television and video are to blame, citing the example of other, advanced societies.

REWRITING ARAB HISTORY

A rather more basic issue was addressed by a veteran historian from Lebanon. "How can Arab history be written in a satisfactory way," complains Nicola Ziadeh, the Damascus-born Lebanese historian, "when there is a religious and ideological veto against the historian?" (in *Al-Hayat* [London], July 19, 1992).

Ziadeh (who died July 27, 2006, age ninety-nine), a Christian, started his academic career in 1933 as a history teacher at Rashidiyya College, in Jerusalem, and after 1947 taught in many Arab and foreign universities. The author of thirty works of history in Arabic and English and translator of seven books from English and one from German, Ziadeh spoke from experience when referring to the religious and ideological veto wielded against Arab historians. In a series of autobiographical fragments and reflections published in the London-based daily *Al-Hayat,* he speaks of the exclusion of historians from writing Arab history, either for not being Muslim or for refusing to adhere to a particular ideology.

Ziadeh recalls that several committees had recently been formed specifically to rewrite Arab history. One such group, formed in Kuwait, was all Muslim; another, assembled in Iraq, contained one Christian Arab, but only because he was a leading follower of a certain ideology—an obvious reference to the pan-Arab Ba'th Party; yet another, whose members were selected by the Arab League, included no Christians. The only committee with a Christian as a member was based in Damascus; though the poorest materially and with the least access to resources, it was the most productive. The one Christian in the Damascus group was Ziadeh himself, who, though a lifetime resident of Beirut, accepted the offer after some hesitation.

Asked why he chose to concentrate on the early stages of Mamluk history and avoided writing on post–World War I Arab history, Ziadeh said that one ought not to forget that when an Arab student of history arrives at some findings and draws certain conclusions from them, he or she may find it advisable to refrain from making these public, owing to the suppression of freedom of thought. "When you cannot express your thoughts in freedom," he explained, "you cannot possibly present your public with a true version of events, lest the price you would then have to pay proves to be too high for you to afford. . . . This is why I decided to devote my research to the study of an earlier period of Islamic history."

Not that Nicola Ziadeh was in any way lacking in Arab-nationalist or pan-Arab sentiment. Like many of his generation of Greek Orthodox Arab writers and thinkers, he can even be said to have been one of the early advocates of the doctrine. In a two-volume 600-page tome titled *My Days (Ayyami)*, published in 1992 in Beirut and London, he writes: "When one contemplates the doctrine of Arab nationalism and pan-Arabism—especially those of us who believed in and advocated it—the idea seems to have passed through phases as confused and confusing as those who bore its banner" (quoted in *Al-Hayat* [London], July 19, 1992).

He then enumerates these phases, starting with the idealistic pre–World War I period, when Arab nationalism was a hope that filled every thinking Arab's heart with a vision of a future pan-Arab union, and then moving through its later phase, in the period between the two world wars and after. During this latter phase, he writes, the creed became a sort of rescue board and last resort. Whenever some setback occurred or some damage was done to the Arab body politic, Arab nationalism and Arab unity were presented as the panacea. "Writers dwelt on them at length; poets sang their praises—and we read and heard all this and became intoxicated by the beauty and the lofty dreams they evoked," he laments.

To illustrate this point, Ziadeh cites the case of Palestine and the Palestine question. When this problem came to the fore, he recalls, resort was habitually made to the Arab-nationalist and pan-Arab ideology. The Palestinians held to it with great hopes; others went on bearing its banner, intoning its slogans, and scattering promises—"and between those and these the issue kept losing momentum and clear purpose, while everybody swore they would, come Friday, pray in the Mosque of Al-Aqsa in Jerusalem, appealing to the spirit of Arabism and Arab unity to make that possible."

"A CRISIS OF RESPONSIBILITY"

A number of Arab thinkers who have delved into this and similar aspects of their people's predicament tend to attribute these mainly to what they deem a pervading lack of "a sense of responsibility." The "crisis of responsibility," as some of them call it, is seen by these writers to pervade not only Arab governments and political leaders in their relations with those whose affairs they have taken upon themselves to manage, but also the Arab individual himself in the discharging of his duties toward himself, his family, his society, and his country. Anis al-Qasim, author of *Maʿna al-Hurriyya fi al-ʿAalam al-ʿArabi* (The Meaning of Freedom in the Arab World), in fact considers a citizen's possession of a sense of responsibility "the most valid and accurate yardstick of [social] consciousness." The present generation of Arabs, he continues, bears the burden not merely of taking its own share of responsibility but also of disseminating and deepening a sense of responsibility in others (24).

Al-Qasim then enumerates the reasons for the Arab's present lack of such a sense. From a scrutiny of these reasons, one can obtain an idea of the societal shortcomings about which many Arab writers complain. Al-Qasim gives these in the following order:

1. Foreign rule: Centuries of foreign dominance robbed the Arabs of the opportunity to develop an adequate sense of responsibility. Imperialists naturally looked askance at anything likely to cultivate such a sense in their subjects, since a responsible citizen is perforce an opponent of foreign rule and refuses to carry out orders from overlords. For this reason, the imperialists chose to create a group of loyal local leaders with whose help they consolidated their rule. Needless to say, members of this group in turn had no interest in seeing a sense of civic responsibility grow among the populace.

2. The schools: Arab schools refrained, and many of them still refrain, from giving their pupils any practical training in collective action and the bearing of responsibility, concentrating instead on the job of memorizing lessons and passing examinations. Civics was taught as just another subject on the curriculum, and student groups and associations—in which pupils learn how to run representative bodies—were absent from schools.

3. Political organizations: Where these existed, they were not of the kind that could help citizens develop a sense of responsibility. In most

cases they were built around the name and personality of a leader rather than on clear principles.

4. Anomie: Lack of contact between government and the governed led to indifference toward what takes place in the public sphere, the feeling that the affairs of government are not of interest to the ordinary citizen. Even where political parties existed and elections took place, these parties reached out to citizens only at election time.

5. Poverty: This too contributed to the prevailing state of things. Those who spend all their time and energy making both ends meet materially cannot be expected to display much interest in public matters.

6. Ignorance: Knowledge and a correct appraisal of the facts are essential for the acceptance and appreciation of responsibility—and in this sense, ignorance about public affairs is a clear impediment to accepting responsibility for them.

7. Conscription: Compulsory military service was applied selectively and easily evaded—by means such as paying a fixed sum of money. This led to a situation in which citizens did not feel a responsibility for their homeland and its defense. (24)

Al-Qasim is aware of new developments and activities calculated to alleviate this situation, but he insists that a sense of responsibility will be cultivated not through preaching or the spreading of the right sociopolitical doctrines, but through practical training in the actual discharging of such responsibility. Social theories, he writes, "live and die within the framework of the life and the circumstances with which they have to deal" (24). Social ideas must be in keeping with the society's specific circumstances and its capacity to resolve its problems.

Qadri Hafiz Touqan too dwells on this subject of responsibility. In his view, the strength of a sense of responsibility in groups and individuals alike "is a criterion of society's progress and of its vitality" (*Maqam al-ʿAql ʿind al-ʿArab* [The Place of Reason in the Arab World]; the quotations in this paragraph and the next several are taken from pages 45–46). A well-developed sense of responsibility "denotes maturity and breadth of mind," while an undeveloped one "spells backwardness and limited goals and aspirations." Referring to the state of affairs in the Arab world, Touqan adds: "There is no doubt that the weakness of the sense of responsibility in the Arabs was one of the main reasons which landed them in failure and disaster. This weakness resulted in limited aims confined to a narrow compass of private interests, which made the individual view things and problems exclusively from the viewpoint of egotism and selfishness. There was thus no attempt to anticipate results or the grave and far-reaching effects of events."

The sense of responsibility "restrains the actions of the individual and his activities and makes him feel that he is not free in his movements," Touqan asserts. It restricts the various forms of his freedom and requires him to conduct them within the framework of the public interest.

> The nation or the group cannot elevate its life or make it mature and fruitful unless its members are guided by the limitations imposed by God and the interests of the homeland, and unless they are conscious of the responsibilities and burdens falling on their shoulders. They should feel that their faculties and what they produce are the property of the homeland and of mankind, and that they have to spend time in such a way as to improve the lot of the community and save it from ills. It is the duty of educational institutions and of thinkers and writers to work to make the individual aware of his responsibilities and the duties imposed on him by the general interest.

There is no doubt, too, that silence in the face of injustice, misrule, and disregard of the community

> is a crime toward the homeland, since this silence can only result in still more harm to the country and to the citizenry. The national duty and the general interest make it incumbent upon the individual not to sit still, and require him to direct his efforts and energies toward eliminating injustice and promoting reform and a respect for human rights. This is one of the elements of a sense of responsibility as well as one of its requirements; otherwise this sense loses its content. . . . We are nowadays in need of a strong sense of responsibility, which can give us enough strength and courage to resist abnormal conditions and do away with prevalent injustice. And this will not come about unless each of us believes in himself and in the homeland, and unless he realizes that life in its essence is a struggle for the good of the community, its progress and reform—and that struggle on any other basis is fruitless and can bring no progress and no good whatsoever.

While most of the Arabic literature of self-interpretation cited in these pages is written in a basically polemical, somewhat emotional way, more scientifically based sociopsychological writings on the subject are not completely absent. Such writings, however, ordinarily come from the pens of Arab scholars who received their training abroad and who, in the majority of cases, teach at Western universities. The most ambitious inquiry into Arab behavior undertaken by such a scholar is a book published in the United States and written by Sania Mahmoud Hamady, a Lebanese Muslim who finished her studies at the American University of Beirut in 1946 and worked as an assistant professor in the Department of Human Relations at the University of Miami. The book, entitled *Temperament and Character of the Arabs* (1960), covers a wide variety of sociopsychological aspects of Arab life and behavior.

It is not within the scope of this work to ask whether there is altogether such a thing as a fixed, immutable national character, or whether one can confidently speak of an ingrained, seemingly unchanging national temperament. Hamady is, however, of the opinion that all those reared in the same social institutions tend to exhibit the same salient regularities of behavior, i.e., characteristic "central tendencies towards common ways of thinking, acting and feeling" (3). Hamady was aware of the audaciousness of attempting the difficult task of studying the character and temperament of the Arabs. However, she justifies the venture by "the magnitude of the crisis in the Arab East" and the dire need to get acquainted with the behavior of a people whose moves she considers as carrying great significance for the international balance of power.

Only an idea of the scope of Hamady's investigation can be given here. According to her, for instance:

- The Arab promises more than he can give or do; he relates fantastic stories about himself and his family and asserts himself by boasting, without feeling any shame.

- The Arab is arrogant. He talks with a marked air of superiority and haughtiness. A proverb well describes Arab vanity: "Thousands of ladders do not reach his head."

- Praise of one's self and of one's family occupies a large part of Arabic poetry. It best illustrates this inflation of personality through self-praise and exaggeration. Glorification of the self or that of one's family disregards references to truths or events.

Of course, such finalistic assertions have to be taken with a good deal of caution. The risk involved in making them is obvious. For while it is true that people growing up in certain environments and under certain social institutions tend to have the same characteristics, these environments and institutions are themselves subject to change, and they vary at different times and in different localities. Thus, while it is quite legitimate to generalize from a fixed point in time and space, Hamady tends to generalize on the basis of selective evidence both from history and from the considerably variegated environments in which the Arabs in their various groups have lived throughout the ages. For instance, in support of her claim concerning the Arab's habit of self-glorification and his disregard for truth, Hamady offers quotations from the poems of Saif al-Dawla and ʿAmr ibn Kulthum—both of whom lived and sang their poetry centuries ago.

However that may be, Hamady has a number of very insightful things to say on her subject. In the chapter "The Arabs' Outlook on Life," she describes the Arabs' fatalistic attitude of mind. "The prevailing view," she writes, "is that the events of a person's life are determined from the very beginning. This is true to such an extent that he really has only to go through the course of events which have been written down for him in God's book to the smallest detail" (29). Holding such a thoroughly deterministic outlook, the Arab believes that "not even in everyday life can man do anything to hasten or otherwise influence what is going to happen to him" (31–32).

Of more interest is Hamady's chapter titled "Identification and Loyalties." The relevance of this chapter to the subject of Arab nationalism and Arab unity is evident. With his loyalty commanded only by personal relationships, the Arab sets his goal not in the interest of his nation; the improvement of the position of his family or, at most, his religious group is the Arab's primary aim; to serve one's family is the first prerequisite for gaining approval. The real problem of Arab nationalism, therefore, is how to help the Arab develop a sense of responsibility toward the public and find enough motivation to give his final loyalty to the larger group, the nation.

As an Arab, Hamady finds it necessary to give some explanation for her decision to embark upon her ambitious and outspoken investigation. The gist of it is her conviction that the times make it imperative for the Arabs "to submit to this critical self-analysis." She believes that it would not suffice for the Arabs merely to free themselves from "the corrupt authorities and institutions that have been inhibiting their human development." They need, in addition, "a simultaneous liberation in the psychological, social and ideological spheres." This type of emancipation will be the hardest, she believes, since it involves "liberation from self." To effect such a liberation, however, "one must know oneself well in order to determine which characteristics need to be changed and which should be preserved" (2).

Obviously, it is easier to talk about such a "liberation from self" than to state clearly what its precise attainment involves—not to mention actually bringing it about. One Arab writer who comes nearest to defining the implications of this "liberation" is Eli Salem, a Western-trained Lebanese Christian who taught in American and Lebanese universities. Pointing out that the problems of man and his responsibility are basic to Arab behavior, Salem asserts that there is in Arab society "a lack of belief in the capacity of reason to create, achieve, shape or even destroy man." In relegating all acts of creation to God, man is relieved of responsibility; "the need for understanding man, therefore, his purpose and his responsibility in promoting his personality, is most imperative in the Arab world; for without this understanding there is no hope for the modulation of the human problem." Salem continues:

> If the state is to undertake this function, it first must be governed by men who appreciate these values and who are in turn courageous enough to embark on radically new plans. They must be sincerely convinced of the seriousness of the task and of their accountability to the people and to history. Since we Arabs are not steeped in democratic heritage, it is natural for our leaders not to comprehend fully their role in service; and many of our leaders are not really convinced that they are the servants of the people. It will be some time before this political philosophy is actually believed and followed. For our world has had the misfortune of breeding masses who were always so poor, so ignorant, so reduced, so crushed by nature, religion, and society as to accept their lot without question. For the Arab world, indeed for the whole of Asia and Africa, the problem of the masses constitutes the deepest and most challenging problem of government. . . . The problem of "man" is the fount from which all the major conflicts in Arab life flow. This theme must be pondered again and again before the other problem, that of nature, is considered. (Salem, "Form and Substance: A Critical Examination of the Arabic Language," 22–23)

Al-Qasim and Salem, like al-Husaini and Touqan before them, were only continuing a somewhat novel chapter in the Arabs' pursuit of self-appraisal and self-view. It would indeed be no exaggeration to speak of the beginnings of an overall intellectual revision in the Arab world starting in the late 1960s. The Beirut monthly *Al-Adaab,* which at the time was the foremost politico-cultural organ in Arabic, called editorially for continued self-examination and reappraisal and produced a special issue titled "The Arab Cultural Revolution." One of its Iraqi contributors, Fadil al-ʿAzzawi, gave the new trend a fuller expression when he called for "a revolutionary thought with cultural dimensions" and for discarding "frozen intellectual frameworks" (*Al-Adaab,* January 1970, 14).

Speaking of "the new Arab generation," ʿAzzawi suggests that yesterday's modernists and revolutionaries were now obsolete—and that the new generation must supplant them in the same way that they themselves supplanted an older, intellectually more stagnant generation. One of the shortcomings of this "middle" generation, he writes, is that its men speak with those of the older one in the latter's own terms of reference, implying acceptance of their premises. What is really needed, however, is a total revision of concepts. This must be done, ʿAzzawi argues, "not in order to win one or two battles in this war but in order to build a homeland to which we may not be ashamed to belong—and in order to build a new Arab man."

The call implicit here for an overall, total revision of accepted concepts and values—a call for what amounts to a re-creation of "the Arab human being"—became widespread in Arab intellectual circles after the 1967 war. Louis ʿAwad, a veteran professor of English literature at Cairo University and literary editor of *Al-Ahram* at the time, described the prevalent cultural mood in Egypt in a book he published early in 1970. ʿAwad's position made his sentiments especially instructive and revealing. He was a literary critic and cultural historian of note; among other works, he translated Shelley and Keats into Arabic, wrote extensively on the theater, published a two-volume study of modern Egyptian intellectual history, and contributed hundreds of papers and articles on literary-political subjects.

ʿAwad's book, entitled *Al-Funun wal-Junun fi Auropa* (The Arts and Lunacy in Europe), is, on the face of it, an account of the author's trip in May 1969 to France and Britain—a kind of exploration of Europe's cultural moods and foibles, commissioned by his newspaper. Since he was particularly interested in the theater, the bulk of his book is devoted to a superficial enough survey of some fifteen European and American plays, including works by Bertolt Brecht, Arthur Miller, Peter Weiss, and others—as well as such ultramodern plays as *Hair.* As if in passing, ʿAwad also deals with the revolt of European youth, the student movement, and the hippies (7).

For our purposes, however, the most instructive part of ʿAwad's book is the opening chapter, entitled "A Spring Journey for Drying the Tears," in which he gives a candid and deeply felt account of the perplexities and soul-searchings that had plagued him since those days in June 1967. He describes his trip as "a journey of convalescence"—convalescence not from any physical ailment, but from the terrible shock of the events of June 1967, "which turned our hours into days, our days into years and our years into generations and generations" (8).

The shock, he continues, had "shattered the nerves, broken the heart with shame, and darkened the soul with despair." 'Awad then tries to define the nature of his country's present predicament: "Briefly, I believe that our predicament is neither military, nor political, nor economic, nor social, nor moral nor yet spiritual; it is all of these—it is a 'cultural' predicament." 'Awad continues:

> Egypt is like an iceberg, of which only an eighth is seen on the sea's sur-face, while seven-eighths remain in the deep. Our life is like an iceberg—an eighth of it is out in the light of the 20th century, seven-eighths in the darkness of the Middle Ages. We are in the same stage as Europe was during her age of transition from medieval times to the Renaissance; we were in labor in the 19th century . . . but the baby was stillborn—and when the embryo again took shape at the turn of the century, it was again mercilessly aborted. Our real battle is one between the old and the new, between reaction and progress; even democracy and socialism seem impossible to attain in the absence of a movement towards humanism, religious reform, and a cultural revolution. (9–10)

FIVE

CALLS FOR "CRITICAL SELF-ANALYSIS"

DEPENDENCE AND FATALISM

Variations on the themes of responsibility and morality are to be found in most Arab writings on self-interpretation and self-appraisal, though mostly in a political vein. George Hanna—a Marxist of sorts, a Lebanese Christian, and an advocate of revolution and socialism who was often excited by the Egyptian revolutionary experiment of the 1950s and 1960s—wrote a good number of books and pamphlets exhorting contemporary Arabs to take matters into their own hands and start freeing themselves from the many fetters that impede their movements and their progress. Some of these fetters are self-imposed or at least "homemade," Hanna says. He believes that the primary cause for the prevailing backwardness of the East are its two age-old maladies—"dependence and fatalism." The most harmful aspect of dependence, he writes, is that the people "throw the burden of responsibility upon their rulers and leaders." The leaders "bend under the burden because they are not [true] leaders, but imposed leaders only, eager to shirk the responsibility wrongly entrusted to them by the people, who, in turn, entrust responsibility to those who value it only as much as it is of benefit to themselves" (Hanna, *Maʿna al-Qawmiyya al-ʿArabiyya* [The Meaning of Arab Nationalism], 60).

The strange thing is that the people and their imposed leaders "busy themselves with wailing and lamentation while dependent on the merciful, benevolent foreigners so that they might volunteer to relieve us and ward off catastrophe from our people and country" (60). What Hanna finds even more startling is that "the imposed leaders continue to impose their leadership and the people continue—inwardly or outwardly—to believe in that leadership, burning incense before them, clamoring for them, keeping quiet about their imposed leadership, submitting to their orders and instructions, waiting for aid to come from them or through them via those who furnish such aid—or, more correctly, via those who sell such aid at the price of dignity and pride" (61). How good it would be for both the people and their leaders to know that asking for help is a sign of weakness, that the donation of aid is a trap set up by the strong for the weak so that the weak will continue to be weak, rendering their subjugation and control of their work rather easy!

According to Hanna, the Palestine catastrophe, "from A to Z," can be summed up as follows:

> During the battle and after our defeat in it, in the conferences held for studying it and in the conferences that are still being held for the purpose of solving it or pretending to solve it, in the contemplation of the hardship that had befallen our homeless and bereaved brethren, in the demonstrative charity made by the charitable politicians, in the propaganda behind which they hide the aims and intentions they want to achieve through these acts, in the promises made by those who do not set any store by promises and declarations: I say this catastrophe, in both its external and internal manifestations, is only one of a thousand proofs of the evasion of responsibility by those who are responsible, and is a true illustration of a dependent soul. It is impossible for this nation to stand on its feet if its youth will not act. (61–62)

Addressing members of the new Arab generation, Hanna continues:

> I have described the age in which you will live as the age of liberation and emancipation. I have called it the age of liberation and not the age of freedom because I have grown tired of this word, since so many speak it, manipulate its meanings, pay it lip service, and sing its praises in their speeches while in their hearts they harbor a great grudge against it, sacrificing it through their acts, and assaulting its values while they falsely and untruthfully claim to be protecting it. Cursed be such a freedom if those responsible for it are subjugated! Cursed be such a freedom if those speaking in its name are liars and deceivers! I warn you, O young man, against a freedom that is subjugated mentally, materially, and ideologically. I warn you against a false, deceitful freedom afraid of emancipation, whose heroes are in fact afraid of any movement that would lead to liberation and emancipation . . .
>
> The first, and most important, and probably the only factor that counts in a movement for liberation and emancipation is that of reason, which distinguishes man from all other creatures. This creative reason—

and reason is creative in its very nature—is the supreme supervisor and regulator of man's life.

Hanna continues his warnings about false teachers: "They talk to you about idealisms and abstract philosophies that reason cannot grasp. . . . They recite to you what the philosopher of Ma'arri, Abul ʿAlaa, had said: 'They have lied: there is no Imam but reason, which is the everlasting guide.'"

"In the past," he adds,

> man lived in ignorance, dominated by spiritualism and superstitions and vacillating between contented fatalism and aimless revolt. Man remained in his deplorable condition until the nineteenth century dawned and human reason began to liberate itself from its age-old fetters. Since then, a savage war has been raging between reason and spirit. Now, in our own age, there is no doubt that the spiritual trend is weakening, chiefly because the spiritualists cling to an abstract metaphysical philosophy incapable of being grasped by reason. Now, if we divide the world into East and West—the first saturated with spirituality and insisting on it, the second actually discarding it, though pretending to adhere to it in words—we would find that spiritualism was the most important single factor responsible for the backwardness of the East and its subjugation by the West. (60–62)

This subjugation, according to Hanna, started "when the West began to turn away from its spirituality and gave its place to a philosophy of knowledge and of creative reason" (62).

Hanna continues in his own rather verbose manner:

> Spirituality and knowledge do not go together except in a small—a very small—measure. Spirituality belongs to the unfathomed and the unknown. . . . I shall anticipate attacks by the clergy and say right away that spirituality is not religion. More than that, I would say that spirituality humiliated religion when it made of it a convenient instrument in the hands of those who feign zeal for it. In essence, religion is a humanist and social philosophy that the ancients related to the unknown because science had not reached the level it has reached in our present age. (62–63)

Concluding his passionate call for the supremacy of reason and the discarding by the East of its spirituality, Hanna beseeches his young listeners:

O young men, they have lied, those who claim that mental emancipation is a blasphemy. Verily, it is they themselves who are blasphemous. If they believe that there is no religion without reaction, fanaticism, dependence, fatalism, and narrow-mindedness, we pity them, because they are misled. But if they uttered what they did not believe out of motives of propaganda, politics, or deception, it would be better for us to disown them, because they mislead. Yours, O young men, is a liberated and liberating mission. It is your duty to your country; nay, it is your duty to yourselves to accomplish this mission most thoroughly. (63)

"WHAT'S WRONG WITH MY MIND?"

In an earnest search for answers to the multiplicity of complex questions asked so frequently in the Arab world, Dawood Sayegh, an enterprising reporter on the staff of the Lebanese weekly *Al-Usbuʿ al-ʿArabi,* in 1975 asked a number of Arab psychologists, sociologists, neurologists, and educationalists such unusual questions as "What's wrong with my mind?" and "What is the Arab mentality?"

The first to whom Sayegh addressed his questions was ʿAlaeddine el-Duroubi, a well-known Syrian psychiatrist working in Beirut. For many years he had been examining and treating scores of fellow Arabs with one sort of mental disorder or other. Did he know what was going on inside the Arab psyche? Here is his answer as recorded by Sayegh: "Once upon a time something big happened to the Arabs, some enormous accident known as the Great Conquests [which followed the rise of Muhammad, in the middle of the seventh century]. Round this past chance happening revolved, and continues to revolve, all the Arabs' notions and sentiments—the Glorious Past, the Great Heritage, and such like. Today the Arabs huddle together and reminisce about this great event that took place in the far distant past" (Duroubi and the others interviewed by Sayegh—Barakat, al-Wardi, and Shamʿun—are quoted in *Al-Usbuʿ al-ʿArabi* [Beirut], July 12, 1975).

However, if we stop to consider the condition of the Arabs today, what do we find? "Why are the Arabs today so disunited?" Duroubi asked. His own reply: "Because of ignorance!" And what is the cause of this ignorance? Poverty! And the cause of the poverty? Backwardness! And backwardness, of course, is caused by . . . And so on and on, "until we find ourselves caught in a whirlpool. And then we start blaming it all on the foreigner. But this is wrong, since weaker nations than the Arabs have managed to get rid of the foreigner."

What was to be done then? Duroubi's answer was unambiguous. He believed that the key to future action and to regeneration lay in "ignoring the past and starting from the present—ignoring that enormous accident which has so far symbolized a whole world, and starting to grapple with present realities and problems, which tend to get bigger and more complex because of our inability to deal with them, which itself results from our being preoccupied with a past coincidence that is fast evaporating."

But, the bewildered reporter wondered, if the past and its accidents and coincidences were to cease to be the unifying factor in the Arab world, what would become the great common denominator? Duroubi admitted he did not know. He declared: "I doubt whether the major differences can be made to disappear by less than major trends. For what are the basic factors that can bring the Arabs together? Arabism? This term needs four dictionaries to explain its meaning. Religion? It does not seem to unite us. Leaders? They tried and succeeded not. A defeat? It happened to us more than once, and yet we remain disunited. Language? We all know that it is not the much sought-after common denominator. Speaking quite candidly, I am rather pessimistic about the whole state of affairs."

Somewhat disappointed, Sayegh went to Halim Barakat, professor of sociology at the American University of Beirut. "To know what goes on inside the Arab mind," Barakat said, "we have to know the sources of the Arabs' values. These sources are three in number: religion, the family, and class."

Religion is by far the most important of the three sources, Barakat explained. The values derived from it are absolute rather than relative, since they are seen as emanating from God: "It thus becomes difficult to distinguish between ends and means—and our thinking is consequently reduced to slogan mongering, since it leans on the absolute." These values are also backward-looking rather than forward-looking—which makes the Arab excessively preoccupied with the past. They are also fatalistic, leading to a view of man as creature rather than creator, powerless in the face of his pre-ordained condition, which, in its turn, is to be accepted rather than fought against. Finally, these values tend to stress charity and mercy as against justice and right: "To be charitable to those whose fate it is to be poor is more rewarding than to try to change their condition."

The family is the source of other, no less objectionable values, Barakat continued. Chief among these is the one that makes the individual a member of his family rather than a person in his own right. "As member of a family," he explained, "you have to carry the burden of the behavior of any of its members—hence the traditions of vendetta and of protecting family honor by eliminating those who violate it."

Lastly, there are class values. "Two-thirds of all Arabs work in agriculture," said Barakat, "and this is the source of many values that can be linked to those derived from religion and the family. Fatalistic notions, for instance, are most widespread among the deprived classes." Accepting prevalent conditions and obeying authority are some of the values taught by Muslim religious savants and philosophers close to the powers that be, Barakat concluded.

ʿAli al-Wardi, professor of sociology at Baghdad University, is a renowned social anthropologist and author of two much-quoted studies of Iraqi society. He told Sayegh that he believes the Arab of today lives through an ebb-and-flow duality of nomadism and civilization. Whenever an Arab country is strong and stable enough to ensure the security of its citizens and put various safeguards into place, nomadic values suffer a setback; but as soon as weakness prevails, nomadism makes a comeback, with all its drawbacks and fanaticisms.

From time immemorial, el-Wardi added, Arab society has given more weight to words than to deeds. The most striking social value of the Arab, past and present, has been heroic performance in war and the predominant role of the word. Another shortcoming of Arab society has been the huge gulf separating rulers from ruled. The eradication of these shortcomings will not be accomplished by force or through coercion, but through the introduction of a rational educational system that would stop looking backward, el-Wardi concluded.

Finally, Sayegh sought the help of an educational psychologist, Maiz Shamʿun. The mentality of the Arab, Shamʿun asserted, has certain characteristics that differ from those, say, of Western man. One of these traits is "the supremacy of emotion," which makes it difficult for the Arabs to gain objective scientific knowledge. Then there is this lack of confidence in the self, which itself is part of a general inferiority complex.

Another Arab personality trait is what Shamʿun called "compensatory behavior," such as an excessive preoccupation with sex and, more important, the use of words and slogans as a means of concealing realities. Finally, fatalism—which results from fear and a lack of self-confidence. "A fatalist is he who waits for change to take place without doing anything to bring about such change," Shamʿun explained.

But the Arab personality has some positive traits too. In Arab culture, for instance, man is seen as being above political regimes and administrative barriers. The concept of time, moreover, is such that an Arab does not consider himself its slave, according to Shamʿun.

While Sayegh and his interviewees were agitated by such topics as the "Arab mentality" and what had gone wrong with it, others tended to aspire to higher things. Ghalib Halsa, for one, writing in the Beirut cultural monthly *Al-Adaab,* asserted that what the Arabs needed most was "an all-embracing Arab philosophy reflecting the phase through which we live and furnishing, at the same time, a program to guide us in our path" (Halsa's observations are quoted in Nissim Rejwan, *Nasserist Ideology: Its Exponents and Critics,* 80–81). Halsa submits that the most serious obstacle to creating such a philosophy is the Arab's insistence on rejecting all ideas derived from the experiences of other peoples, "on the ground that they are imported ideas born in surroundings different from ours and invoking values and ideals foreign to our own." This attitude, he says, springs from a "failure to distinguish between what is positive and what is negative in the human heritage." A healthier attitude toward the creation of a fertile Arab philosophy would be "to consider the positive aspects of all philosophies valid and useful for us."

Halsa lays part of the blame at the door of the intellectuals. Failure to formulate such a philosophy, he claims, is nothing but "an expression of the intellectuals' despair of themselves and of their intellects." He accuses the Arab intellectual of betraying his true mission. For him, the intellectual is by definition a revolutionary "who speaks of the future and proclaims a state of permanent protest against the present. . . . The intellectual who concentrates on praising what exists is a traitor to his mission." Halsa then demands candidly that the intellectual be permitted to play his role in full. Citing the case of Stalin's Russia, he warns, "The consequences will be grave and terrible if we fail to give the intellectuals an opportunity of performing their role properly and in a positive manner." This means, he explains, that the intellectual cannot be an official thinker serving the immediate ends of any regime. He deplores "the prevalent belief that the best way of treating the intellectual is to flood him with privileges and make of him a well-to-do man." What helps spread this belief is that many intellectuals "reach for material gains with great eagerness and are willing, for the sake of these gains, to surrender everything."

Yet, despite the damning indictment, all the more striking for its frankness and candor, Halsa in the end fails to outline even in the broadest terms the all-embracing Arab philosophy that he says the Arabs so direly need. This is rather typical of most of the discussions periodically conducted in Egypt and other Arab countries about the meaning of the Arab cultural heritage and the need for an authentic Arab culture and outlook. A most perceptive comment on the subject was made by Fuad Zakariyya of Cairo University, the doyen of Egyptian philosophy professors and author of numerous books on modern and contemporary Arabic thought. Commenting on Halsa's plea for Arabs to accept the positive aspects of all philosophies as valid and useful for them, Zakariyya reflects that although the plea sounds quite reasonable, it presupposes that the Arabs in their present condition can distinguish between what is positive and what is negative in other philosophies. Yet to be able to make such distinctions, you have to have a basis for judging. In other words: "In order for the Arabs to have a philosophy, they must have a philosophy!" (quoted in Rejwan, *Nasserist Ideology,* 81).

CONSPIRACY THEORIES UNDER ATTACK

One aspect of Arab culture said to influence Arab behavior, and that has come under attack, is a reliance on conspiracy theories. Belief in conspiracy theories, or what one might term the conspiratorial interpretation of history, is as old as known human history and is not peculiar to any race or culture. However, rightly or wrongly, the phenomenon in more recent times has been increasingly associated with the political culture of the Middle East.

And with good reason, too, as far as appearances go. During the past several decades, and especially since the defeat suffered by Arab armies in the first Arab-Israeli war (1948–1949), Arabs have perceived virtually every setback as being the result of some Western-Zionist conspiracy. To cite a recent example, the late Iraqi president Saddam Hussein responded to the imposition of a "no-fly" zone over southern Iraq by accusing the United States, Britain, and France of conspiring to break up the Iraqi state and seize control of its oil.

The phenomenon has not escaped students of psychology and the social sciences. One of these, Jon W. Anderson, lists a number of what he calls "master narratives" that "perform yeoman interpretive service in indigenous political analysis in the Middle East" (Anderson, "Conspiracy Theories, Premature Entextualization, and Popular Political Analysis"; quotations from this article are drawn from pages 98–99). Among these are widespread conspiracy theories related to the United States and Israel, neo-imperialism, and Western economic interests. The last one, says Anderson, "has supplanted dashing nineteenth-century uniformed imperialists with grey-flannel and blue-serge financial ones." Local conspiracy theories focus on internal events, such as "fixed elections." In the world of the conspiracy theorist, indeed, "the only things that happen by chance are how one discovers the conspiracy; the only mistakes are those of the losers."

Anderson's observations throw further light on this fascinating subject:

> Such kinds of conspiracy theories, and an overall prevalence of the genre, index less psychological fear than interpretive confidence. The confidence is placed first in certain master narratives, of stories well known "already," and very familiar, perhaps too familiar, so rooted in experience as to be experienced repeatedly and thus to have taken over experience. In such a setting, then, the story takes on the characteristics of an art form: it has an aesthetic, which first sets a standard and then, through competition, invites exceeding or perfecting the standard. At this point, conspiracy theories have the characteristics of literature. . . . Classically, traditionally, literature in the Middle East is marked as being imaginative, whether as epics or as morality tales. . . . It is marked, literally, as "expressive" culture—that is, of a sensibility that refines everyday consciousness, experience and routines. This is a literature that exaggerates more than mimics (simulacra are not its forte) in order to reveal a hidden behind the apparent, [an] inner meaning behind outer experience that turns the latter into a parable, which in turn draws its power from its aesthetic properties.

So, too, may conspiracy theorizing, writes Anderson: "This is a field not just of imagination but of competition in interpretation, and there are prizes in the form of authority and influence for adept interpreters. The tests here are less tests of truth, in the philosopher's sense, than of adherence or correspondence to additional, other, not initially apparent information."

Inevitably, the conspiracy theory gradually became something of a national obsession, and many publicists, propagandists, and scribblers in the Arab world have gotten used to the convenience of attributing momentous events of the recent past—especially those that ended in failure or defeat—to plots carefully and darkly engineered by Zionists, Western imperialists, or both in unison.

One of the more systematic examples of this approach to contemporary Arab history is a book published in the mid-1990s in Beirut by a little-known outfit boasting the name Arab Center for Research and Documentation. The 407-page book is entitled *The West's Conspiracy against the Arabs: Signposts in the Phases of the Conspiracy and the Resistance to It,* and the author is Brigadier-General Dr. Yassin Sweid, described as "a prominent intellectual and revolutionary scholar" (excerpted in Nissim Rejwan, "Arab Conspiracy Theories," 40).

The book comprises five parts. The first enumerates the phases of the conspiracy, starting with a conference held in London by the European powers in 1905, a meeting that Sweid dramatically calls "the conspiracy of the age." Then come, in succession, the Sykes-Picot Agreement (1916), the Balfour Declaration (1917), the failure of the Syrian uprising against the French Mandate (1925), the UN Partition Plan for Palestine (1947), and the armistice agreements that Israel signed with Lebanon, Egypt, Syria, and Jordan in 1949.

The other four parts are devoted, respectively, to Arabs' resistance to Western-Zionist plottings against them, starting with the Arab Revolt of 1917 and ending with the Palestinian intifada of the late 1980s; the Gulf War of 1991 and the Arab-Israeli peace conference in Madrid later the same year; Lebanese resistance to the Israeli invasion of 1982; and an outline of what the author perceives as "Futurist Trends." A selection of documents is appended.

An even more exotic illustration of just how far the conspiracy-theory imagination can be indulged is provided by a work purporting to deal with Zionism and Islam. In a book bearing that title, a well-known Egyptian Islamist polemicist, Anwar al-Jundi, sets out to show that Freud's invention of psychoanalysis coincided with the birth of the Zionist movement; that psychoanalysis is not a science, "as Freud claimed"; that "it has had close relations with the Jewish-Zionist mind and heritage since the emergence of the Jewish Bible"; that Jews and Zionists launched a tremendous propaganda campaign aimed at spreading Freud's teachings; and that "it has been conclusively proved that Freud was in fact a Jew, that he was active in certain organizations, and that he was a personal friend of Herzl's" (quoted in Rejwan, "Arab Conspiracy Theories").

It is interesting to note that al-Jundi, a Muslim fundamentalist, in making these claims, cites the writings of a Christian writer, a certain "Dr. Sabri Jurjus," who is also quoted (never with any references or footnotes) as saying that "the organic, mutually-beneficial and fateful relation between Judaism, Zionism, and imperialism on the one hand and Freudian psychoanalysis on the other hand has made these three movements [sic] a trinity consisting of racialism, superiority, and corruption—a trinity which constitutes a challenge and a threat to mankind and its future."

From these wild claims, al-Jundi finds it rather easy to go on to show that Zionism has a blueprint for the destruction of the world. Among "the many books and documents" said to provide proof positive of this, he claims, is a book entitled *The World after Zionism*, written by one Commander William Carr, which includes this passage: "Zionism is behind every revolution that has been staged and every war that has been waged. It is behind all corruption, behind all subversive ideologies—Communism, Nazism, Fascism, and Freemasonry—and its aim is the destruction of religions and the domination of the world so that the kingdom of Satan can be established."

Despite purporting to deal with Zionism and Islam, this tract contains little, if anything, on the former's alleged attitude to the latter. Toward the end, al-Jundi quotes freely from the same Commander Carr to the effect that by establishing the state of Israel in Palestine, Zionism aims to make that state a starting point for a total war of destruction whose arena will be the Islamic world. This is because Zionism "seeks to destroy Islam, as Islam is the last force being confronted by the forces of evil." This war, al-Jundi writes, has already started; it is what is taking place now, what with the campaign being waged to destroy the Islamic creed and to contain it by way of spreading foreign ideologies.

Though published in the post–Yom Kippur War period and after Sadat's peace initiative, *Zionism and Islam* properly belongs to what can be called the anti-Semitic phase of the Arab literature on the conflict. It is also to be noted that the pamphlet is number three in a series of ten—all written by al-Jundi—under the general title *On the Road to Islamic Authenticity*, which was brought out by an obscure publishing firm called Dar al-Ansar. Other titles in the series include such purely Islamic topics as the concept of civilization in Islam, Islam and the idea of history, imperialism and Islam, Islamic education, and "one thousand million Muslims on the threshold of the fifteenth century to the Hijra." There is almost no doubt, in fact, that much of the contents of this pamphlet—as well as others in the same series—are a rehash of something written by the author some years or even decades back.

Brigadier-General Sweid's—like al-Jundi's—is what might be called the habitual or classic Arab-nationalist approach to contemporary Arab history. However, in the wake of more recent developments—the end of the Cold War, the war in Iraq, the almost unprecedented inter-Arab splits and conflicts, and the prospects of peace with Israel—new voices are calling for a comprehensive reappraisal of the Arab situation. No aspect of Arab behavior or thinking is being spared—Arab nationalist ideology and Arab unity; ethnic and religious minorities in the Arab world; the position of women; human rights; the prospects of democracy in the various Arab states.

Among several other such sensitive topics—until recently treated as sacred cows—the conspiracy theory too has come under fierce criticism. A few striking but fairly typical examples will be cited here. In two well-argued and carefully documented articles in the London-based Islamist weekly *Al-ʿAalam* (widely thought to be sponsored and financed by the Islamic Republic of Iran), Mahmoud Muhammad al-Naqooʿ, a Libyan, warns eloquently of the dangers of conspiracy theories. In the first, entitled "The Conspiracy Theory in Contemporary Muslim Thought," Naqooʿ outlines the tenets of the theory, its widespread use in Arab and Islamic political writings, and the ways that it has been exploited and manipulated in futile attempts to explain away and justify the failures and setbacks experienced by Muslim Arabs since the late nineteenth century (quoted in Rejwan, "Arab Conspiracy Theories," 40–41).

What Naqooʿ finds especially alarming is that the conspiracy theory gradually expanded to cover not only the alleged machinations of the West and the Zionists but also certain recent phenomena within the Arab and Muslim worlds—such as the modernist movement in Islam, its founders, and its leading proponents.

In the second article, "The Conspiracy Theory in Muslim Thought and Its Negative Dimensions," Naqooʾ goes a little further, enlisting the support of no less an authority than Islam's holy book, the Qurʾan. Quoting chapter and verse from a work by the Muslim scholar ʿImad al-Din Khalil, *The Islamic Interpretation of History,* he infers that the conspiracy theory is tantamount to a heresy. The Qurʾan, Naqooʿ argues, adopts and teaches a wholly different approach from that advanced by exponents of the conspiracy theory—an approach of "lection, contemplation, reflection, open-mindedness, reasoning, cause-and-effect, and strict accuracy"—in short, "the approach of active intellectual effort in search of the truth." The conspiracy theory, Naqooʿ concludes, usually gains ground when nations pass through periods of weakness, frustration, and decline—"when society is unable to meet challenges, fails to resolve its problems, and loses confidence in its potential, so that it turns to forces outside itself in search for explanations and justifications" (41).

A rather more focused and systematic assault on Arab conspiracy theories comes from Egypt. In an article in the Kuwaiti monthly *Al-ʿArabi,* the aforementioned philosophy professor Fuad Zakariyya takes his cue from a long summary-review that appeared in Cairo's leading weekly, *Al-Musawwar,* of Paul Kennedy's best-selling book *Preparing for the Twenty-first Century* (Zakariyya's observations are quoted in Rejwan, "Arab Conspiracy Theories," 41–42). In that article, whose author Zakariyya does not name, Kennedy is praised very highly for his erudition, his insights, his mastery of his subject, and the overall validity of his conclusions.

What Zakariyya finds inexplicable, however, is that the praise so generously heaped on Kennedy suddenly turns to abuse when the *Al-Musawwar* reviewer deals with those passages in the book concerning the Arab and Muslim worlds, finding it especially vexing that Kennedy "is influenced by the classical Western approach in these matters," arguing as he does "that the majority of Arab and Muslim states are unprepared for the 21st century since they remain stuck in the 19th."

When Kennedy deals with the Middle East, the *Al-Musawwar* reviewer continues, "he abandons his neutrality and his erudition in history and in strategies, replaying the old and broken gramophone record to which we have grown so weary of listening; for he suggests that the Arab states lag behind in the march of civilization, that they are weighed down by rivalries and competition, that the terror groups place the future of Algeria, Morocco, Jordan and Egypt in grave danger, and that what has lately taken place in Lebanon constitutes an object-lesson in the uses of sheer force, an illustration of how the strong swallows up the weak."

After citing these damning remarks, Zakariyya writes that he finds it astonishing that the thought never seems to have crossed the reviewer's mind that Kennedy's depictions of the Arab situation might be accurate. He reminds the reader "that the Muslim reformers and leaders of the modernist movement in Islam of the late 19th century kept warning their fellow-Muslims that the same problems besetting the Muslim world at the time would continue pursuing [them] through the 20th century."

Nay, he adds, the situation has even worsened: "We continue to consider the veil and women's going out to work a problem. We still differ on the day a lunar month starts, thus casting doubts on the usefulness and accuracy of science and its tools. We continue to be skeptical about the sciences themselves, expending great efforts in convincing people that the universe is governed by fixed laws. Indeed I do think that our intellectual standard at the end of the past century was higher than it is today."

Coming closer to the main subject of his essay—curtly entitled "The West: That Eternal Conspirator"—Zakariyya dwells on what he terms "the everlasting suspicion with which Arab intellectuals keep viewing the West and everything Western—so much so that the very name West has become almost synonymous with that of the devil." To be sure, he adds, suspicion of the West is understandable—"this West that has reduced us to colonial status and continues to try to impose its hegemony on us by a variety of means. However, when this frame of mind becomes merely a search for ways that are diametrically opposed to those of the West, suspicion becomes a sign of sickness that calls for serious soul-searching on our part."

Enumerating a few such symptoms ("a considerable sector of Arab intellectuals seems ready to deny the fact that the sun rises every morning if this truism is uttered by a Westerner!"), Zakariyya argues that at the root of all this "lurks the idea of the eternal Western conspiracy against the Arabs and Islam—an idea of which we convinced ourselves and with which we feel quite comfortable." The idea is convenient because "it performs a number of useful roles in our lives: It absolves us from confronting our drawbacks and from making the efforts needed to amend them . . . it gives us a cozy feeling of self-importance, since it is we, and no one else, who are the target of that conspiracy which the West keeps busy engineering day and night— we and not Japan, China and the rest—we alone who sow fear in the West and deny it sleep."

"Consider Paul Kennedy, for example," writes Zakariyya.

Kennedy was an eminent professor and an objective, keen scholar when he dealt with any part of the world. However, as soon as he turned to dealing with our part of the world he became a liar, shallow and an automaton reiterating those tired prejudgments currently prevalent in his environment. There is no doubt that what made Kennedy do this is the fact that we are more dangerous, greater, and more important than the world's mightiest giants—otherwise why should the West keep losing sleep in an effort to perfect the conspiracy against us of all the rest!

Zakariyya concludes:

Lastly, this widespread belief in the existence of a global conspiracy the West has been engineering against us, and us alone, tends to fire the imagination of the masses and give them a feeling of happiness unsurpassed by the effects of any hard drink or drug. For the fact, you see, is that everything is just fine with us, and the fault is wholly that of the conspiratorial West—and here is our opportunity to avenge ourselves in this seemingly unending historical vendetta.

In my personal experience, anyone who plays this melody in the course of a lecture or a symposium in any Arab country is hailed with resounding applause from the public, whereas one who tries to awaken a sense of responsibility in his listeners or shake them out of the ecstasy of the alleged conspiracy causes them anxiety and discomfort.

Another example of the current assault on Arab conspiracy theories, brief but no less unsparing in its self-criticism, comes from the pen of the Saudi writer and thinker Turki al-Hamad. Writing in the Saudi-owned London-based daily *Al-Sharq al-Awsat,* al-Hamad dwells on four "illusions" that he says contemporary Arabs entertain—"sovereignty," "conspiracy theories," "the leader-as-savior," and "uniqueness" (quoted in Rejwan, "Arab Conspiracy Theories," 42).

In their current political discourse, al-Hamad laments, the Arabs invariably place the blame for every failure, every mishap, every setback, at the door of some outside force: "We failed to have our renaissance because outside forces were on the wait for us everywhere and at all times. We failed to attain sovereignty because of plots engineered in the dark of night against us. Israel defeats us [in the battlefield] as a result of some conspiracy. Resolutions are adopted against us because of innate hostility and endless plotting. . . . None of the blame for any of this is attributable to us; all comes from the outside."

Another fierce assault on the conspiracy theory came from a somewhat unexpected source. Ghazi Algosaibi, a Saudi politician and diplomat, in his book *The Gulf Crisis: An Attempt to Understand,* refers to the prevalence of conspiracy theories in the Arab world, asking rhetorically, "An American conspiracy or a New World Order?" (excerpted in Nissim Rejwan, "Unfinished Business," *Jerusalem Post,* May 20, 1994). While the "American conspiracy" theory now prevails in the Arab world, he explains, there was a time when it was usually a "British conspiracy." Everything that happens or does not happen can be attributed either to colonialism or to the servants of colonialism, the latter being former Egyptian president Jamal Abd al-Nasir's addition to the theory.

At the height of British influence, Algosaibi relates, there was a widespread saying in the Arab world to the effect that "the only reason why fish die in the sea and birds fall from the sky is British colonialism. The saying was not in jest." Then came the "Communist conspiracy," and "with the retreat of British and Soviet influence, the atmosphere was cleared for the American theory, which became 'the mother of explanations' during and after the (1990 Gulf) crisis."

SIX

UNITY IN DIVERSITY

THE RISE OF "LOCAL NATIONALISMS"

The death of Arab nationalism and Pan-Arabism has been proclaimed so often during the past thirty years that one cannot help being reminded of that other much-celebrated demise—the alleged death of the novel. However, while the novel seems to continue to thrive despite recurrent ups and downs, pan-Arab nationalism and aspirations for an all-Arab unity have both gone into something like a coma.

One of the first to announce the death of Pan-Arabism was Fouad Ajami, a Shiʿi Muslim scholar from Lebanon who lives and teaches in the United States. His thesis was that Pan-Arabism, both as an idea and a movement, had lost out to the polycentric reality of multiple Arab states.

Momentous events in the Middle East since 1978—the year in which Ajami's article "The End of Pan-Arabism" was published in *Foreign Affairs*—were to reinforce his thesis. Chief among those were the peace treaty that Egypt signed with Israel amid unanimous Arab condemnation, and the Gulf War of 1990–1991, in which a number of leading Arab states—including Egypt, Saudi Arabia, and Syria—joined in an alliance with the United States and the West to fight against "a sister Arab state" and a leading member of the League of Arab States (Ajami, "The End of Pan-Arabism," 355–356).

Ajami's thesis remains valid, and its validity is not likely to diminish for some time. This, however, in no way affects Arabism as a cultural and existential reality: Arabic is the language of all Arabs, and Muslim Arabs have the same history, share the same cultural and literary heritage, and feel pride in a common, glorious past. However, as a living tongue, Arabic cannot be said to constitute a single language. There are dozens of different Arabic vernaculars, some of which are unintelligible to speakers of the others. Culturally, too—in the current sociologically accepted use of the term "culture"—there are almost as many Arabic cultures as there are vernaculars, and it is not at all rare to encounter among Arabs cultural differences that sometimes entail estrangement and even hostility.

Over and above these differences, too, is an often shocking degree of ignorance about one another among Arabic-speaking peoples and groups. Common people in the countries of the Arab East, *al-Mashriq,* know next to nothing about their opposite numbers in the lands of the Arab West, *al-Maghrib*—Libya, Tunisia, Algeria, Morocco, and Mauritania. In the heyday of the Egypt-Syria merger and the United Arab Republic, 1958–1961, the Syrians openly resented the many instances in which their Egyptian partners misspelled and mispronounced some very well-known names of Syrian persons and places both in their printed and broadcast literature.

This phenomenon has led a number of Arab writers and thinkers to air their views on this lack of cultural cohesiveness among their peoples, some of them hinting that some sort of coordination, cooperation, and exchange of information in the cultural sphere ought to precede practical measures for any full-fledged union or federation of Arab states. Writing in the ideological organ of the Arab Socialist Union in the aftermath of the Egypt-Syria merger, George Jabbur, a Syrian writer and a former advisor to the Syrian president, spoke of the many "gaps" that he said plagued inter-Arab cultural life and relations (excerpted in Nissim Rejwan, "Why Arabs Can't Unite," 19–20).

One of these gaps, according to Jabbur, is the difficulty of knowing about the books published in some Arab countries, since such works are not advertised or reviewed in the press of sister Arab countries. A reader living in one of the lands of the Mashriq, for instance, would know virtually nothing of the products of any publishing house in any of the countries of the Maghreb or the Arabian Peninsula. One of the more distressing outcomes of this state of affairs, Jabbur points out, is that information concerning the Arab countries of North Africa is usually obtained by Eastern Arabs mostly from books published in Western Europe, especially Britain and France.

Another gap in this sphere is the lack of a comprehensive index or list of books published in Arabic; Arab students or researchers wanting to know about the works of a certain Arab author are obliged to write to or meet the author personally. The League of Arab States, which has been trying to fill this gap since 1946, has so far done nothing concrete despite the fact that its Cultural Committee laid down the necessary theoretical solutions a long time ago.

Worst of all and most urgently in need of treatment is the lack of cultural coordination between the various Arab countries. Take, for instance, the field of translation into Arabic. In the present chaotic state of affairs, it is not rare to see one foreign-language book translated two or three times into Arabic; in some cases, indeed, some Arab quarters—official and unofficial—have ordered a book translated from a foreign language when a good Arabic translation of the same book was for sale in local bookstores.

This lack of cultural coordination is badly felt also in research. For an Arab scholar engaged in literary, social, or scientific research, it is well-nigh impossible—outside of a narrow circle of personal acquaintances—to find out about the work a fellow scholar is engaged in, even if the two scholars live in the same city. No framework exists for the exchange of information between Arab academic institutions.

Finally, Jabbur deplores Arab professionals' unfamiliarity with their colleagues in other Arab countries. True, occasional all-Arab "congresses" bring together such professionals as lawyers, physicians, engineers, or pharmacists. But outside of these professions—and especially among academics working in the humanities and the social sciences—contacts between Arab professionals are often confined to chance encounters at academic gatherings held in Europe or the United States.

In the early 1960s the Nasserist regime in Egypt gave Pan-Arabism a substantial push forward when it defined "the Arab world" as one Arab "nation" now artificially divided into separate sovereign states but destined to be united into one all-Arab state. The Nasserists were not the first to introduce this version of the Arab world and Arab unity. The formation of the Syria-based Ba'th party, with its slogan of "One Arab Nation with an Eternal Mission" (*umma 'Arabiyya wahida dhat risala khalida*), preceded Nasser's rise to power, in 1952.

For many years now, however, since Nasser's pan-Arab drive of the late 1950s and early 1960s caused a serious cleavage in Arab ranks, any sign of rapprochement between the Arab states has been received with acclaim and a great deal of jubilation. Even a summit conference bringing together leaders of member states of the Arab League was perceived as a veritable breakthrough—something transcending by far any passing political considerations or ideological differences and affinities. Strange as it may sound, some Arab observers have continued to use quasi-Nasserist terms and slogans since the early 1970s, when Arab nations and regimes of widely disparate outlooks and with deep-rooted historical rivalries somehow came together and conducted an open, meaningful dialogue among themselves.

For how many centuries—asked an awed commentator in the Beirut weekly *Al-Sayyad*—had a rivalry for Arab leadership been going on between Cairo and Baghdad? For how many centuries had relations between

Egypt and the regimes of the Arabian Peninsula been tense and often non-existent? And for how many hundreds of years had enmity between Arab and Persian, Iraq and Iran, been an established fact of Middle Eastern life and politics? (reported in the *Jerusalem Post,* October 13, 1987).

The elation often bordered on euphoria. However, what with the open rift and the noisy recriminations that followed the signing of an interim agreement between Egypt and Israel in 1978, disappointment soon set in, and things were back to the usual climate of discord and rivalry. The Arabs again seemed disunited, and the old perplexities were again aired concerning this and other aspects of Arab behavior and the telltale "Arab mentality" and "Arab mind."

Those phenomena—and others like them—have of course far deeper roots in Arab history. A nationalist self-view among the Arabs began to emerge, according to C. Ernest Dawn, "with the adaptation to Near Eastern conditions of the European concept of patria and patriotism" (Dawn, "The Origins of Arab Nationalism," in *The Origins of Arab Nationalism*). The appeal of the European concept of patriotism to Egyptian and Ottoman intellectual bureaucrats resulted from their desire to overcome the perceived deprivation of the Islamic countries or the Ottoman Empire, Dawn writes: "They had direct contact with European civilization as a result of occupying positions of authority and responsibility in the governance of their polities. They were painfully aware that the European countries and the Christian Franks were far more advanced in civilization than the Muslim countries. They fervently wished to bring the Islamic countries up to the level of the West." Dawn continues:

> The perception of the Self as deprived relative to the Other often injures the self-view, and Arab and Turkish intellectuals and statesmen were no exception. . . . The pain caused by the invidious comparison was eased, as is commonly the case, by noting some virtues possessed by the Self and lacking in the Other and by finding hope for the future of the Self in its past. The Muslims were still blessed with the perfect religion, while the Franks, Christian in name only, relied on reason alone. Moreover, in the past Muslims had been the teachers of the Franks in the natural sciences, as some of the Franks admitted. Thus, the Muslims should borrow the Western sciences from the Franks and hold fast to the true religion. In doing so, it was thought, the gap would soon be closed. (4–5)

The obvious need to imitate the West, Dawn adds, "intensified the injury to the Ottoman and Eastern self-view." The literature produced after the 1860s had an emotional intensity that was absent from the writings of the previous generation: "The government was attacked in the strongest terms for betraying Islam and the fatherland to the Christian West, which was depicted as a determined and unprincipled enemy." The starting point was a bitter lamentation for the lost power and glory that had once been Islam's but had now passed to the Christian West. Islam and the East had not always been in such a sad state: "The glories, military and cultural, of the Islamic past were recalled, and the reputed debt of European civilization to Islam was emphasized." In fact, it was declared, the modernity of Europe was of Islamic origin, borrowed from the Muslims and used to advantage, while the Muslims deviated from the original true Islam and consequently suffered stagnation and decline. The correct path, these critics decreed, was "to eliminate the corruptions in the heritage and return to true pristine Islam, which would establish constitutional representative government, freedom, etc., which were of Islamic origin even though their current best manifestation was in the West. In this way, Islam would recover its lost power and glory."

Dawn briefly and succinctly describes the process through which this disillusionment was to lead to the formation of a nationalist self-view among the Arabs:

> The Muslim Arab reaction to the West that culminated in [Muhammad] ʿAbduh's Islamic modernism was shared by many Christian Arabs, including most of those commonly called the creators of secular Arab nationalism. Far from expressing feelings of kinship with the West, their writings share the Muslim defense of an injured self-view. Butrus al-Bustani, like many Eastern Christians, resented the perceived patronizing arrogance of Anglo-Saxon Protestant missionaries, and warned against borrowing Western blemishes and vices, as did Ahmad Faris al-Shidyaq and Adib Ishaq. Criticism of excessive "Frankification" became a commonplace of Christian Arab writers. Finally, none of them were Arab nationalists. Bustani, Shidyaq, and Ishaq were Ottoman patriots, as were later luminaries, such as Sulayman al-Bustani, Shibli Shumayyil, and Farah Antun. (5–6)

Many, perhaps all, of the early Western-influenced intellectuals of the Ottoman territories and Egypt "held overlapping self-views without any sense of contradiction," Dawn concludes. Bustani and, to a lesser extent, Ishaq did call themselves Arab and take pride in their Arab heritage: "But so did Tahtawi. None of them, Christian and Muslim, attributed political consequences, or even ultimate cultural consequences, to Arabism" (6–7).

Dawn here breaks what is considered new ground and—as Rashid Khalidi, one of the editors of *The Origins of Arab Nationalism,* writes in his introduction—provides "perhaps the most convincing clarification of a question that has most vexed historians of Arab nationalism: What was the impact of the nineteenth-century literary *nahda,* or renaissance, on Arab nationalism, and in particular the contribution of the mainly Lebanese Christians who played such a large part in this literary revival" (xii).

In his own contribution to the volume, "Ottomanism and Arabism in Syria Before 1914: A Reassessment," Khalidi refers to the work of those historians of Arab nationalism who downplay "the extent of Arabist feeling before 1914," and asserts that these seem to be arguing against three categories of primary evidence—namely, foreign diplomatic and consular archives, contemporary material contained in the press, and recollections of those involved in the prewar Arab movement.

Khalidi admits, however, that it is possible "that our view of this period is influenced by the post-1918 success of Arab nationalism as an ideology in the *mashriq.*" This criticism, he adds, has been leveled in particular at Arab nationalist writers such as Amin Saʿid, Asʿad Daghir, and Antonius, "whose recollections of the pre-1914 period may well have been colored by later events and by political preferences." Against the weaknesses in the analysis of these traditional writers, however, must be set the evidence of the other two categories of sources: "Scores of consular and diplomatic dispatches in the British and French archives document a rising Arabist trend in Syria after 1910, frequently with specific references to events, individuals, and groups, reaching the point by 1912 or 1913 where it is described as a majority tendency. For all their flaws as sources, whether due to their authors' ignorance of local languages and conditions, or their own biases, these dispatches paint a consistent and convincing picture, particularly when checked against other types of sources." Similarly, "the most prominent, forceful, and apparently popular Arabic-language papers of this period, whether those published in Beirut, Damascus, or Cairo, were Arabist in tone" (quotations in this paragraph are from pages 52–53).

Another and certainly more topical aspect of this subject is the phenomenon of local nationalism in the Arab world. Muhammad Muslih deals with this in "The Rise of Local Nationalism in the Arab East," his contribution to the same collection, in which he traces the phenomenon back to what he terms "the group of early Palestinian nationalists, or 'Palestine First.'" Local patriotism and political interests were at the heart of the ideological preferences of these older elites, he writes: "Seeing Palestine put under a separate military administration and alarmed at Britain and its pro-Zionist policy, they chose to focus on Palestine first and other Arab matters second. From their perspective, therefore, Palestinian nationalism was the appropriate response because the British and Zionists were a direct danger to Palestine in particular" (quotations from this paper are drawn from pages 180–181).

Moreover, "the short-run goal of monopolizing local political power on the part of the traditional Palestinian elite enhanced their emphasis on local political independence for Palestine. Familiar as they were with the local political game, they foresaw the challenge that the elite of such Syrian cities as Damascus and Aleppo would pose to their positions of local control." Compared with Palestinian cities, Damascus and Aleppo had much larger populations and greater commercial importance, and "equally significant was the fact that Damascus had a decisive ideological edge by virtue of being the birthplace of Arab nationalism." Therefore, the Palestinian elite argued, were Palestine to merge with a greater Syria, it was likely that the Syrian notables would overwhelm their Palestinian counterparts, a scenario the older Palestinians managed to avoid. And so by 1920 the conflicts and differences in the order of priorities were sufficiently pronounced to create permanent lines of division in the Arab-nationalist movement.

> The pull of Palestinian nationalism ultimately prevailed. The inhospitable universe of the traditional Syrian elite exposed the vulnerability of the doctrine of pan-Arabism. Painful as they were, the assaults by members of this elite on the Arab "foreigners" provided a recipe for the reorientation of the politics of the Palestinian pan-Arabists. If an important segment of the Syrian body politic was too preoccupied with domestic concerns and priorities, then why not a Palestinian focus on Palestine before anything else? Did not the Syrian Arab nationalists themselves put the Syrian question at the top of their action agenda, in the process relegating the Palestine cause to a secondary position? Zionism and the imposition of the Mandate system provided the spark and added to the fuel that had already been there. . . . Indeed by the end of 1920 nationalism in Palestine had acquired a rather narrow focus. Palestinian independence became nationalism's highest aim. The Palestinian pan-Arabists came to concentrate all their efforts on achieving this goal before all else. They had already learned their lesson in Damascus.

"Thus," Muslih concludes, "in keeping with the tenor of inter-Arab politics after the war, the Palestinian pan-Arabists made peace with Palestine's new 'national' situation and accommodated the particularism of the Palestine cause within the 'universalism' of their Arab nationalist doctrine."

CAUSES OF THE FAILURE

A far less balanced and somewhat polemical appraisal of the subject is supplied by Munif Razzaz, a Syrian Ba'th Party ideologue, in a paper entitled "Arab Nationalism." Razzaz starts by asserting that Arab nationalism is "the driving force behind the Arabs in their struggle to create a progressive nation that can hold its own with the nations of the world" (in Adams, ed., *The Middle East: A Handbook;* quotations are drawn from pages 359–360). Tracing "the sense of belonging to an Arab entity" back to pre-Islamic days, Razzaz supplies a brief account of the confrontations the Arabs had with "Western colonialism," the first occurring "in the Arabian Gulf [i.e., the Persian Gulf] and the Indian Ocean at the beginning of the 16th century."

After providing a brief account of confrontations that followed, Razzaz turns to the Arab-Israeli dispute and the impact it has had on the Arab-nationalist stance. The 1948 war, he writes, "which brought the humiliating defeat of the Arabs by a handful of Jews, was the last straw that destroyed any remnants of confidence between the ruling classes on one side and the masses on the other." For, in addition to their other faults, these ruling classes had shown themselves incompetent as well: "Resentment against the Western powers for creating and supporting Israel, which could never be forgiven by the Arabs, was only enhanced by the defeat. The demand for an end to all Western tutelage, for the abolition of military bases and the abrogation of treaties, with a refusal to join in any military pact, became the common theme of everyday life at the popular level." In conclusion, Razzaz writes:

> Gradually, the masses began to discover the pattern in which the ruling classes, the pro-Western politicians with their vested interests in the liberal bourgeois economy, represented the agents of Western capitalism. The whole of political life began to crystallise around two centres. One was that of a ruling class at the same time reactionary, corrupt, inefficient, afraid of the emancipation of the masses, and connected directly with Western governments and capital. The other centre was that of the masses who were definitely anti-Western, anti-imperialist, anti-capitalist, anti-Zionist, and in favour of unity, freedom, socialism and neutralism. This was called, in general, "Arab Nationalism". The history of the Arab world during the last 20 years is the history of the conflict between these two forces.

The Arabs are fond of calling the collectivity of Arabic-speaking countries "the Arab homeland" (*al-watan al-'Arabi*), preferring this to the more common "Arab world," Arab states, or Arab peoples. In the post–Gulf War era, however, even diehard followers of Arab nationalism and Pan-Arabism became wary of indulging in such manifestly empty rhetoric.

And no wonder. A mere glance at the situation of the Arabic-speaking lands in the mid-1990s would make any thinking Arab nationalist wonder. Iraq, the most advanced of the Arab states and one of the richest in resources and manpower, became virtually a pariah state with hardly any Arab connections; Egypt, Saudi Arabia, Kuwait, and the Gulf states refused to have any dealings with Jordan and its king; Libya under Muᶜammar Gadhafi was left to fend for itself in its ongoing confrontation with the United States and the world at large; and suffering Somalia, a sister Arab country and bona fide member of the Arab League, got hardly more than a passing mention in the Arab media. This sorry state of affairs has led a number of erstwhile pan-Arab ideologues to do some fresh contemplating, and questions are today being asked about fundamental issues—questions that only a few Arab writers and thinkers had the courage to raise or even contemplate in the recent past.

To be sure, there have always been dissenting minority opinions, but such dissidents were invariably treated as freaks. One of the more interesting political groups that advocated a different opinion on the subject—and is now virtually defunct—is the Syrian Nationalist Party, founded and led by Anton Saadeh (1904–1949), a Lebanese. Among other propositions, the Syrian Nationalists argued that rather than being one nation, the Arabs comprise four distinct "nations": the Syrian nation, comprising Syria, Lebanon, Palestine, and Jordan; the Maghreb nation, including Algeria, Morocco, Tunisia, and Libya; the Nile Valley nation (Egypt and Sudan); and the Arab Gulf nation, comprising Iraq, Saudi Arabia, and all the other countries of the Arabian Peninsula.

That such a division of the Arab world should come from what is generally considered a fringe group is not surprising. Similar ideologies sharing the same skepticism about the feasibility of an all-Arab union have always come and gone, but they were never taken seriously, and did not achieve popularity or mass support. What is new, and surprising, is that similar voices are now being heard from a number of Arab writers and thinkers whose adherence to and advocacy of Arab nationalism and Pan-Arabism has never been in doubt.

One of these was Lutfi al-Khuli (1928-1999), the left-leaning Egyptian political writer and analyst and veteran editor of Egypt's onetime leading political monthly *Al-Taliᶜa*, now long defunct. In a programmatic article headlined "One Arab Homeland or a Number of Homelands in One Arab

World?" this faithful follower of Nasserist ideology dwells at some length on the factors that led to the failure of the various attempts made since the 1950s to attain even one of the proposed Arab unions: Egypt and Syria; Iraq and Jordan; Libya and Egypt; Egypt, Libya, and Syria; the Arab states of North Africa; and others (excerpted in Nissim Rejwan, "How Many Arab 'Homelands'?" *Jerusalem Post,* August 28, 1992). Many of these attempts, Khuli reminds us, were made between the years 1955 and 1970, a period generally recognized as the heyday of the modern pan-Arab movement.

There have, however, been two successful attempts at union—both accomplished after 1970. These were the unification of six Gulf entities into the United Arab Emirates (Abu Dhabi, Dubai, Sharjah, Umm al-Qaiwain, Ajman, and Fujairah) in 1971, with Ras al-Khaimah joining the following year, and the more recent union between the Yemen Arab Republic (North Yemen) and the Democratic People's Republic of Yemen (Southern Yemen).

Proceeding from the assumption that the success of these two union plans was due to the uniqueness of the characteristics as well as the circumstances shared by the states concerned, Khuli draws a future scenario in which such shared characteristics and circumstances lead to four equally successful unions, what he calls "homelands." These are to comprise the following:

• Saudi Arabia, the United Arab Emirates, Kuwait, Bahrain, Qatar, Oman, and Yemen

• Iraq, Syria, Lebanon, Jordan, and Palestine

• Egypt, Libya, and Sudan—with the possible addition of Somalia and Djibouti

• Morocco, Algeria, Tunisia, and Mauritania

While these schemes of union are almost identical to those envisaged by the Syrian Nationalists, they differ decisively from them in two significant ways. For one thing, they draw their legitimacy from a bona fide Arab-nationalist ideology, whereas the Syrian Nationalists' program seems too close to the Greater Syria plan and ultimately to an ideology whose adherents have often professed and even boasted of Phoenician ancestry. For another, Khuli's scenario places Iraq properly where it has always been seen to belong: with the countries of the Fertile Crescent. It also has the advan-

74

tage of bringing together Libya and the two Arab states of the Nile Valley, Egypt and Sudan.

It is worth noting here that Khuli, a convinced Arab nationalist, writes almost in passing that his reflections and conclusions about the fate of Arab unions in the past do not amount to an obituary of the pan-Arab ideology. Present-day realities and past legacies, he asserts, show conclusively that Arabs everywhere share "a unity of fate." He refrains, however, from clearly defining the nature of that common fate.

A "common fate" of a certain kind does indeed seem to have brought two countries of the Levant, Syria and Lebanon, to a state of virtual unity, though one that is incomplete, not fully recorded, impermanent, and, above all, unequal. The link, in fact, is more in the nature of a protector-protectorate relationship than of a union between two sovereign entities. What seems to be the last bit of this remarkable design was filled in on May 22, 1991, when a document called the Treaty of Brotherhood, Cooperation, and Coordination between Lebanon and Syria was signed with much pomp. Ironically enough, the treaty contains a provision binding the two countries to respect each other's "independence."

How this feat was achieved is told from the point of view of a true Lebanese patriot in a book published shortly before the treaty was signed. The book, characteristically entitled *A Homeland's Curse,* was written by Karim Baqraduni, a Lebanese lawyer and publicist of note. Hafiz al-Assad, Baqraduni writes in his bitter polemic, "will never rest until 'the Syrian solution' for Lebanon is finalized and sealed" (reported in *Al-Hayat* [London], May 5, 1991).

In Assad's view, in fact, "a solution in Lebanon has to be a Syrian solution or it's no solution at all." Assad's patience is inexhaustible, Baqraduni adds. "The Lebanese have themselves gotten bored with their crisis but he hasn't. The whole world has tired of it but he hasn't. For him, Lebanon is a Syrian protectorate, and his whole political-military strategy is centered on a unified leadership of Lebanon, Jordan and the Palestinians under a Syrian umbrella."

And, indeed, Assad and many of his predecessors conceived of the situation always as a "Greater Syria"—*Bilad al-Sham,* best translated into English as Lands of the Levant. This was based on the claim that Western imperialism had fragmented this geographic and political unit, establishing the three states of Syria, Lebanon, and Jordan and promising Palestine to the Jews.

This apart, it is evident that nearly a century of talk about Pan-Arabism and Arab unity, as well as a few decades of trying to achieve it even partially, has failed to produce any concrete results. Walid Khalidi, an astute observer of the Arab political scene and an Arab himself, touched upon some of the basic reasons for this state of affairs. In an essay from the late 1950s entitled "Political Trends in the Fertile Crescent," he traces the changing attitudes and stands the advocates of Pan-Arabism adopted during the years preceding and succeeding Western dominance in the region (in Laqueur, ed., *The Middle East in Transition;* quotations are drawn from pages 122–123). Because of "the aristocratic and feudal background of most of them," he writes, holding office became to the traditional Arab nationalists "synonymous with the protection and expansion of the particular land or commercial interest which they represented," so that "their triumph over the foreigner was erroneously taken by them as proof of their own importance and placed them in a false moral position vis-a-vis their public. They felt that they had satisfactorily fulfilled their duties to the people and that they could now start attending to themselves."

None of this, Khalidi adds, was lost upon the rapidly growing educated classes and the people in general, who now "began to look upon the traditional nationalists not as leaders but as targets." Subsequently,

> the gap between the ruling classes and the people was further widened by the Arab, or rather non-Arab, policies of the rulers. Before independence the traditional nationalists were pan-Arabists. After independence they became jealous particularists. To satisfy the popular feeling for pan-Arabism the Arab League was formed as a half-hearted attempt in that direction. But the Palestine war of 1948 exposed the bankruptcy not only of the Arab League but also of its authors . . . The unpreparedness of the armies and the humiliating terms imposed upon them by the armistice agreements inevitably caused them to turn against their governments.

The Arab officer thus "became the spearhead of all the pent-up feelings of the educated people and the masses against the traditional ruling classes."

SEVEN

THE QUEST FOR DEMOCRACY

Despite their protestations that democracy is not a purely Western creation fit only for Europe and North America, Arab political intellectuals were slow to realize that the road to a democratic system of government in the Arab world would be long and difficult. A recent example from Iraq is worth citing, although the democratic experience in that country is seen as vastly different from that of any other Arab country. In the course of a meeting he held with representatives of the Iraqi press shortly after the end of the war with Iran, Saddam Hussein assured his listeners that henceforth newspapermen and authors could write whatever they liked, since press censorship had been lifted. "We want you," he added, "to expose the drawbacks, the wrongdoings and the mistakes committed by the government—and in cases where you are in error we will just point out your mistakes to you without any resentment on our part" (quoted in the *Jerusalem Post*, March 17, 1991).

This was not the first time Saddam's regime had made such promises. Similar assurances had been given to the press two years previously by the minister of culture and information. Needless to say, these pledges did not come to much; all that one noticed in their wake were occasional criticisms of the work of some minor officials and of certain aspects of local government, some of them no doubt officially inspired. Nor was this in the least surprising. Fear of recrimination and punishment aside, Iraqi newspapermen and editors had for so long been subjected to censorship and intimidation that they must have lost the habit of honest newspaper work—and in all probability they had never known the practice.

The subject of press censorship and freedom of expression is of course closely related to that of democracy and the multiparty system—and both were promised to the Iraqis by the regime time and again after the end of the Gulf War. The habitual Western reaction to these promises was that as long as Saddam Hussein was in power, no such changes could possibly be effected and no promises could be taken seriously. Altogether, the received wisdom at that time was that nothing of consequence could be accomplished there while Saddam continued to rule Iraq uncontested.

This was at best only half true—especially concerning the subject of democracy. The argument, in fact, rested on the erroneous and simplistic assumption that democracy and the democratic way of government could be introduced and implemented by fiat—by revising a constitution or by promulgating a new one. The truth, though, is that in the absence of a tradition of government by consultation and consent, such impromptu measures can mean very little indeed. This has been made abundantly clear by the experiences of many countries of the Third World, among them almost all the Arab states, during the past six decades.

Shortly after the Gulf War ended, former Egyptian prime minister Kamal Hasan ʿAli, who had also served as defense and foreign minister and had been one of the chief negotiators of the peace treaty with Israel, told a reporter in Cairo that the aftermath of the war would witness many and far-reaching political changes in the Arab world: "I believe that after the war is over democracy will prevail in the Gulf states and in the Arab world as a whole." He added that these changes would not come as a result of military coups or revolts, but "gradually and in a natural, constitutional manner" (quoted in the *Jerusalem Post*, March 17, 1991).

The veteran Egyptian politician was not the only experienced observer in the Arab world who was breaking the good news; he was, in fact, one among many. Nor were his predictions either new or confined to this juncture in recent Arab history. Rumors of change and of some impending march toward democracy have been heard periodically and have accompanied all the major crises in the recent history of the region—largely, of course, because democracy is perceived by most Arabs as the solution to all their people's problems.

Whether or not things will eventually be different and working democratic institutions will be introduced, one aspect of this subject seems always to escape these observers' and pundits' notice. This is that democracy and representative government constitute the proclaimed political system of practically every Arab state. In fact, universal, free, direct, and secret suffrage is guaranteed in the constitutions of all Arab states with the exception of Saudi Arabia and a number of small Persian Gulf emirates and sheikhdoms.

In the constitutions of Syria, Jordan, Iraq, Lebanon, Egypt, Sudan, Kuwait, and the countries of North Africa, a clear and complete separation is drawn between the legislative, judicial, and executive powers; in all these constitutions, legislative power is said to be vested in the people and their elected representatives; and in the case of monarchies, that power is shared by the king. That these assurances and guarantees and safeguards almost never acquired real meaning in practice will become plain from a brief summary of the experiences of three Arab countries during the past few decades.

The constitution of the Kingdom of Jordan, as amended in 1955, vests the legislative authority "in the King and the National Assembly, consisting of the Senate and the Chamber of Deputies." It further stipulates that the Chamber "shall consist of members elected by universal, secret, and direct suffrage," while one-half of the members of the Senate shall be appointed by the king. In November 1989, legislative elections were held—the first Jordan had had in twenty-two years. Up to that date, little was heard about Islamic fundamentalism in Jordan, or about the Muslim Brethren (also known as the Muslim Brotherhood) there.

The Brethren's existence was brought to the fore, however, when the results of the elections were announced. Together with a few much smaller Islamic organizations, they won a stunning thirty-one out of the Chamber's eighty seats; the Brethren alone occupied twenty-two. When the results were made known, many observers in the Arab world and outside it thought the Islamic groups constituted a grave danger to the Jordanian regime and to the throne itself. As he had done so often before, however, King Hussein was able deftly to weather the storm, somehow making the Brethren and their allies feel at home in the Chamber and keeping them out of harm's reach. On November 17, the Brethren's chief spokesman, Abdul-Latif Arabiyyat, was elected speaker of the Chamber, and finally, late in December, the Brethren's position was stabilized further when they were given five cabinet seats, including the education portfolio, thus becoming practically part of the political establishment.

In Egypt, a country in which parties and parliaments had existed for almost a century before its constitutional monarchy was overthrown by a military coup, in 1952, a huge gap still yawns between theory, written legislation, and actual practice. Even in post-1952 Egypt, where, in effect, some revolutionary command council or other ruled the country uncontested for nearly three decades, elections and popular plebiscites were held regularly, the results invariably showing well over 95 percent of the populace opting for the powers that be. As one prominent Egyptian lawyer who is also active politically put it so eloquently, the famous separation of the three powers about which he learned some four decades before, in his student days, was never in evidence. Instead, he lamented, the only power of which he was made aware was the executive, which always reduced to the status of mere puppets and tools both the legislature and the judiciary (quoted in Nissim Rejwan, *Arabs Face the Modern World*, 195–196).

According to the Lebanese constitution, promulgated in 1926 and last amended in 1947, "All Lebanese should be equal in the eyes of the law. . . . The legislative power shall be exercised by the Chamber of Deputies." The Chamber, it is stated, is "to consist of elected members chosen by every Lebanese citizen who has completed his 21st year and fulfills the conditions laid down by the electoral law." The situation on the ground in 1991 was quite different, however. It is true that in 1990, after fifteen years of civil strife, during which all pretences of democratic or representative government had been abandoned, there continued to exist in Lebanon something called a parliament. Since 1975, however, this shadow of a legislature had seldom managed actually to meet or to have the required quorum.

What is more, the chamber had been elected back in May 1972, and of its original ninety-nine members, thirty were no longer among the living by mid-1990, when, in accordance with an agreement reached in the Saudi city of Taif in 1989 by the warring parties, nine more Muslims were to be added to the chamber to attain some sort of fair distribution of seats among the various communities and denominations—besides the need to elect successors to the thirty dead deputies.

Elections for a new house—since named the National Assembly—had originally been scheduled for November 1975. Because of the civil war, they were first postponed for twenty-six months, but on the appointed day, the term of the house was further extended until June 1980. In December 1987, after four additional postponements, the term was extended to 1990; further dates for the actual voting were fixed, but it was not held until early in the summer of 1998.

While only Jordan, Egypt, and Lebanon have been cited here as examples, the situation in the other Arab countries differs only in a few details, and is almost invariably worse. This gap between written legislation and actual practice has of course been evident for everyone in the Arab world to see, and is often remarked upon and deplored—and the merits of "true democracy" are endlessly enumerated with longing and nostalgia.

During and directly after the Gulf War there was much talk about "a new Arab order" that would follow the end of hostilities. One of the changes envisaged for the Middle East was the institution or restoration of democracy in those Arab countries where the absence of democracy was acknowledged as well as seen.

Blueprints for new orders, however, have almost always tended to be either too ambitious or misguided or both. And at least this particular part of the blueprint for the most recent new order was no exception. For several decades now, all attempts at instituting any sort of meaningful, workable democratic system in the Arab-Muslim world have come to naught. While perfectly democratic rules and provisions figured in every written constitution in the region, formulated by some of the best minds in the field, the situation on the ground remained the same: no truly representative government of any kind has been seen, and no real separation of powers achieved. If anything, changes that were effected turned out always to be for the worse. The executive always had the upper hand and manipulated both the legislature and the judiciary. Several observers and students of the Arab scene, Arabs as well as Westerners, have tried to explain the reasons for this failure to accept and adapt to the democratic system of government. Needless to say, deep socioeconomic, political, cultural, and historical factors lie at the root of this state of affairs. These factors are often ignored or dismissed as irrelevant by theorists, well-wishers, and planners of all kinds.

"A PLANT OF SLOW GROWTH"

One of the few students of the region to address himself to this subject is Charles Issawi, an internationally acknowledged authority on the economic history of the Middle East and a Middle Easterner by birth and upbringing. Some years ago Issawi set out to examine what he calls "the economic and social foundations of democracy" and to relate them—or the lack of them—to the subject of democracy and its fortunes in the Arab world.

Taking as a yardstick those countries in the West, chiefly in Western Europe and North America, where democracy is practiced, Issawi reaches the conclusion that "democracy does not thrive in the Middle East because the economic and social basis which it requires is as yet non-existent" (quoted in N. B. Argaman, "Looking for an Arab Democracy," *Jerusalem Post*, March 17, 1991). That basis, he adds, embraces the following aspects: the size of the territory and population, the level of economic development, the distribution of wealth, industrialization, the homogeneity of language and religion, the degree of education, and the habit of cooperative association.

It is Issawi's basic assumption that for democratic institutions to develop and for the democratic spirit to flourish, two conditions seem necessary: "the community must be bound by a strong social solidarity; and at the same time it must contain enough diversity to produce tension between its constituent parts." In practically all these spheres, Issawi implies, the Arab world is at a disadvantage. What is needed, he asserts, "is a great economic and social transformation which will strengthen society and make it capable of bearing the weight of the modern state." Mere constitutional or administrative reforms, or just a change in government machinery or in personnel, he emphasizes, would not be enough—"not even the adjustment of an obsolete political structure to bring it in line with a new balance of forces reflecting changing relations between various social classes" (quoted in Nissim Rejwan, "Arab Regimes Still Unripe for Democracy," *Jerusalem Post*, December 27, 1991; the quotations from Issawi in the next several paragraphs are drawn from this article).

Other explanations have been advanced for the shortcomings of Middle Eastern democracies. One of these used to be the standard explanation offered by Arab nationalists and local patriots, who argued that no real democracy could develop in countries such as Iraq, Syria, Egypt, Jordan, and Lebanon as long as British and French armies of occupation were the determining factors in all political matters, and, as Issawi notes, "as long as the population continued to be preoccupied, not to say obsessed, with the problem of its relations with the foreign power."

Another explanation, current in the West, is that democracy is a plant of slow growth, which gradually developed over several centuries in the congenial climate of Europe and North America. It could not possibly be expected to thrive when suddenly transplanted to an alien Eastern soil that since the dawn of recorded history had bred nothing "but the thorns and thistles of despotism." The absence of democratic traditions, Issawi explains, and of the historic customs, habits, and attitudes required to make democracy work, "was one of the first aspects of the East to strike nineteenth-century Europeans, and no one has expressed this better than Lord Cromer: 'Do not let us for one moment imagine that the fatally simple idea of despotic rule will readily give way to the far more complex conception of ordered liberty.'"

A third explanation, also cited by Issawi, has been prevalent in both the West and the Middle East. It is that Middle Easterners generally "are incapacitated, by their extreme individualism, from achieving the degree of cooperation required for the successful functioning of democracy." Middle Easterners, he argues, tend to develop "intense loyalty to certain small units, such as the family, the clan, the tribe, or the religious sect, but they do not seem to be able to transcend those groups and feel towards any larger body, for example the city or the nation, enough devotion and responsibility to subordinate their individual selfish propensities to some common goal."

Issawi goes all the way back to Ibn Khaldun, who wrote in his famous Introduction (*Muqaddimah*): "Every Arab regards himself as worthy to rule, and it is rare to find one of them submitting willingly to another, be it his father or his brother or the head of his clan, but only grudgingly and for fear of public opinion." It is interesting to note that while arguments regarding these shortcomings of traditional ways and political forms originated mostly in the East, Western-oriented reformers and revolutionaries in the Arab world have reiterated them since the late nineteenth century, and in several cases tried to emulate the ways of the West.

However, Western-style democracy and parliamentary forms proved unworkable and, as the experience of almost all Westernizing Arab politicians showed, raised numerous problems and, in the end, proved to be these politicians' own undoing. The examples of Iraq, Syria, Egypt, Libya, and Algeria are the first to come to mind. The question, in fact, is whether democracy can work smoothly in these countries within the framework of a multiparty system, fair elections, and the other trappings of representative government. The answer to this question can best be given indirectly. In an interview published in the Spring 1990 issue of *New Perspectives Quarterly,* Sir Ralf Dahrendorf, rector of St. Antony's College, Oxford, said that the major problem in Eastern Europe was "finding ways to sustain the open society by constructing a civil society" (quoted in Rejwan, "Arab Regimes Still Unripe for Democracy").

By civil society, Dahrendorf added, he meant "on the one hand, the established rule of law and, on the other, the broad development of autonomous institutions—that is, institutions that are not run by the state but that act as agent of the will of the people, [such as] political parties, trade unions, independent industrial enterprises, social movements like local ecology groups, free churches, liberal professions, autonomous universities." Writing a nice constitution will not be enough to sustain an open society, Sir Ralf explained: "You have to create . . . the general social reality in which the constitution can live." The trouble, he added, is this: "It takes six months to create new political institutions, to write a constitution and electoral laws. It may take six years to create a halfway viable economy. It will probably take 60 years to create a civil society. Autonomous institutions are the hardest thing to bring about. I don't want to sound like Jeanne Kirkpatrick, but when she says that only Britain and the United States have developed civil societies, she is not being unreasonable, only extreme."

IS DEMOCRACY A STARLET?

It is interesting to note that when faced with this and similar theses, Arab writers and commentators generally take this to mean that only in the West can the democratic system work. In January 1993, a column by the Lebanese writer Raouf Shahouri appeared in the Paris-based Lebanese weekly *Al-Watan al-ʿArabi* under the loaded headline "Is Democracy a Blonde?" The gist of his complaint is that democracy is generally depicted as being "with blonde hair, blue eyes, slim and well-shaped, affluent and demanding, and is good only for developed, advanced peoples." She is also said to be "totally incapable of dwelling in desert tents or inhabiting the alleyways of backwardness, since she would then be overwhelmed by microbes and bacteria and ultimately become disfigured and wither away!"

Lest he be misunderstood, Shahouri proceeds to sing democracy's praises. The democratic system, he writes, is "a medicament that can do no harm even when it doesn't help"—and while democracy has its drawbacks, dictatorship has no merits whatsoever. Nor does Shahouri care for the idea of "the just tyrant," an idea accepted in the East as the shortest way between backwardness and progress, when in reality it is an evil, deceptive, and self-contradictory theory.

While a number of the points he makes are valid, Shahouri ultimately fails to convince, especially since the only example he cites to prove his thesis is how the democratic process in Lebanon is finally reaching fruition. It is, he admits, a long uphill struggle; but it can work—if only as a way to educate people toward a truly working democracy. It may well be that democracy is not a blue-eyed blonde, since in certain European countries where real-life blondes abound, democracy has not proved workable. However—to follow Shahouri's novel metaphor—so far democracy has mostly fit that description, even though, like some blondes, this particular one is by no means perfect.

THE KUWAITI EXPERIENCE

Experiments in democracy and representative government were made also in the Gulf States. In Kuwait, for instance, the National Assembly has always included a small minority of opposition elements—active radicals such as pan-Arab nationalists, Nasserists, and socialists. The elections held in February 1985, to give one example, produced an Assembly that, though still with a conservative majority, had a vocal and active opposition group of radicals and independents, exceeding in number any that the house had had in the past. This led to a series of crises until the cabinet resigned on July 1, 1986, on the grounds that it was no longer possible for the government to carry on with its work. Two days later the emir ordered the Assembly dispersed and suspended articles in the constitution stipulating that elections had to be held within two months after the dispersal. In an address to the nation, the emir spoke of the danger of foreign-inspired subversion and the pitfalls of sectarianism; but his main complaint—and the real reason for the Assembly's dispersal—was directed against the deputies, whom he accused of obstructing the government's work, among other things. Another measure taken by the regime was the imposition of press censorship (this account of Kuwaiti politics was reported in the *Jerusalem Post,* February 24, 1991).

After the eight-year Iran-Iraq War ended, in August 1988, pressure was renewed for the restoration of the Assembly and the lifting of press censorship. Adding to the intensity of the calls and the movement for reform were the winds of change issuing from Eastern Europe, which reportedly made the Kuwaiti radicals—representing as they did an electorate drawn from the upper stratum of the society, the elite of an already privileged minority—more vociferous in their demands. In 1989, calls for change became loud and persistent, and also increased in number—and toward the end of the year a group of fifty citizens organized a petition to the emir, asking for the Assembly's recall. They managed to mobilize 25,000 signatories to the petition—an extremely impressive figure, considering that it was the equivalent of about 40 percent of the country's entire electorate.

In response, the emir appealed for calm, saying in a speech to the nation, "Let us always remember that we are members of the same tiny community which cannot tolerate dissension, . . . and where it is easy to come to terms given good intentions and open-mindedness." For his part, prime minister and crown prince Sheikh Saʿad al-Abdullah as-Sabah promised that his government would sound out public opinion, adding that the problems of the old Assembly required some new forms of democracy, though the principle of public political participation was not in question.

The emir then came up with a compromise of his own. He told the nation on April 22, 1990, that after taking into account all the opinions expressed by a wide spectrum of society, he had decided that a provisional National Assembly would be established, consisting of seventy-five members, fifty of whom would be elected by secret ballot while the remaining twenty-five would be appointed "on the basis of qualifications and experience." Moreover, during the four years of its mandate, the new Assembly's main task would be "to study the reasons for the difficulties that arose between the legislative and executive branches of the government with a view to finding ways of avoiding them in the future." He added, however, that the Assembly would also have the power to question ministers on government policy and to debate the budget before it was approved. The emir also set the date for elections—June 10, 1990.

Reacting to the emir's compromise offer, many of the former deputies claimed that he was using a device to alter the parliamentary system stipulated by the constitution—a charge that apologists for the regime tried to refute by claiming that what the emir was really doing was to place the onus of reforming the system on members of the provisional Assembly, and that he was making it clear that Kuwait was not about to abandon the principle of elected representative institutions. Considering the limitations he himself had placed on the size of the new Assembly and how it was to be established, however, it is clear that the emir was indeed trying to change certain crucial rules of the democratic game as set out in the constitution.

The election of fifty Assembly members duly took place, and the remaining twenty-five "qualified and experienced" others were named by the emir. As luck would have it, however, the new house of deputies was to prove far more provisional than it had been meant to be. It had held only one or two meetings before the Iraqi army invaded the emirate on August 2, and Kuwait was proclaimed the nineteenth province of the Iraqi Republic literally overnight. It is remarkable that, conservative or radical, pan-Arab nationalist or Kuwaiti patriot, capitalist or socialist, no Kuwaiti citizen of note, and certainly no National Assembly member, went on record as welcoming the Iraqi intruders.

This came as no surprise to observers. Tribal and paternalistic in character though it is—the Sabah clan boasts some 1,000 princes and princesses—the regime of the late Emir Jaber (1926–2006) was easily the most enlightened, most benevolent, and most prudent in the region. As soon as oil started flowing in strength, just after the end of World War II, the Sabahs decided to set aside about one-third of the revenues as reserves for the future, and the rest was largely used for building infrastructure and supporting a welfare state unsurpassed in its benevolence and the comprehensiveness of the services it offers citizens.

While the experience of Kuwait is highly instructive as a case study, the future prospects of democracy in Saudi Arabia, the major Arab state on the Gulf, are clearly more crucial to the subject. During the months of crisis preceding the Gulf War, indeed, a good deal of attention was given to the Saudi political scene, both in and outside the Arab world. One of the subjects on which speculation became rife was that of change in the desert kingdom, change that had already been considered overdue but that the crisis and the war were deemed to have made inevitable or at least to have hastened considerably.

On the subject of democracy, Abdullah Rashid, a columnist for the United Arab Emirates daily *Al-Ittihad,* published a scathing article on October 27, 2003, titled "Long Live Dictatorship," in which he asks a series of questions that seem to contain their own answers. "The entire world is perplexed about us," one of these questions asserts. "Do we really seek our freedoms and attempt to rid ourselves of ages of oppression, and domination? Do the Arab peoples really want to extricate themselves from the claws of repressive regimes?" By way of answer, Rashid writes that in light of ongoing events, "it appears that the Arab peoples, all of them, have become completely addicted to dictatorship, oppression, and regimes that beat (the people) on their heads with their shoes and hit them below the belt."

THE SAUDI EXPERIENCE

Along with other monarchs and rulers of traditional Arab-Muslim nations, the Saudi ruling family has for some time been aware of the existence in its midst of increasingly vocal minorities calling for basic personal freedoms, an equitable distribution of the national income, a free press, and democratically elected governments. With the exception of the Hashemite Kingdom of Jordan, however, where an earnest and (so far) successful leap was taken in that direction, responses to such calls have been far from encouraging.

Saudi Arabia is no exception. On November 8, 1990, three months into the Gulf crisis, King Fahd announced that a *shura* council would be set up in the kingdom and that other laws—including "a constitutional law"—would soon be promulgated. Spokesmen of the regime went on record as saying that these measures constituted "a new policy based on free choice and the wishes shared by the leadership and the citizen" (*Jerusalem Post,* April 3, 1992).

Grand enough talk, this was—and just as grandly reassuring. What it all amounted to, however, was far less clear. Plainly, the operative word here is the Arabic term *shura.* When they refer to a shura council, Saudi spokesmen and Arab observers generally equate the term automatically with "parliament." The sole point of similarity between a Western-style parliament and a Muslim shura council, however, is that both are places where people "speak" and tend to discuss and consult about things—in this case, affairs of state.

And indeed the word "shura" means "consultation," and a shura council or assembly (*majlis al-shura*) is a gathering of representatives of a people or a community, and can also be the supreme legislative authority for that people or community. But the shura council the Saudi monarch promised his subjects differed in one cardinal point from a parliament as the term is understood in a democracy: rather than being popularly elected, the promised majlis was to be rooted firmly in the rules of Islamic shariᶜa (law), which the Saudi monarchy is pledged to be "absolutely and permanently committed to follow equally as a faith, a program, and a basis for government, and from which there can be no deviation." The difficulty here, of course, is that the exact nature of the shura way of government—which some Muslim writers have called "Islamic democracy"—has never been properly defined as a working system with clearly defined rules.

THE EGYPTIAN EXPERIENCE

In Egypt, where a limited democratic tradition exists, almost everybody admits—the regimes of the day not excluded—that the election process leaves much to be desired and that the road to "real democracy" remains long and strewn with stumbling blocks. Until recently, however, there was a consensus among political intellectuals about the need for a system that would ensure the democratic process, complete and in one quick leap.

However, after events in Algeria in the early 1990s—where democratic elections threatened to bring to power Islamist elements openly announcing their intention to ban such "Western heresies" as free elections once they assumed power—Egyptian advocates of democracy started having some serious second thoughts on the subject. Indeed, the topic of a symposium held in Cairo shortly after the Algerian episode was "Democracy—in One Lump or Piecemeal?" Five political intellectuals participated, of whom two advocated "full-fledged democracy now" and three reasoned for "applying democracy in installments" (the proceedings were reported in *Al-Hayat* [London], April 15, 1992).

The advocates of "democracy now"—curiously, both were right-leaning liberals—argued mainly that democracy was an "indivisible whole" and could not be dispensed piecemeal, and that what had happened in Algeria was not likely to happen in Egypt, because "circumstances" differed substantially in the two countries. The advocates of "democracy by installments," two left-leaning journalists and a historian, argued that democracy had never anywhere in the world been applied in one go; that on the two occasions when democracy was practiced in Egypt—through 1923–1952 and in 1981—difficulties arose; and that all in all and on every such occasion, repressive measures had had to be taken to curb disorders and foul play.

Judging by the performance so far, the facts seem to favor the gradualists. Since the Free Officers came to power in July 1952, indeed, what have passed for parliaments in Egypt have been no more than tools of the regime. Egypt's ruling party today—the National Democratic Party, which holds around three-quarters of the seats in the Assembly—is in reality not much different from the various organizations Nasser created to give his regime a semblance of democratic rule; the last of these, the Arab Socialist Union, was dissolved in the early 1970s when Anwar el-Sadat decided to allow some semblance of a multiparty system.

Another approach under attack by the gradualists can be called the legalistic one. In many Arab countries, as in Egypt, political groups in search of democracy argue that existing legal and constitutional barriers need to be removed, allowing political groups and parties to be formed—and ensuring freedom of action to them. In Egypt, specifically, the call has always been for an amendment to the existing law regulating the formation of new political parties—a law that has allowed the authorities to withhold a license from such a powerful organization as the Muslim Brethren, denying it the opportunity to take part in parliamentary elections on its own rather than being appended to one of the legally recognized political parties.

One answer to this approach was offered by Usama al-Ghazzali Harb, director of the Center for Political and Strategic Studies of *Al-Ahram*. In a well-argued article in the London-based Lebanese daily *Al-Hayat* (April 15, 1992), Harb asks two questions: What changes could legislation for a free multiparty system bring? What would happen if, say, the existing constitutional restrictions in Egypt were removed? His answer: Nothing much! The political climate might improve, to be sure, as every political group formed its own party, free to do and say whatever it liked. However, the thirty or forty parties that would emerge overnight would not be likely to effect any substantial change in the political scene—or even in the existing division of political opinion and trends.

"In sum," Harb concludes, "the vitality of political party life in any country is a function of the interaction between suitable legal and constitutional conditions and objective socio-political forces. In the same way as these forces cannot work without a suitable legal framework, the provision of such a framework cannot ensure a satisfactory political party life. When a specific political force capable of attracting mass support emerges, however, it will not wait for some official license of legal recognition but will impose itself on the authorities as a fait accompli."

ANTIDEMOCRACY: THE COUP D'ÉTAT

As against the democratic process and a system of representative government, the Arab world of the post–World War II period witnessed a seemingly endless series of military putsches and counterputsches that left these countries in most cases with one-party one-man governments, some of which remain in power today. A somewhat convoluted exposition of the "ideology" of the coup d'état is offered by Ghassan Tweini, a veteran Lebanese political writer and journalist. In *The Logic of Force: The Philosophy of the Coup d'état in the Arab East* (1954), Tweini sets out "to extract the historical principles lying behind the Syrian and Egyptian coups d'état, and to use these principles as a guide for evaluating the shifts and changes which our Arab world is witnessing" (quotations are drawn from pages 5–6 and 11–12). These historical principles dwell in two sets of contrasts that drove the course of events in Syria and Egypt through "five tightly knit phases coming in what looks like necessary and inevitable succession."

The first of these contrasts is that Egypt and Syria had been governed in accordance with democratic rules but had lacked the civic, economic, and social foundations without which democracy cannot work or survive— much less succeed: "The people cannot really govern themselves by themselves if they are not freed from the fetters that impair the election of their representatives and the bringing of them to account—fetters that in fact make these representatives impose themselves on the people whether they like it or not."

The second contrast, which springs from the first, is that these two countries are independent only in theory: "they enjoy the benefits of national sovereignty from the juridical point of view, but because of their shaky political systems, the weakness of their social and economic structures, and the poverty of their civilization, they are unable to resist imperialism in its peaceful forms and are helpless in the face of its political and military might."

It is from these two sets of contrasts, Tweini writes, that comes the first phase in the coup d'état sequence—the phase that Husni el-Za'im called the Hamidian phase (naming it after the Ottoman caliph Abdul Hamid, known for his despotic ways). This is a phase characterized by tyranny, despite any supposed democracy. It is followed by eruption, a stage in which the people start moving without having realized the causes of their discontent or having probed the way sufficiently: "The symptoms of the people's discontent and their awakening vary in their scope and seriousness; sometimes they take the form of demonstrations staged for negligible reasons, sometimes they are given expression through assassinations; they always lead to continuous and prolonged cabinet crises—and they follow each other in so regular a succession that observers usually describe them as 'the crisis of the system' or the rule."

Then comes the third and decisive phase—that of the military coup against the rulers. The army, in the name of the people, seizes power and sets up a temporary administration with the partial cooperation of politicians opposed to the Hamidian conditions or to the regime just overthrown. But, according to Tweini, "this cooperation soon results in antagonism, either because it shrinks too much or because it unduly expands, or as a result of differences of opinion between the military and the civilians—between the actual master and the nominal one who possesses legal or semi-legal authority."

It is from these contradictions that the fourth phase follows—"the phase of the search by the ruling group, in the completeness of its revolution against the old regime, for popular bases on which to erect its rule, in order to be able to dispense with the services of the civilians with whom it had cooperated. . . . In this phase the army enters the political arena by way of the new civilian apparatus, through which it wrestles with the authentic popular movements and the old political parties, and in this way tries to introduce planned democracy."

In the fifth and final phase, the weakness of a system based on naked force is exposed, though this force, whether impromptu or having the elements of permanence, may be disguised as a popular movement. This is what Tweini perceives as the logic of force: "it constitutes the historical basis of the events that the Arab world has witnessed and is witnessing, and of which the most prominent is the Syrian coup or coups, and the Egyptian one [of July 1952]."

EIGHT

RESOURCES AND DEVELOPMENT

T he question of how to set themselves and their society free from the fetters of what they variously call the West's "cultural imperialism" or "mental invasion" has exercised the minds of many Arab writers and intellectuals in recent years. The problem, as most of them formulate it, has been that since the Arabs have finally managed to liberate their lands from the political and economic dominance of the West, the time is ripe for them to try and do away with the cultural, psychological, and intellectual manifestations of that dominance.

There has been no uniformity of views about how best to accomplish this feat. There are those who argue that the break with the West should be total, since there is an intrinsic, unbridgeable difference between the culture of the West—its norms and its civilization—and that of the Muslim Arabs. Another school of thought has advanced the thesis that since much of what is now taken to be Western culture owes its origin and flowering to elements borrowed from Arab and Islamic culture back in the Middle Ages, such a break would be unnatural as well as unreasonable, impractical, and harmful. Finally, there are those who advocate full-scale Westernization as the only way to meet the challenge of the West—and of Israel as part thereof.

THE TECHNOLOGY FIX

With certain slight differences, most of those writers and scholars who tackle the subject nowadays can be said to belong to the second group—i.e., those who neither reject the West and its ways totally nor accept them unconditionally. Muhammad Husni ʿAbbas, an Egyptian professor teaching commercial and maritime law at the University of Kuwait, is a good example. In "The Arabs' Road to the Era of Technology" (*Al-ʿArabi* [Kuwait],

January 1992), ᶜAbbas does not bother to go into the pros and cons of bor-rowing from or even imitating the West, but takes it quite for granted that if they are to get anywhere, the Arabs must emulate the West. "We are," he writes, "a nation possessing all the requisites of progress—money, raw ma-terials, scientists. All we need is openly and seriously to tackle the subject of our backwardness . . . so as to discover the real reasons for this state of affairs. This is the first step in any scientific enterprise."

After diagnosis, he goes on to say, comes prescription—and after the pre-scription has been given, the role of the scientist and the scholar ends and a third phase starts: the governments must furnish the tools required for the healing to be successful. According to ᶜAbbas, technology is all. To stress this point, he asserts that what exercises the mind of Israel most is the ques-tion "What will [the Israelis] do when the Arabs attain progress . . . when they enter the era of technology?" He then cites both the defeat of the Six-Day War and the gains of the Yom Kippur War as proof that the Arabs can be ingenious and inventive—and concludes: "Thus it becomes obvious that our fate and the fate of our civilization both depend on technology. Our destiny is linked with technology in every respect—the economic, the sci-entific, the practical, the military and the political. This is the main prob-lem facing the Arab nation today."

In attempting to show how backward contemporary Arab civilization is, ᶜAbbas compares the number of patents registered by Arab scientists with those registered in developed countries. (According to the figures he cites, only 147 Arab patents were registered in 1974—compared with 50,642 in the United States, 41,070 in the USSR, 30,873 in Japan, and so on.) What then is to be done? ᶜAbbas is convinced that technology is the answer, and that the road to the era of technology must be paved by the state first and foremost. He lists five spheres in which basic reforms and legislation are needed:

- Reform of the laws governing industrial ownership

- Administrative reforms and innovations in all those bodies whose job it is to deal with science and scientific research and technology

- New legislation regulating the registration and safeguarding of patents

- A basic review of educational policies

- Joining the Paris Agreement pertaining to the protection of industrial property; the Washington Treaty of international cooperation in the field of industrial protection; and the Strasbourg Agreement on the registration of patents and inventions

It will be noted that almost all the reforms demanded by ᶜAbbas fall within his own academic discipline—legislation. Indeed, he goes so far as to claim that "regulating the transition to the era of technology is a legislative-economic problem; it is the legislators who are to blame for our technological backwardness—and no one can open the way of the legislators toward the era of technology except the State, since the whole problem pertains to legislative and administrative reform."

The complaint most generally made by Arab intellectuals in this regard focuses on another aspect of the subject. The argument goes as follows: Arabs cannot reasonably continue to import information about themselves and their lands from abroad and thus to acquire an understanding of themselves only through others. There are, both in the Arab world and abroad, Arab experts and specialists in all the scientific pursuits, and they can establish the largest and greatest of institutes in the field of strategic studies or in any other area. They add, however, that scholars and experts taking part in such enterprises should be allowed to participate without having to become officials or employees of the state.

ECONOMIC CONSIDERATIONS

Not least among the important factors at work in Arab life and politics during the past five decades has been the long and painful legacy of sheer economic backwardness, with all that that implies about poverty, disease, and illiteracy. This backwardness had very solid historical and physical reasons having little to do with the peoples of the area or their culture; the economic decline of the Arab world started some seven centuries ago. In "Decline and Revival of the Middle Eastern Economy," which serves as the introduction to his *Economic History of the Middle East, 1800–1914,* Charles Issawi tries to discern the causes of the long period of decline, stagnation, and isolation that befell the region from the twelfth century until the nineteenth. This is a relevant topic at a time when, despite one and a half centuries of recovery and steady growth, the peoples of the Middle East still appear to labor under the crippling effects of the decline.

Plainly, it is impossible to explain everything in purely economic terms. Strictly economic factors played their part, to be sure; Issawi mentions "the grave deficiencies in three major resources of the Arab Middle East: forests, minerals and rivers." In the Arab countries, he explains, forests were always scarce, and they shrank steadily with the passage of time, thus depriving preindustrial Arab society of one of the most fundamental raw materials—

wood. The general scarcity of minerals and the acute sparseness of rivers were among the lesser causes of decline, but they contributed their share.

The causes were not strictly economic, however. By the beginning of the twelfth century, "the scientific and intellectual life of Islamic society was already showing signs of fatigue and rigidity"; Islam itself "was becoming more dogmatic and intolerant." Furthermore, there was what the author terms "the lack of mechanical inventiveness of the Islamic civilization." To be sure, certain important processes and products were adopted or developed in the region between the eighth and the thirteenth centuries, "but Islam has nothing comparable to the remarkable technical advance of the Graeco-Roman civilization in the period 400 BC–100 AD or to the no less impressive progress registered in Western Europe in the 11th and 12th centuries" (4–5).

Thus, the causes were not all internal ones having to do with intrinsic attributes and characteristics of Islam or its civilization. As Issawi points out, prolonged warfare with the Crusaders, Mongols, and Tatars caused much destruction in Iraq and Syria, and "what was no less serious, in the course of repelling these invaders the Arab countries transformed themselves into militaristic, 'feudal' societies whose institutions were much less conducive to economic and social development." Moreover, the Turco-Persian wars, which dragged on for nearly three centuries, impeded the economic recovery of Iraq, and the breakdown of authority in the Ottoman Empire in the seventeenth century wrought further damage to economic and social activity throughout the provinces.

Has the Middle East really recovered from the aftereffects of this centuries-long process of decline? Issawi speaks of the beginning, in the nineteenth century, of "an upward movement which [since then] has steadily gained momentum and scope." Indeed, he considers it no exaggeration to say that during the last 150 years the Middle East "has compressed, in some regions and branches, the process through which Europe passed between the Middle Ages and the end of the 19th century" (11–12).

But there are differences as well as similarities in this parallel economic development, and it is in the differences that one can trace the reasons for the Middle East's apparent failure during the past century and a half to attain the measure of economic and technological advance achieved by Europe in its first centuries of growth. Issawi lists three spheres in which these differences were to influence later developments. In the first place, "the Middle East, although much more stagnant technologically and intellectually than Europe on the eve of the Crusades, was more urbanized, made much wider use of money in its internal transactions, and had less of a subsistence economy—with obvious consequences for its future course of development."

Second, "the high technical level and the great economic and political power of Europe, when it impinged on the Middle East in the 19th century, not only accelerated but also drastically changed the nature of the evolution of the latter." Lastly, "whereas the agents of economic change in Europe were natives, in the Middle East they were primarily foreigners. This not only gave a particular character to economic relations but meant that whereas in the medieval period the capital accumulated, the experience gained, and the external economies achieved benefited the backward area [Europe], in the modern period they accrued to the more advanced area [again Europe] and not to the Middle East." As a result, in several parts of the Middle East, foreigners performed most "middle-class" economic activities, and a "national bourgeoisie" emerged, slowly and painfully, only in the last few decades.

It was only in the nineteenth century that the process of decline and stagnation began to be reversed, Issawi concludes. In the history of the Middle East, that century forms a transitional period between the so-called medieval and the modern periods. The nineteenth century was, for the economy of the region, a period of gradual transformation, which took several forms and was at work in a number of fields. Among these, Issawi includes the integration of the region into the international commercial and financial network; the investment of foreign capital; the development of mechanical transport; the transition from subsistence-based to market-oriented agriculture; the decline of handicrafts; the growth of the population; and the attempts to establish modern industries. Yet, while this transformation, as Issawi points out, was part of the wider changes in the political, social, and cultural life of the region, more than a century of it has somehow failed to make the change real and effective (12–13).

Regarding the regional economy, Kenneth Pollack, former director of Persian Gulf Affairs at the National Security Council, maintains that although the economies of the Arab states are generally seen as "more or less broken," "some of the Gulf oil states are still doing reasonably well, but the big state that matters, Saudi Arabia, is doing very poorly. And for the rest of the Arab world, there really isn't an economy to speak of; there isn't any kind of a cash crop like oil that they can use to subsidize these massive populations" (Pollack, "America and the Middle East after Saddam," January 2004, available at http://www.fpri.org/fpriwire/1201.200401.pollack.aftersaddam.html).

The result of all this is deep frustration. The people of the region, Pollack believes, "understand that the rest of the world has taken off with globalization; even places like East Asia, which forty or fifty years ago was poor and worse off than they were. How did East Asia go from being behind them to being so far ahead of them? In every other part of the world, even in Africa, they see states that seem to be doing better than them." When they complain, they are told things like "we have to stay mobilized to go to war against the Israelis," or "it's because the Americans are manipulating our economy."

POLITICS AND DEVELOPMENT

Clearly, what the Arab world needs most is development. As Issawi puts it, "while it is futile to lament the absence of democracy in a region still un-prepared for it, it is absolutely necessary to set in motion the forces which will transform Middle Eastern society in the desired manner" if political democracy is to put down firm roots in the area. This much is fairly univer-sally accepted. But the obstacles to this kind of transformation are not easy to surmount. Yusuf Sayegh, a professor of economics at the American Uni-versity of Beirut and director of its Economic Research Institute, dealt with one aspect of the problem in a paper titled "Development and Democracy," read at the annual conference of the Middle East Institute in Washington in May 1963.

It is Sayegh's conviction that while large-scale development is eagerly desired in all Arabic-speaking countries, "this widespread concern for de-velopment is not generally accompanied by an equal concern for political democracy" (quotations are from the text of Sayegh's lecture). The truth is, he adds, that so far development and democracy have on the whole been sought and thought about separately, "although it is clear that the ordinary Arab hopes for political rights along with his hope for material and social welfare." It is therefore both timely and essential to ask what relation exists between the political ideology in force in the Arab world and the content of development, as well as how development in turn influences the ideology and locus of political power.

The relation, Sayegh believes, is neither simple nor clear, and is best ex-amined within the pattern of the distribution of power in Arab society. This is so because "the determination of the content of development, and likewise of the categories of population likely to benefit most from development, is clearly a function among other things of the identity of the group that has the authority to design and promote development." In the final analysis, "supreme economic authority resides where supreme political authority re-

sides in Arab—as in other underdeveloped and Eastern Bloc—countries."
This coincidence of political and economic power is one of the most important differences between the social systems of the more-developed countries and those of almost all other countries. In less-developed societies the
decision-making process is highly concentrated in both the political and
economic spheres, while it is diffuse and widely based in more-developed
societies.

This is no mere accident, Sayegh asserts: "Quite naturally and ratio-
nally the group that until recently enjoyed the concentration of one type
of power in its hands in the Arab world saw to it that the social system assured it of the other type of power too. It is obvious that economic power
is precarious when not protected by political power, and political power is
precarious when not supplemented by economic power, in countries like
our own where little room is allowed for the concept and the mechanism of
countervailing power familiar to Americans, Britishers, or Dutchmen."

The Arab social system has not lent itself comfortably to the application
of Western-style democratic institutions:

> The attempts have been numerous but their failure is a well-known story
> by now. Where the parliamentary system has been retained, it has done
> so as a legalized and more respectable form of oligarchy which has had
> the appearance of Western democracy but maintained the reality of con-
> centrated power. In monarchies and republics alike, the application of
> Western-style democratic institutions has done little to give the citizen
> the freedom and the power of political choice, the power to hire and to
> fire governments so to speak, which is the essence of modern Western
> democracy. In brief, when the vote failed to satisfy the real masters of
> political power, it was usually the vote that was changed; the element of
> constancy was thus the group in power, and the variable was the elector-
> ate's will which had to be bent to the accommodation point.

The first step toward the correction of the social imbalance, Sayegh concludes, is to give development a social component to go along with its economic and technological components:

> Development cannot be satisfactory if all it means is change in the pro-
> duction function and a rise in national income per head. It must mean
> something beyond more and better factories and a larger flow of goods
> and services. It must be associated with a fairer distribution of income;
> but it must also aim at a fairer distribution of ownership of wealth and

capital. And, along with these largely material advances for the masses, it must involve more and better schools and health services, more opportunities equally open to all, a reasonable measure of economic security, and above all the evolving of the legal and social institutions that will safeguard, for the formerly underprivileged individual, his newly found dignity and material betterment. With such a content, development benefits the population at large, so that no group that contributes to the realization of material progress will be deprived of the rightful rewards of its efforts.

Numerous books have been written by Arab and Muslim scholars and commentators on the causes of underdevelopment, the factors that tend to perpetuate it, and the reasons why nearly all the innumerable plans and projects drawn up by governments to rectify the situation remain largely ink on paper. Two of these are worth mentioning here in brief.

In *From Here We Start* (1950), Khalid Muhammad Khalid (1920–1996), an Egyptian Muslim scholar of note and well-known for his generally liberal stands, deals with the causes of rural poverty in Egypt and the centuries-old lethargy and submissiveness of the peasant population. (The work of Khalid and al-Qasim, below, is summarized and quoted in Sa'id B. Himadeh, "Social Awakening and Economic Development in the Middle East," in Laqueur, *The Middle East in Transition*.) Stressing the need for social change, Khalid proposes a just socialism as the only solution to Egypt's problems. Khalid's main theses:

- A sound understanding is needed of the spirit of religion.

- "Sheikhcraft" (priestcraft) has misinterpreted religion and its mission, held the people in chains of superstition, and defended poverty and ignorance.

- Religion is essentially democratic and humane, contrary to the teachings of sheikhcraft, which denies freedom of thought and opposes democracy.

- Women should be emancipated and granted full civil and political rights.

- The toiling masses, long forgotten, are beginning to wake up.

Another Muslim scholar, Abdullah 'Ali al-Qasim, in a book entitled *These Are the Chains*, makes the following points:

- Western civilization has some merit.

- Traditionalism has kept Arab and Muslim society in chains.

- Arab societies should adopt the spirit of Western civilization.

- The essence of modern man's greatness is his intellectual daring, which has harnessed nature and conquered such enemies as poverty, disease, and ignorance.

- Through an erroneous concept of religion, religious leaders have indoctrinated the people with a defeatist attitude toward life, with unquestioning acceptance of authority and resignation to their miserable lot in this world.

- The mission of Islam is to redeem people from the enslavement of mind and will; from submission to the tyranny of leaders and governmental systems that inflict poverty, distress, and misery; and from the grip of fixed doctrines and beliefs that hinder people from liberation and stunt the development of their creative faculties.

- Men's tyranny against women is deplorable, and women's degraded status can be ascribed to a false interpretation of religion.

NINE

THE SOCIAL SCENE

THE STATUS OF WOMEN

Observers generally treat the status of women in the Arab world as if it were uniform or at least very similar all over the area. Islam's perceived rulings concerning that status are habitually cited, and generalizations made accordingly. The actual situation, however, is vastly different, as the experience of one Arab country, Yemen, shows. In Yemen, whose two "parts" were reunited in 1990 after two centuries of separation, a new law of personal status was passed in May 1991, driving women of former South Yemen (Aden) to the streets in protest.

The new law, while in part a considerable improvement as far as women of the former North Yemen were concerned, robs Adeni women of rights and privileges they had enjoyed under the Marxist regime there since 1974. Changes introduced by the new legislation put Adeni women under obvious disadvantages. Under this law, men are no longer barred from taking a second wife (which they had been allowed to do only in cases in which the wife was terminally ill or barren); divorced women cannot keep the house they had shared with their husbands; and the maximal limit put on dowries—$215—was lifted, with the result that brides will henceforth be given to the highest bidder, as in the North, where a dowry can be as much as $5,000. (The per capita gross domestic product in Yemen in 1990 was approximately $545; data is available at "Yemen Economy—1991," http://www .theodora.com/wfb1991/yemen/yemen_economy.html.)

Other regressive features of the new law include the provision that a girl can be wed "when she reaches maturity"—which can mean that she could be as young as thirteen or fourteen, whereas the existing law in the South put an age limit of sixteen. The legislature eventually adopted an age limit of fifteen for males and females.

If anything, the gap separating the respective positions of women in the two parts of this one country shows how risky it is to generalize about the status of "Arab women." To take another example: whereas women in the former South Yemen functioned as judges and worked in other judicial capacities, and joined the police and the armed forces, all these occupations were strictly out of bounds for women of the North. Among Adeni women there have been also many apprehensions about the future. It is feared, for instance, that when the many ailing state companies decide to lay off workers, the first to go will be their female employees. Again, educated women of the South fear that if the Islamists of the North get the upper hand in government, women will be forced to give up work outside the home and be confined to their kitchens, a course of action that they say is not in keeping with the teachings of Islam.

We all know that we live in "a man's world," but the term "male morality" is at once more poignant and less familiar. The Lebanese poet Adonis coined the phrase in Arabic in a book that dealt with the nature of Arab culture and Arabic literature, pointing out that Arab society is governed by "a male morality." Needless to say, wherever male morality rules, sexual customs and mores tend to perpetuate double standards, generally requiring women to observe the strictest rules of chastity while allowing men unlimited sexual freedom. The phenomenon was commonly known and recognized in nineteenth-century Europe, especially in Victorian England.

Things, however, are not as bad as they seem. Colette Khuri, a Syrian novelist who shocked the Arab literary world in 1959 with the publication of her first book, *Ayyam Ma'ahu* (Days with Him), an unusually frank and daring narrative by an emancipated young woman, told a Lebanese reporter that as far as their place in society was concerned, the women of today have very little to complain about. They no longer have to wear the veil; they work in factories and offices side by side with men; they mix more or less freely socially; and they are economically far less dependent than they were even ten years ago.

However, Khuri was aware that all these gains have so far failed to affect "the essence of the problem," which she summed up as "How can woman fulfill her humanity in a stealthy, backward society?" Economic emancipation, she added, is just not enough: it does not automatically give women the self-assurance they need—"This will take time" (quoted in Nissim Rejwan, "Arab Women's Long Road to Liberation," 15–16).

Khuri certainly knows what she is talking about, and part of the trouble no doubt lies in Adonis's characterization of male morality. Ambiguity and double standards still seem to be the rule, and the general Arab attitude toward the emancipation of women continues to suffer from glaring inconsistencies. More than one Arab writer and sociologist has remarked on the wide difference between the contemporary young educated Arab male's intellectual image of his female friends and associates and his actual behavior toward them.

With all his education and liberal views, they point out, this young man continues to subscribe to the age-old belief that a woman outside the safe walls of the home is in mortal danger of losing her chastity, and that she has no business exposing her charms in modern dresses unless she means to sell them or give them away. Moreover, he automatically disqualifies as a wife any girl who would give herself out of wedlock, even to him.

This disparity is paralleled by another, no less pronounced one: young men and women, going through the same educational system, attending the same universities, and imbibing the same modern notions of the West about women and their place in society emerge from their training with widely disparate attitudes and expectations. In many cases, this results in disappointment and disillusion—sometimes even with tragic consequences.

Fatima Mernissi, a professor of sociology at the University of Rabat, is a true feminist—candid, articulate, and persuasive. One of the most fascinating and instructive features of her book *Beyond the Veil* (1975) is the way she approaches her subject, and the distinction she draws between sexual inequality in the West and in Islam. In Western culture, she argues, this inequality is based on a belief in women's biological inferiority. "This," she writes, "explains some aspects of Western women's liberation movements, such as that they are almost always led by women, that their effect is often very superficial, and that they have not yet succeeded in significantly changing the male-female dynamics in that culture" (*Beyond the Veil;* quotations are drawn from pages 176–177). In Islam, by contrast, there is no such belief in female inferiority. "On the contrary," she adds, "the whole system is based on the assumption that women are powerful and dangerous beings. All sexual institutions (polygamy, repudiation, sexual segregation, etc.) can be perceived as a strategy for containing their power."

According to Mernissi, this belief in the potent powers of women is likely to give the evolution of the relationship between men and women in Muslim settings a pattern entirely different from the Western one. If, for instance, there are any changes in male-female status and relations in Muslim society, these changes "will tend to be more radical than in the West and will necessarily generate more tension, more conflict, more anxiety, and more aggression." This is because, while the women's liberation movement in the West focuses on women and their claim for equality with men, "in Muslim countries it would tend to focus on the mode of relatedness between the sexes and thus would probably be led by men and women alike." Because men can see how the oppression of women works against men themselves, "women's liberation would [in Muslim society] assume the character of a generational rather than sexual conflict." Mernissi indeed maintains that this could already be seen "in the opposition between young nationalists and old traditionalists at the beginning of the century, and currently it can be seen in the conflict between parents and children over the dying institution of arranged marriage."

Not that Mernissi is unaware of the plight of women in the Muslim societies of today. As she sees it, one of the distinctive characteristics of Muslim sexuality is its "territoriality," which reflects a specific division of labor and a specific conception of society and power. "The territoriality of Muslim sexuality," she explains, "sets patterns of ranks, tasks, and authority. Spatially confined, women were taken care of materially by the men who possessed them, in exchange for total obedience and sexual and reproductive services. The whole system was organized so that the Muslim umma (community) was actually a society of male citizens who possessed, among other things, the female half of the population." She quotes with approval a Lebanese writer—a man—who remarks bitterly that while people generally say that there are 100 million Arabs, in fact there are only 50 million, the female population being prevented from taking part in social responsibilities: "Muslim men have always had many more rights and privileges than Muslim women, including even the right to kill their women."

It has often been said that women's liberation is ultimately men's liberation. Referring to the article in Morocco's family law that defines the man as the sole provider for the family, Mernissi propounds this same thesis in more practical terms. "To define masculinity as the capacity to earn a salary," she writes,

> is to condemn those men suffering from unemployment (or the threat of it) to perceive economic problems as castration threats. Moreover, since the Code defines earning a salary as a man's role, a woman who earns a salary will be perceived as either masculine or castrating. If the privileges of men become more easily accessible to women, then men will be perceived as becoming more feminine. . . . The authority of males, traditionally embodied in their ability to provide for their families, is seriously jeopardized by their present situation. . . . Modernization, in these terms, clearly appears to be a castrating phenomenon. (12–13)

ISLAM'S STAND: TWO VERSIONS

It would be wrong, however, to infer from Mernissi's account that the situation of women in all Islamic societies is uniform or even similar. Judith E. Tucker, who spent some time in Egypt researching the subject and had access to primary sources, is vigorously critical of this approach. In a long introduction to *Women in Nineteenth-Century Egypt* (1985), she rejects that part of the Orientalist heritage that perceives Middle Eastern history as the embodiment of "the Islamic spirit" rather than as the outcome of a complex interaction of material forces and ideological formations. "Faced with a dearth of information on the historical reality of women in the region," she writes, "many writers simply revert to 'Islam' for both description and cause of women's position. 'Islamic' concepts, customs, and sexual mores both dictate and define women's role in society" (3–5). Tucker considers this argument tautological and therefore totally unverifiable: Muslim laws and customs reflect women's reality. That is, we can know how women lived and worked from a study of the rules, formal and informal, applicable to them; these same rules, however, also function as the main instrument of women's oppression, for they assign women an inferior position in society and limit their activities.

The actual situation is rather different, and evidence points to the diversity and complexity of women's roles in societies in which Islam is the dominant religion. Tucker's carefully researched account makes it abundantly clear that women in nineteenth-century Egypt did not live in some sort of timeless privatized world untouched by historical change, for women "were affected by and, through their own actions, helped to shape, the sweeping changes of the period." To define the position of Egyptian women in the period covered—1800–1914—Tucker seeks to explore four interlocking dimensions of women's position and power: women's access to property; their position in the family unit; their participation in social production; and the prevailing ideological definitions of their roles. Each of these dimensions is discussed "against a backdrop of broad economic and social changes arising, in part, from the ongoing integration of Egypt into an economic system dominated by the West."

Another Western student of the subject, Nikki R. Keddie, has drawn a number of far-reaching conclusions. In a paper entitled "Deciphering Middle Eastern Women's History," she writes, "Feminists disagree about whether they should continue trying to interpret Islam in reformist ways or rather should stand foursquare for secularization, saying that Islam should be a matter for private belief and worship only" (in Keddie, *Women in Middle Eastern History,* 19). Those who stress the more liberal interpretation hope to meet some of the cultural needs of ordinary women, including Islamists, while the more radical reformists say that approach would serve only to prolong the repressive life and practices of political Islam.

The truth, as Keddie sees it, is that faced with the rising Islamist wave, both the feminists who are convinced that Islamic theory can be reinterpreted in favor of their cause and those who say this would be playing into the hands of the antifeminists are trying to find the most promising way "to bring back a situation in which women's rights may be actively furthered." How realistic is such a prospect? Keddie is understandably rather wary. "It may be," she concludes, "that both the Islamic reformist and the secularist paths can contribute to this, especially if they concentrate more on the needs and desires of popular-class women."

Delving more deeply into the subject and going back as far as the first years of Islam, Nabia Abbott, a Middle Easterner herself, writes about ᶜAisha, the prophet's favorite among his wives. In *Aishah: The Beloved of Mohammed* (1942), she tells the story of this remarkable woman. The daughter of Muhammad's right-hand man (and successor) Abu Bakr, ᶜAisha, "with her lively temperament and pert charm," brought a refreshing air of romance into the closing years of the Prophet's life (quotations are drawn from pages xvii–xviii).

But it is ᶜAisha the widow and her activities that occupy the bulk of the biography. At Muhammad's death, ᶜAisha was still a young woman: "How she made herself felt in the life of the prophet and how, after his death, she continued, for something like half a century, to exert her influence on the affairs of the new Muslim state are major and lively themes of early Islamic history." Drawing on a wealth of oral traditions and other sources, Abbott produced a work that is both scholarly and a pleasure to read. Although Abbott wrote it in the early 1940s, her attitude toward the women's movement in the Middle East is enthusiastic as well as hopeful, calling it "the most significant single factor in changing the Middle East, even as the status of woman is everywhere the most significant measure of civilization and human progress."

We learn from Abbott's book that the status of women in Islam has undergone many changes and revisions since the time of Muhammad. Muhammad's own attitude did not favor complete equality. For, as Abbott points out, although he did initiate certain improvements in the legal and socioeconomic status of all Muslim women, other aspects of his practice "left women forever inferior to man, placed one step below him." In the religious domain, Abbott concedes, women were readily accepted by the Prophet as converts and received encouragement and honors. She insists, however, that "the crucial test of woman's real position is to be looked for in the field of active leadership: Was she allowed to fill all or any of the public offices associated with the new religious life?" No uniform answer to this question either is or can be given: what is certain is that while women in early Islam were able to exert considerable influence (Muhammad made no objection to a woman acting as a prayer leader in her own house, for example), the role of Muslim women in the public aspects of religion gradually diminished.

The position of women in Egypt today offers a partial illustration of their situation in several other Arab countries. In 1979, as a result of efforts by women's organizations and the interest taken by then-president Sadat's wife, Jihan, certain substantial amendments were made to the country's personal-status law of 1920, which had first been amended in 1957. A detailed account of these efforts, and of their results, is given in Nadia Hijab's *Womanpower: The Arab Debate on Women at Work* (1988; quotations in the following paragraphs are drawn from pages 32–33).

When the amendments to the law were being advocated, Hijab reports, there was some criticism of the role played by female deputies in parliament, who, many writers said, had remained strangely silent. (Under the electoral law in force at the time, there had to be a minimum of thirty women in parliament.) Some of the female deputies defended themselves by saying that they were working behind the scenes, and had left the talking to the men so that they would not be accused of defending the law simply because it was a woman's law.

Concurrently, the debate about women's rights in Islam heated up. The respected columnist Ahmad Bahaeddine wrote in *Al-Ahram* (May 8, 1979), "The articles of the law should be taken up by a deputy and presented to parliament anew, and woman, who has the right to vote and be elected, and to serve as minister, must give her opinion on such a law." He added on May 12, "Those who interpret the rulings of Islamic Shariᶜa are men, and those who pass laws of all description are men. The world has been a man's world for thousands of years, and even if the message of heaven comes to bring women justice, the world of men listens a little, then goes back to its previous ways."

Not all writers were so liberal, Hijab adds. Ahmad Bahgat, also writing in *Al-Ahram* (May 6, 1979), asserted that he had had objections to the law from the start: "The amendments did not bring justice; indeed, they brought unintended injustice. The amendments were contrary to Islamic Shariᶜa in more than one area." He added on May 7, "What Almighty God has allowed should not be described as harmful," referring to the article whereby polygamy was judged to be harmful and grounds for divorce.

Another columnist cited by Hijab declared in *Al-Gumhouriya* (May 18, 1979) that there was "a difference between women's freedom and women's liberation. Islam gives women many rights, and more freedom and respect. But it does not recognize the wave of liberation which some ladies are calling for. Islam protects the Muslim woman who is decent and who respects her home, her husband and children. Islam does not give rights to the woman who rebels and who is nashez [who leaves her husband's house and refuses to return]. Islam protects the veiled woman, but it does not look at the woman in a bikini."

Some writers were critical of what they saw as women's half-hearted efforts to remedy their position. In *Al-Musawwar* (May 17, 1979), Hussain Ahmad Amin, a columnist noted for his liberal Islamist views, declared,

> As for our women, in spite of my sympathies for their plight, I say frankly I am not sorry to see them lose rights that were not the fruits of real efforts on their part. How easy it is to lose rights that come without struggle. The conditions of women all over the world were similar at one time, no better than those of slaves. The European or American woman only got her rights after a bitter fight and as the fruit of centuries of development and struggle. As for our society . . . these rights came because of two or three books written by men earlier this century, because of the struggle of some wives of prominent men, and because our governments want the West to look upon them as enlightened. They are always rights that are given, not rights that are taken.

Addressing himself to the dozens of women who had urged him to write in favor of restoring the law, Amin declared,

> Crying and complaining never won rights, nor does wailing and breast-beating ever erase injustice. Organize yourselves; register your objections; raise your voices so that people may know you have voices. Write to your deputies in parliament; convince one of them to present the law anew. Above all, let the educated among yourselves, and this should be easy, strive to prove that the rulings of this law are not in conflict with the Shariᶜa as some claim. Let them try, and this is harder, to put an end to this miserable holier-than-thou bargaining and trading with religion that has become such a heavy nightmare. (33–34)

In fact, Hijab adds, there were divisions in the women's ranks, and personality and political clashes surfaced at meetings. One columnist wrote in *Al-Gumhouriya* (May 16, 1979) that the cancellation of the law "revealed the lack of unity in women's ranks and the absence of an organization to speak in women's name." Referring to a women's meeting that had taken place, she said sarcastically that nothing had come of it but the decision to hold another meeting. "If the women of Egypt cannot unite over the question which affects the life and future of each and every one of them, they will never unite," she declared.

As the days passed, Egyptian women began to work together a little more effectively than before, according to several women who were involved in the campaign to restore the law. As Aziza Hussain, a longtime campaigner for women's rights, described it to Hijab in July 1985, "We decided we had to get this law back because the decision was a setback and other setbacks would follow if we did not act, although most of us did not think the law was good enough. We went to the head of the constitutional court, and to everyone involved including the minister of social affairs. We dug out copies of 1979 law with the accompanying explanations for the Shariʿa and passed them round so everyone could understand it."

Hijab further quotes Malak Zaalouk, a social scientist who had also been active in the campaign, from an interview:

> We learned to work together. We worked round the clock to educate people. At one meeting we drafted a law and were careful not to be too extremist. Some of the men and some religious scholars said we were being too careful; they said polygamy should be abolished completely, without beating about the bush. We formed a committee to defend the Egyptian woman and family, and we have decided to continue its work. We will not be restricted to this issue but will take up political rights and consciousness-raising. The people on the committee are not narrow feminists but can make the link between the political, economic and social spheres. (34)

How much the women would have achieved, and how much further they would have been prepared to go, had the government not been on their side is another matter, Hijab reflects. The Hosni Mubarak regime, which replaced Sadat's in 1981, clearly wanted to see the law restored. The female minister of social affairs, Amal Othman, was most active in this respect. Within days of the constitutional court's decision, an official committee was formed to conduct a quick study on the rights of women in Islam. Some days later the parliament speaker convened a meeting of female deputies to discuss preparing a new draft of the personal-status law.

Just weeks after Law No. 44 had been scrapped, a new personal status code was passed by parliament for the first time in Egyptian history: the 1929 and 1979 amendments had been passed by royal and presidential decrees. The new law was passed just in time for the UN End-of-Decade conference in Nairobi in July 1985. This, cynics said, was deliberate so that the Egyptian Government would look "modern" at the meeting. The 1985 Law kept the basic amendments of the 1979 Law, with some changes. For instance, it made the judge responsible for deciding whether a wife had been harmed by a second marriage; in Law No. 44 this had automatically been grounds for divorce. On the other hand, the new law provided for penalties to enforce its provisions, which the 1979 Law had not done. (35)

"As can be seen from all of the above," Hijab concludes,

the issue of family law and of women's personal rights is debated almost entirely within an Islamic framework by both conservatives and liberals. What should be noted is that, in the case of Algeria and Egypt, it proved difficult for the Government to ignore both the need for reform and the number of people seeking reform, even if this displeased the conservatives. Significantly, in many of the debates we have examined above, women were fairly vociferous, and female lawyers were able to argue the issue of women's rights on solid grounds. As Al-Awadhi declared, women must know their legal rights as a first step towards achieving them. Moreover, people were willing to go public with their grievances, and to organize demonstrations, petitions and media campaigns. True, this was done on a limited scale, but considering that most serious political opposition has been crushed in the Arab world, the extent of the response was dramatic. (35–36)

EDUCATION AND ILLITERACY

It is estimated that the population of the twenty-two members of the League of Arab States totaled 300,000,000 in the year 2005. The range of problems this unprecedented population growth poses is staggering. Many of these can be grouped together under the heading, "educational, scientific and cultural," and it was to deal with such problems that the Arab Educational, Scientific and Cultural Organization was established in the early 1980s.

An idea of the kind of problem tackled by the organization can be found in a lengthy interview with its then-first secretary, Fuad Nas'hi, conducted by the Beirut weekly *Al-Sayyad* and published on January 17, 1991. Citing an old Chinese proverb—"If you want to make your harvest in a year, go for wheat; if you want it in 10 years, plant a tree; and if you want a hundred years' harvest, teach the people"—Nas'hi called for long-range planning to combat illiteracy, undoubtedly the most acute problem facing the Arab world today and the source of many others.

According to Nas'hi, if the Arabs continued to combat illiteracy as they had done in the 1980s, it would take them some forty years to eradicate it. Statistics from the early 1970s, he explained, showed that 61 percent of all Arabs age ten or older were illiterate; that the proportion was far greater among females; and that during the previous decade the total number of illiterates had increased, despite a drop in the percentage of the population unable to read. He attributed these deficits to the steady growth in population, the failure of many Arab governments effectively to implement compulsory education, and lack of both adequate tools and sufficient allocations for the campaign to combat illiteracy.

To remedy this state of affairs, Nas'hi suggested that all youngsters who read and write be mobilized to spend three years helping in the campaign, "so that illiteracy will be totally eradicated." In another part of the interview, however, he sounded far less optimistic. Speaking of the obstacles facing Arab society in its march toward modernization, he listed a number of "negative aspects of the Arab character" that he thought constituted such an obstacle:

- Disdain for manual work and a "worship" of clerical jobs, which leads to inflation in administrative jobs and bureaucracy

- Insufficient public spirit and "collective consciousness" as well as too much fatalism and a propensity to trust in mystical concepts

- Lack of appreciation for the value of time and a refusal to be punctual

This being the case, Nas'hi said, any serious attempt to deal with the problems at issue in his organization, whether in the social, economic, educational, or cultural sphere, "ought to stipulate ways of creating a positive breed of Arab citizen capable of contributing to the reconstruction of society."

In this drive, efforts to improve the lot of the Arab woman and increase her participation in the reconstruction of society should take a prominent place. This situation has already improved considerably: in legislation as well as in theory, Nas'hi pointed out, women now enjoyed equality with men in most Arab countries. Egypt was perhaps the most advanced in this respect. At least one cabinet post, that of social affairs, was held by a woman; several women were members of the People's Assembly, each representing one Cairo constituency; and more girls than boys were enrolled in the Arts College at Cairo University.

At the other end of the scale, women's causes face strong opposition on the ground that a woman's proper place is in the home. However, even in Saudi Arabia, for instance, things have improved quite radically. In 1960 the Saudi government decided to open a limited number of schools for girls; ten years later, in the 1970–1971 school year, the number of schools for girls had jumped to 464, catering to 152,000 pupils, and the funds allocated were 242 times the 1960 budget.

Despite such progress, however, Nas'hi admitted that the advancement of women in the Arab world continued to be fraught with difficulties. First, there was the stubborn opposition by Islamic conservatives who oppose women's active participation in public places of work and in public life in general; then there was the illiteracy rate among women, more than 80 percent, higher even than among men; finally, there was the failure of those girls who finish primary or secondary school to move on to vocational and technological schools and colleges, or else to do so in very small numbers.

On the problems of illiteracy, briefly referred to by Nas'hi, Arab leaders, teachers, and educators have for decades been engaged in what has turned out to be a veritable wild-goose chase. In the campaign to eradicate illiteracy—often termed "the war against illiteracy"—all Arab governments took a hand, some more, some less, but invariably to little or no avail. In Egypt, to take one example, not only has the total number of illiterates failed to drop, it has actually increased.

Periodically, whenever new statistics and estimates are released, the subject captures headlines in the more serious weeklies and monthlies. This happened in April 1992, when new figures and forecasts were published by the United Nations Educational, Social and Cultural Organization (UNESCO). The gist of these statistics is that by 2025 the combined population of the twenty-two members of the Arab League will hit 400 million. It is also estimated that if present policies of growth and development are maintained, the resources available in 2025 will suffice for not more than a quarter of that total. (The UNESCO figures and the remarks by Al-Sab^c, below, are excerpted in Nissim Rejwan, "Arab Countries Are Losing the Literacy Battle," *Jerusalem Post*, May 15, 1992).

On the literacy front, the relevant statistics were released to the Arab press personally by the noted Sudanese novelist al-Tayyib al-Saleh, a UNESCO official. Refraining from making forecasts, al-Saleh revealed that of the 230 million Arabs in 1991, 100 million (43 percent) were illiterate. The publication of these figures created an outpouring of lamentation accompanied by cries of disbelief. Yet they should not have been unexpected, as the illiteracy rates in a few of the more densely populated Arab countries demonstrate: Sudan, 60 percent; Egypt and Morocco, 45 percent; Yemen, 40 percent; and Iraq, 30 percent. What drives many Arab observers to distraction is that the situation tends to worsen over the years. It looks like a classic example of the working of the vicious circle: a high population growth rate, coupled with a backward educational system and a low standard of living, leads in turn to a further increase in the number—and percentage—of illiterates; a further weakening of the educational apparatus; and a continued failure to lower the birthrate.

The case of Egypt, where serious attempts have been and are still being made to fight illiteracy, is especially instructive. Toward the end of the 1980s, President Hosni Mubarak announced that the decade starting in 1990 would be devoted to the eradication of illiteracy. This was not the first campaign of its kind to be started in Egypt. Successive governments before Mubarak's had made exactly the same promises and submitted remarkably similar blueprints. Statistics, however, can sometimes be misleading. Mubarak asserted, for example, that the total number of illiterates in Egypt was 9,750,000. But that figure included only citizens between the ages of fifteen and forty-five. When it comes to Egyptians age ten and older, the total nearly doubles, and the percentage rises to almost 45.

Several factors are cited as being responsible for this situation, the most decisive being the inability of the Egyptian educational system to accommodate the potential school population—not even all those age 6–15, who are officially covered by the compulsory-education law. And so, year after year about 20 percent of the children who are supposed to attend school fail to do so, or are simply not admitted for lack of classrooms. Of those eligible for secondary education (age 15–18), moreover, hardly a quarter of the total are actually enrolled, the number of dropouts being estimated at 300,000.

The situation is by no means better where the Arab world as a whole is concerned. According to figures released by UNESCO in 1995, the total number of illiterates among those fifteen and older was 61 million, while the number of illiterates among those age 6–15 was 23 million. In the mid-1990s, moreover, the number of Arab children age 6–11 who never attended school was about eight million, in addition to several million dropouts. Among these, a substantial majority are females.

These figures have led to a number of reappraisals and a good deal of soul-searching and self-criticism. One commentator, Hasan al-Sab^c, ridicules what he perceives as the Arabs' preoccupation with the West's alleged conspiracies against them, the perils of the New World Order, and the obsession with arms and armaments. What, he asks, is the relation between these so-called anti-Arab designs and the war against illiteracy or long-range planning for growth and development?

The problem, al-Sab^c asserts in an article in the London-based daily *Al-Hayat*, is not that the outside world—"always the West"—is busy conspiring against the Arabs. "The trouble is that the West is deserting us, does not pay us due attention, and fails to save us from our current state of indecision, backwardness and chaos," he writes. "The situation has become such that we ought now to be apprehensive lest, with the onset of the twenty-first century, some international trusteeship council be appointed to handle the affairs of 300 million Arabs!"

The subject of illiteracy, al-Sab^c concludes, is as crucial for the Arabs as the Palestine question, "and in the long run possibly even graver." It is high time the Arabs started tackling such problems as the population explosion, shortages of food and water, and others threatening a veritable calamity. "The problem," he concludes, "is not that there are 100 million Arabs who neither read nor write. The problem is that there are 100 million Arabs who read and write solely in the books of the past, paying no heed to the present or the future."

THE YOUNGER GENERATION

Taken as a whole, Arab society is one of the youngest in the world; hence the increasing preoccupation of Arab economists, sociologists, and psychologists with the specific problems of Arab youths and adolescents and the proliferation of writing on the subject in recent years. The most visible of these problems are, of course, the socioeconomic and demographic ones—unemployment, emigration, the "brain drain," excessive birthrates, and urban growth.

In 2006, the ten largest cities in the Arab world were Cairo (15.8 million), Khartoum, (5.75 million), Baghdad (5.65 million), Alexandria (5.5 million), Riyadh (4.65 million), Algiers (4.2 million), Casablanca (3.85 million), Amman (3.15 million), Jidda (3.125 million), and Damascus (2.85 million). The movement from villages to urban centers has involved tens of millions of souls, with the result that the percentage of city dwellers in the Arab world as a whole has jumped from 38 in 1970 to 53 in 2000—and it is expected to go up to 65 percent by 2030 (see *World Urbanization Prospects: The 2001 Revision,* United Nations, 2002).

The percentage of urban dwellers in 2000 was especially high in oil-rich countries like Iraq (68), Saudi Arabia (86), Kuwait (96), Algeria (57), and Libya (88). In the other Arab countries the situation was only relatively less critical: Lebanon had 90 percent of its population living in urban centers; Syria, 51; Egypt, 43; Tunisia, 66; Sudan, 36; and Yemen, 25.

Suggestions for solutions to these problems are usually offered in plenty by all and sundry: cuts in the colossal expenditures on arms and armaments, and, by inference, increased efforts to resolve the Israeli-Arab conflict; job creation for the armies of unemployed, thus discouraging the emigration to Europe of hundreds of thousands of young men in search of employment; large-scale reclamation of land for agriculture as well as other measures to stem the tide of agricultural workers streaming to the cities; and creating opportunities for scientific research, to prevent the continuing flight of doctors, engineers, and scientists from the Arab world to Europe and the United States.

In addition to these basically material problems, there are, according to some Arab observers and scholars, even more crucial issues in the sphere of psychology and human relations. One of these is the set of problems confronting the Arab teenagers and youngsters now reaching maturity in the millions. Are these problems peculiar to Arab youths? If so, how? More than six decades ago Salama Mousa, an Egyptian writer and thinker with opinions and practical proposals so advanced that they proved unacceptable to his contemporaries, wrote a short essay in which he enumerated the points of contrast between the young males of Egypt and Europe. When we compare the two, he wrote, we find them equal in intelligence and perhaps in training and education—but there the comparison ends (Mousa's essay is summarized in Nissim Rejwan, "Arab Youths and Their Discontents," 17–18).

Among the disabilities that Mousa found in the young Egyptian when compared to his European counterpart were:

• Unlike his European contemporary, the young Egyptian male is beset by an inability to be at ease with members of the opposite sex, to confront his superiors on equal terms, or to act without fear and feelings of weakness and helplessness.

• While the European youth enjoys freedom of action within the home, his Egyptian counterpart grows up in an atmosphere of coercion and submission; he kisses his parents' hands instead of their cheeks; he notices that his mother wears the veil and learns from her a fear of forwardness and directness.

- In school the Egyptian boy finds that his teachers are concerned more about exams than about the formation of his personality, that they demand obedience rather than affection. After spending his boyhood and adolescence in an all-male environment, moreover, the boy leaves school assuming a world in which the sexes are separated, so that a young man of twenty will in all probability have had no experience of dealing or discoursing with a woman other than his mother and sisters.

Mousa's observations were made in the early 1940s. Since then the world has undergone some profound changes, of which the revolution of the young has not been the least significant. In greater or lesser measure, the Arab world was duly affected by these changes. However, a number of field studies of the Arab world tend to indicate that the basic problems posed by Mousa in his short sketch continue to beset the young Egyptian—as well as other Arab youngsters, male and female. This emerges from a perusal of the proceedings of conferences regularly held in the Arab world, mostly in Cairo, by psychologists and social scientists from different Arab countries. One such gathering dealt with the topic "The Arab Adolescent: His Life and Problems"; it was organized by the National Center for Social and Criminological Studies, Egypt's foremost institute of its kind (the proceedings are summarized in Rejwan, "Arab Youths and Their Discontents").

To the observer interested specifically in the problems of Arab youngsters, the symposium was partly disappointing, since almost half the experts dwelt on adolescence generally, concentrating mostly on the emotional conflicts experienced by the adolescent and explaining how these conflicts are the result of an inability to express newly developed needs in a socially acceptable manner.

On the problems of the Arab adolescent in particular, his feelings and patterns of behavior, a number of papers were read, consisting mostly of the results of "preliminary" research conducted among samples of young men and women in certain parts of the Arab world. One of the most interesting of these was the paper submitted by Othman Farraj of the American University of Cairo, in which he surveyed "the problems of the Arab adolescent" on the strength of a questionnaire distributed among first-year students at the American University of Cairo and the American University of Beirut.

The study revealed a huge "gap" between the adolescents and their parents: 72 percent of the male students said they did not like the way they were treated by their fathers, while 84 percent of the girls admitted they hid their emotional problems from their mothers. However, the question whether these percentages were higher or lower than those prevalent among the adolescents of Europe and the United States was not dealt with.

A little more helpful was Khalil Shihab, who summarized the findings of a questionnaire on which his PhD dissertation was based. The dissertation, which won him a degree from Columbia University, dealt with "the social, psychological and personal problems of the Arab adolescent" and was based on research conducted among samples of Egyptian, Iraqi, Algerian, Sudanese, and Syrian young men and women. Shihab's findings revealed that the Arab adolescent's acutest problems were, in rank order, "the hardships of school life, the problem of absorbing the material taught, lack of freedom in choosing a profession or discipline, sexual problems, bad health, and lots of leisure time which the adolescent did not know how to pass."

Again, we do not know how these findings compare with those of other studies conducted in other parts of the world. Munira Ahmed Hilmi, whose paper dealt with the psychological crises suffered by Arab adolescents, found that 40 percent of them were beset by such crises and that the source of these was "the persistent frustration experienced by the Arab adolescent in his scholastic career."

By far the most informative paper was one based on research conducted by the center itself. Drawn from responses by students from various parts of the Arab world and processed by computers, the study revealed that in the paramount field of leisure, 61 percent of Arab adolescents did not own a television set, 47 percent did not know how to organize their leisure, and 44 percent said they lived "in a fatal vacuum." On their life at school, 30 percent complained there was not enough coordination between home and school, 35 percent said most teachers were inept at their job, 38 percent claimed that some teachers did not pay their pupils enough attention, and another 38 percent accused some teachers of favoring certain students.

The Cairo symposium surveyed above was basically an academic affair, and the papers presented were prepared by specialists applying their psychosociological tools and insights. More recently, in a series of wide-ranging interviews published in the Islamic-oriented London-based Arabic weekly *Al-ʿAlam,* the same subject was addressed by four ʿulema (religious savants) rather than by specialists. The questions put to these dignitaries were searching and fairly comprehensive: What are the problems besetting Arab-Muslim young men and women today? What are the causes of the perplexity felt by these youths in confronting the challenges by the modern world to Muslim culture and the Islamic heritage? Finally, what measures did the four venerable savants suggest for facing these challenges effectively and preserving Islamic values and the personality of the Muslim intact? (These interviews are excerpted in Rejwan, "Arab Youths and Their Discontents.")

The answers given by the four ᶜulema to these questions, and to others relating to the same subject, make interesting reading. Taking part in the mini-symposium were Dr. Ahmad al-Waʾili, Dr. Ibrahim al-Salqini, Dr. Muhammad al-Zehili, and Shawqi Abu Khalil, all of whom live and work in Damascus. According to al-Waʾili, a Shiᶜite theologian born in Najaf, Iraq, one problem that confronts all youths nowadays, including Muslims, is that of what he called "ideological vacuum," which he believes is a result of the prevailing lack of purpose and "the absence of a sense of mission." This state of affairs, he asserts, has led these youths to concentrate on material gains and the satisfaction of their "animal drives" without paying any heed to morality, ethics, and the life of the spirit. In such an atmosphere, he adds, values become sheer rhetoric, morality a mere device for simulating a distinction between human society and the animal world.

This applies mainly to the nonbelievers among young Muslims, al-Waʾili remarks. The believers among them, for their part, are torn asunder by the multiplicity of schools of thought in Islam. Inasmuch as Muslims generally are divided among themselves, both on the theoretical and the practical planes, a Muslim youth today finds himself totally unable to resolve the problems facing him and his society—starting from the smallest detail and going up all the way to the major issues of the day, such as the kind of political regime best suited for Muslims today. Needless to say, this particular ᶜalim told his interlocutors, all this was a result of the fact that pristine Islam is nowhere observed in the world today.

Ibrahim al-Salqini, Aleppo-born and dean of the Shariᶜa College, Damascus University, concurs; but he has another explanation for the causes that have led to the present sorry state of affairs. The Arab-Muslim world, he asserts, has suffered greatly and at length from foreign incursions since the times of the Crusades. "Military imperialism," however, has been "less harmful and less evil and less perilous . . . than mental and cultural imperialism." According to him, this latter variety of imperialism seeks to isolate the younger generation from Islamic culture and the verities of Islam—"and ignorance leads to hostility."

Shawqi Abu Khalil, a Palestinian who works for the Department of Education in the Damascus area, was more down to earth. To be sure, he agreed with his colleagues about the evils and perils of "cultural imperialism"; but he also wanted to stress the problems facing Muslim youth today in the material sphere, and went so far as to address the sexual aspects of the problem. He also dwelt on the painful subject of the brain drain, lamenting that many young Muslim males today choose to emigrate as soon as they acquire a profession, work abroad, take foreign women for wives, and ultimately acquire another nationality—thus "losing their Muslim identity forever."

Muhammad al-Zehili, a Syrian who teaches at the Shariʿa College, was the only one of the four luminaries to voice slightly dissenting opinions. He was also more coherent, more specific, and better equipped for the task. He first enumerated the problems that he saw confronting Muslim youths, then went on to point out that these problems were never unique to the young themselves but beset society as a whole. Moreover, he said, the problems discussed were not peculiar to our era—or to any other era for that matter. The third important point made by al-Zehili was that the problems facing Muslim youths today are faced not only by them but by all young men and women in many parts of the world, irrespective of their religious faiths or nationalities.

Turning to the issue of "cultural imperialism" and "mental invasion," al-Zehili engaged in a kind of egg-and-chicken debate when he asserted that the ideological, cultural, and mental vacuum preceded and was responsible for, rather than being a result of, the cultural intrusion to which his three colleagues referred. Had that vacuum not existed, he explained, no mental invasion would have been possible. He also implied, ever so subtly, that the other participants were placing too much emphasis on the concept of cultural imperialism, possibly as a way to evade some of the real issues.

This immediately placed al-Salqini on the defensive. Insisting that the root of the trouble lay in the alien intrusions to which Islam and the Muslims have been subjected for so long, he rejected the notion that he and his colleagues were using the term "cultural imperialism" as a peg on which to hang everything that is wrong with contemporary Muslim societies. Abu Khalil too came to the rescue, arguing that military invasion and colonialism followed rather than preceded the mental invasion that he had mentioned and that he described as "missionary," since it preached that Arab-Muslim societies will forever remain agricultural and will resist industrialization in favor of consuming more foreign products.

In the final round of the symposium, al-Zehili again referred to the point at issue, this time launching an attack on "certain Muslim thinkers" who, he said, relate to the problems of Muslim youths with cynicism and demagoguery, and who masquerade as defenders of and spokesmen for these young men and women when in reality they are "totally unfamiliar with the problems and have no real contact with the objects of their alleged advocacy and care."

Thus, whether viewed from a conservative Islamic vantage point or approached scientifically, the problems confronting Arab-Muslim youths and adolescents seem not to differ basically from those faced, say, by their Catholic, Jewish, or Hindu counterparts. The evils decried by the four doctors of religion from Damascus—ideological and spiritual vacuum, knowledge for its own sake, the intrusion of alien cultures and lifestyles, to mention only a few—are as prevalent in Rome, Chicago, Tel Aviv, and Madras as they are in Cairo, Damascus, Amman, and Nablus.

Taking a more general look at the problem, and stressing one aspect of it, Hisham Sharabi breaks down the intellectual crisis of the younger Arab generation into three main phenomena—psychological uprootedness, the loss of moral and religious certainties, and valuational drift (Sharabi, "Political and Intellectual Attitudes of the Young Arab Generation," in Kerekes, *The Arab Middle East and Muslim Africa;* quotations are drawn from pages 50–51). Uprootedness does not affect only the Levantine type of Arab, who is found in all large cities from Beirut to Tangiers and to whom cultural and psychological uprootedness is a normal state of being. It afflicts "the entire literate Arab generation that has come into manhood in the mid-twentieth century to find itself disinherited in a world providing no values or certainties that are not relative and contingent." Islam, the one force that provided the older generation with the necessary assurance to render the world a familiar and habitable place, now holds more meaning as part of the Arab national heritage than as an all-embracing view of man and the world.

Living amidst the ruins of this world of shattered values, Sharabi adds, the Arab intellectual "has so far refused to face the needs implicit in the rebuilding of his world. The vital task of defining and formulating the fundamental problems inherent in his condition . . . he has left to Christian and European scholars whose works are just about all the knowledge the Arab has of himself, of his present and of his past." However, self-knowledge achieved through the eyes of others is external, limited, and inadequate—and so it is in the intellectual atmosphere of the contemporary Arab world, "which lacks real subjectivity and the capacity for self-criticism in any profound level."

Sharabi offers a brief characterization of the present-day Arab intellectual—the writer, the journalist, the teacher, the lawyer, the student, the government official, and the army officer. In his view, this intellectual is

1. a separate individual, since the group to which he belongs possesses no status on the social level;

2. generally solemn and serious and wholly lacking in a sense of humor;

3. capable of great pedantry;

4. endowed with a natural grace of gesture and a verbosity that his rich and beautiful language makes almost imperative;

5. allergic to brevity and precision, usually extravagant and addicted to superlatives in his writings and public pronouncements: his mind, already impregnated with too much color and noise, cannot be impressed except by ever sharper contrasts.

Cut off from his heritage, the young Arab intellectual has also to import his ideologies: "In itself, the impact of the West is dizzying; even greater is the state of intellectual and moral suspension which this impact creates. To a mind hungering for certitudes, multiplicity of values does not contribute to an inner sense of direction; a culture which offers reason and method as normative principles of thought and action rather than philosophic finalities cannot be assimilated without distortion. From this vertiginous tension, there appears to be no easy escape." The solution offered by Kemalist Turkey seems no more satisfactory than that offered by Lebanon or Tunisia. It is now quite obvious that on any profound level Westernization through state legislation is as sterile in the long run as any partial compromise: "There is no evading the fact that nothing can be imposed on the mind from the outside."

Sharabi paints a somber picture of the choices open to the Arab intellectual—who today "finds himself driven either to compliance or to exile, to prostitution or to solitude." To those young intellectuals who strive for harmony between conduct and thought,

exile no longer consists solely of being physically banished from their country; the most bitter kind of exile now assumes the form of domestic acquiescence, of putting the mind under arrest. . . . It is inevitable that those who choose compliance and accept the silence are forced . . . to cultivate the virtues required for success in these changed and changing times. It therefore should not be surprising if in the new hierarchy of wealth, rank and power—where conversation is dead and silence reigns despite the clamor of voices—servility and the bended knee become chief requisites not only for forging ahead but also for earning a mere living. As we all know, new virtues create new vices; for the Arab, the most abhorred of the latter is dishonor. (53–54)

TEN

THE CASE OF EGYPT

IDENTITY AND CULTURAL ORIENTATION

Egypt's cultural orientation, or identity, a subject that in the 1930s and 1940s gave rise to fierce controversies and wide differences of opinion, has all but ceased to be the cause of such debates. Time was when intellectual leaders and pathfinders like Taha Hussein, Salama Mousa, Muhammad Hussein Haykal, and ᶜAbbas Mahmoud al-ᶜAqqad found themselves troubled by the question of where, precisely, Egypt belongs culturally: Europe, the Mediterranean, Africa, or the Arab world. Since the 1950s, however, there has been something very near a consensus that Egypt belongs to the Arab world and, as Abdel Nasser told the Egyptian National Assembly upon his reelection as president in January 1965, "is an integral part of the Arab nation" (*Al-Ahram* [Cairo], January 21, 1965).

What to Nasser seemed obvious, however, had not always gone unchallenged by other Egyptians. Late in 1961, as the dust was settling on the ruins of the Egypt-Syria merger, some voices began to be heard in Cairo suggesting that the whole idea of pan-Arab unity lacked a solid foundation both in history and in reality. One of these was Taha Hussein, who related in a newspaper article how he first encountered the idea of pan-Arab unity. It was from the Syrians, he wrote, that he had heard "the talk about Arab unity" many years before—"and I never heard it for the first, the second and the third time except from the Syrians" (*Al-Gumhouriya* [Cairo], October 7, 1961). Arab unity had been the Syrians' dream when their land, their lives, and their interests were in the hands of the French—and it may have been their dream before that, too, when Syria suffered under the despotic rule of the Ottoman Turks. Syrians hated to hear an Arab speaking of the Syrian "nation" (*umma*); they always hastened to correct one, arguing that there was no such thing as a Syrian nation, an Iraqi nation, or an Egyptian nation: there was only one nation, the Arab nation. They conceded, however, that there was a Syrian "people" (*sha'b*), an Iraqi people, and an Egyptian people—but they added that these peoples will inevitably be united, as they had been united in the past, and merged into an Arab nation, as it had existed in the past.

(This distinction between "nation" and "people" only shows the amount of confusion, intellectual and political, under which the modern Arab nationalist labors. Pan-Arab nationalists would not allow of the existence of an Iraqi, Syrian, Egyptian, or Palestinian "nation," but would gladly concede the existence of an Iraqi "people," an Egyptian or Palestinian "people." The contrary—if anything—would seem to be the case. The term "people" is vague and general enough to be given to such a cultural-linguistic group as "the Arabs" (it has also been given to the Jews, with a certain measure of credibility). For all intents and purposes, however, Syrians, Egyptians, Iraqis, and Palestinians each constitute a "nation"—or a "nationality"—if "nation" is to be seen, as it has always been seen in the West, as a function of geography, citizenship, and international procedure.)

"I remember," Hussein adds, "that I used to argue with them at length on this union; I used to ask them where would the capital of such a union be— in Medina, as in the days of the first caliphs? In Damascus, as it was in the time of the Umayyads? Or in Baghdad, as in the days of the Abbasids? . . . Eventually they accused me, in their newspapers, first of Pharaonism, later of *shu'ubiyya*. Then they proceeded to accuse all or most of Egypt's writers of Pharaonism, which they used to hate exceedingly and condemn root and branch."

Such "non-Arab" sentiments, expressed by Taha Hussein and other Egyptian thinkers following Syria's secession from the United Arab Republic, were soon reciprocated from certain quarters in Damascus—with the result that the Nasserist regime now had to defend its belief in Egypt's Arabness on two fronts. "We have no choice," declared Nasser in an address he gave at a mass rally on February 22, 1962. "We are Arabs, and Egypt will remain Arab because this is nature itself." Nasser was replying to unidentified persons who were making the suggestion, he said, that Egypt ought to let the Arabs alone and start concentrating on its own affairs. Earlier in this address, referring to Syrian charges that the Egyptians were confirmed "Pharaonists" rather than Arabs, Nasser had declared that all this talk of Egypt's *fir'awniyya* was unfounded, since it started "just because Taha Hussein, years ago, expressed the opinion that the Egyptians were Pharaonists."

The point, of course, is that Egypt has had too many and too prolonged contacts with cultures other than the Muslim-Arab one for it to be readily identified as Arab and for its culture to be one of a piece. "Where do we stand in the world?" asked Fat'hi Ghanim, a young Egyptian writer and novelist, not long after the dismantling of the Egypt-Syria merger. "What is our attitude toward the policies and the ideological, cultural, and religious trends surrounding us? . . . The history of our literature in the past twenty-five years is a record of the attempt to answer these questions" (Ghanim, "Perplexing Questions," *Sabah al-Kheir* [Cairo], January 25, 1962). But while in the literary field it was agreed that "we have to create a literature of our own that is not influenced by anyone," the question was harder to answer on the sociocultural level. In fact, the writer says, the question why Egypt should not be a part of Europe and Egyptian society not a part of European society never got a satisfactory answer.

It was this same question that Taha Hussein tried to answer in his well-known book *Mustaqbal al-Thaqafa fi Misr* (*The Future of Culture in Egypt*), first published in 1938 (quotations in the following paragraphs are drawn from pages 62–64). In the first part of the book, he gives his assessment of the nature of Egyptian culture. History, he says, will have to be our guide. From ancient times there have been two civilizations on this earth, whose every encounter was a hostile clash—i.e., Europe and the East. The question: Is the Egyptian mind Eastern or Western in its concept formation, imagination, perception, understanding, and judgment? There is but one test: is it easier for the Egyptian mind to understand a Chinese man or an Englishman?

The answer is obvious, Hussein submits. There is no evidence of intellectual, political, or economic ties between Egypt and the East (i.e., the Far East) in antiquity. Close ties existed solely with the Near East—Palestine, Syria, and Iraq. On the other hand, there is no need to insist on the well-known connections between Egypt and the Aegean, and Egypt and the Greeks, from the very beginning of their civilization down to Alexander. In fact, until freed by Alexander, Egypt resisted Persian invaders from the East with the help of Greek volunteers and Greek cities.

Thus, Hussein continues, all the Egyptian mind's real ties were with the Near East and the Greeks, and insofar as it was affected by outside influences, these influences were Mediterranean. The Mediterranean civilizations, Egypt being the oldest, interacted, but never did the Egyptian mind enter into contact with India, China, or Japan. What he cannot understand, Hussein writes, is why, despite all these well-known facts, Egyptians still consider themselves Easterners.

Had the ready acceptance of Islam, then, made the Egyptians an Eastern nation? According to Hussein, spiritual unity and political unity do not necessarily go together. The Muslims always realized that political organization and faith were matters of different orders; they conceived of government as dedicated primarily, even exclusively, to public affairs. Europe, too, was organized along the same lines, both Islam and Christianity having been influenced by Greek philosophy.

In the modern age, Hussein asserts, Egypt has taken Europe as a model in all aspects of the material life. Egypt's mind, too, is purely European. To support his thesis that Egypt should aim for out-and-out Westernization, he finally turns to the "tales" told about the "spirituality" of the East and the "materialism" of the West. Pointing out that European civilization possessed great spiritual content, though there was a great deal of materialism in it, he argues that the Near East had been the cradle of all the divine religions, those adopted by Europeans as well as those followed by Near Easterners. "Can these religions be 'spirit' in the East and 'matter' in the West?" he asked rhetorically.

Hussein was by no means the only Egyptian of note to express such sentiments. Abdel Rahman 'Azzam, the Arab League's first secretary-general, and an Egyptian, has related how when once he tried to discuss the subject of Arab unity with Sa'ad Zaghlul, this prominent Egyptian nationalist leader interrupted him: "If you add a zero to a zero, and then to another zero, what will you get?" 'Azzam himself, when he was later faced with an increasing amount of criticism of the league and its work, and especially its secretariat, said: "The Secretary-General is only a mirror of the Arab states. . . . The condition which prevails in it now is nothing but a reflection in this mirror of conditions prevalent in the Arab lands" (reported in *Al-Musawwar* [Cairo], April 17, 1953).

In this connection it is useful to recall a controversy started in the 1950s by Fat'hi Radwan, the Egyptian writer and national guidance minister at the time. In a lecture published later in the Cairo weekly *Akhbar al-Yaum* (March 21, 1953), Radwan raised the question of who are the Egyptians. "We are indeed Egyptians," he wrote. "But are these Egyptians Arab? Are they Arab by race, or are they Arab by politics? Or are they perhaps Arab by culture?"

He went on to ask whether the Egyptians were Muslims, in the sense that they ought "to erect [their] politics, education, and constitution on the teachings of Islam"; or Africans, in more than a geographical sense; or Mediterraneans, or Europeans. But Radwan refrained from giving any answers, and contented himself with inviting the politicians, educationalists, and social scientists to answer them "without hesitation or delay." The re-sults were highly interesting. The weekly *Al-Musawwar,* on the initiative of its editor, Fikri Abada, organized a symposium in which the participants were three ministers, former secretary-general of the Arab League 'Azzam, a former dean of Alexandria University, the deputy dean of Cairo Univer-sity, and Abada himself.

The discussion produced no conclusive results, but what was said there was illuminating. 'Azzam concluded his dissertation by saying: "We are Egyptians first and foremost, then Arabs, then Muslims" (the comments by 'Azzam and the other participants appeared in *Al-Musawwar,* April 17, 1953). Husain Kamel Salim, the deputy dean of Cairo University, declared: "We are Egyptians first and last." Fikri Abada ruled: "We are ancient Egyp-tians and nothing besides." William Salim Hanna, municipal affairs min-ister, said: "As we speak Arabic and as our literature is Arab, we can by no means ignore the influence of that literature on our being, our life, our orientation, our plans, and our everyday reactions . . ." 'Abbas 'Ammar, so-cial affairs minister, dealt with many points but gave no answer at all to the question of Egyptian identity, while Radwan contented himself with play-ing the role of moderator. Finally, a former dean of Alexandria University, Mansour Fahmi, complained that he had entered the hall with his head swirling with questions, and his perplexity had only grown after he heard the participants speak.

It is important to bear in mind that all this took place after the Free Officers staged their coup d'état in July 1952, though nearly a year before Nasser emerged triumphant from the struggle for power inside the mili-tary junta. It would, however, be wrong to assume that a belief in the separateness of Egypt from the Arab world or in the uniqueness of its destiny was to disappear as a result of the regime's deep pan-Arab involve-ment during the late 1950s. In a book published early in 1961 in Cairo—*Sindbad Misri* (An Egyptian Sindbad), by Hussein Fawzi—the author in-vokes Egypt's history "as a complete whole" and says that as soon as Egypt awakens, and her eyes open to Europe's civilization, "she will discover something strange, she who has forgotten her ancient history: she will dis-cover that this history that she has forgotten has a place, a very important place, among the bearers of this modern civilization. She will discover that these consider the civilization of the pharaohs the earliest awakening of man's thought—his conscience and his sensibility—that history has ever known. It should no longer be tolerated that Egyptians should remain ignorant of the civilization of their fathers, who are forgotten solely by them!" (115).

'URUBA AND FIR'AWNIYYA: ARABISM AND PHARAONISM

Viewed in the light of this firm tradition of dissent, the prevalence and the sheer endurance of the idea of Egypt's Arab affiliation seems remarkable, in that its validity has often been put to question by the logic of events and circumstances. Yet it becomes understandable when we consider the broadness, the all-inclusiveness almost, of the definition that the Arabs generally have given to Arabness and to Arab nationalism. A few illustrations of this somewhat loose concept of "Arabness" are apposite here. 'Abdel Rahman al-Rafi'i, the historian of the Egyptian national movement, believes, for instance, that Arab nationalism is "a natural movement that derives its rise and existence from the factors that link the Arab peoples together" (al-Rafi'i, "Al-Qawmiyya al-'Arabiyya" [Arab Nationalism], in Al-Hilal [Cairo], November 1961). Explaining these links, al-Rafi'i enumerates language, history, beliefs, common objectives, interests, common aspirations, and geographical contiguity.

More instructively, three Egyptian university professors, in a book written jointly for use in their classes, give these three pillars of Arab nationalism: liberation of the Arab world from foreign dominance; unification of the Arab world within its natural borders; and neutralism in the Cold War. The authors are emphatic in their belief that Arabism ('uruba) is not conditional on either race or religion; for them, Arab nationalism is "a political creed—just like the democratic creed, the socialist creed, or the movement for European or American unity" (Boutros Boutros-Ghali, Mahmoud Kheiri 'Isa, and 'Abdel Malik 'Oda, Al-Qawmiyya al-'Arabiyya wa Simat al-Mujtama' al-'Arabi [Arab Nationalism and the Characteristics of Arab Society], 26).

A most elaborate exposition of the idea that Egypt is Arab first and foremost is to be found in a book published in 1967 and appropriately—and somewhat inconsistently—entitled Shakhsiyyat Misr: Dirasa fi 'Abqariyyat al-Makan (Egypt's Personality: A Study of the Genius of Place), by Jamal Hamdan. Though the first chapter of the book is devoted to a study of "the regional personality" of nations, and though the author throughout the book speaks of a distinct Egyptian "personality," the final conclusion is nevertheless that Arabism is Egypt's "destiny." "Islamism," Hamdan writes, "is a unity of creed and cooperation, not a national unity or a destiny"; the unity of the Nile Valley is "part of a whole"; local nationalism is a "limping, inadequate part of the same whole." This whole, he explains further, "is Arabism and Arabism alone. Our lot is Arab nationalism, and Egypt's destiny [lies] in Arab unity. This is what the Egypt of the revolution has pronounced finally and decisively" (249).

One of the main, and natural, activities through which this reaffirmed cultural identity has been cultivated in Egypt since the late 1950s is the revival of the Arab cultural heritage. The idea is that since the present renaissance has to spring from the Arabs' own environment, their traditions, and their true personality, the best way of establishing these traditions and this personality is to study and revive the cultural heritage of the Arabs and to transmit it into the contemporary Arab's consciousness. The project, however—known as the "Revival of the Arab Heritage"—has presented some difficulties, in both its general approach and its method. These difficulties remain of the essence of Egypt's drive toward cultural revival. For instance, what attitude is to be adopted toward this Arab heritage: unquestioning acceptance and veneration, critical selectivity, or downright defiance? In the words of the late Salah Abdel Sabour, a leading Egyptian poet of the modern school: "Is the heritage going to be a burden or a driving force?" Some of the people who speak of reviving the Arab heritage, Sabour points out in an article in the literary supplement of *Al-Ahram* (January 22, 1963), believe that every withering piece of paper constitutes "heritage," and that every such paper and every ancient manuscript ought to be gleaned and printed on shiny white paper. "They forget that the ancients, too, had their good and bad, serious and frivolous, talented and untalented—exactly like our own contemporaries," he wrote, pleading for critical selectivity in dealing with heritage.

Another Egyptian intellectual, Abdul Jalil Hasan, believes that the required effort does not involve mere compilation and printing, but a conscious, original study of Arab culture and thought by leading Arab experts in the field (Hasan's comments were reported in *Al-Katib* [Cairo], November 1964). For some 150 years now, he complains, the Arab's response to the challenge of Western civilization has been one of extremes: either total rejection or blind acceptance—attitudes that resulted in either clinging to his old heritage or disowning it completely (94). The time has now come for a new approach.

Writing apropos of a book by a German Orientalist on the impact of the Arabs on Europe, Hasan deplores the prevailing attitude on this subject among the Arabs, which he describes as one of self-satisfaction and jubilation each time some Western scholar discovers the beneficial influence that Arab culture has had on Western civilization. The danger inherent in such an attitude is that the modern Arab tends to fall under the spell of a glorious but largely irrelevant past. Besides, those who are engaged in reviving the Arab heritage must bear in mind that these European scholars, "no matter what they write about our history, remain Westerners writing for Westerners." The essential thing is for the Arabs to study themselves and write their own history, for their own sake and for the sake of the truth: "The responsibility is not theirs and the history is not theirs: how can we leave this task for others to do? It is indeed a scandal that we do not find original Arabic studies in this field. It seems to me that we avoid doing it the hard way, since this requires knowledge of many languages, considerable patience, and the ability to conduct research and devote oneself to it" (94–95).

Hasan concedes that the "boastful approach" to the heritage has had its positive aspects, "in that it has helped develop a consciousness of one's identity and increased one's self-confidence—and prevented total defeat in the face of Western triumphs and Western imperialism." Yet "we cannot content ourselves with a state of affairs in which we defend our identity by merely using a cultural weapon and by singing the praises of the past while neglecting the needs of the present." For the fact is that the past, for all its glories, is of little use in facing the problems of the present: "The thoughts of the past and its solutions do not constitute a panacea for our current cultural problems. In addition to viewing the heritage critically, and giving it a continuous, evolutionary form, there is need for rediscovering it completely and opening it to interaction with other contemporary cultures" (95).

Moreover, "we must not allow ourselves to be swayed by finding in our heritage something that proves our precedence over Europe," Hasan continues. "That should not interest us so much as knowing ourselves, our vistas, and the kinds of questions that were raised in our history—and why they were not resolved." What the Arabs want "is not to bring out certain threads and trends and build them up anew. We do not want a new reorganization of old material, or to build a new house from the bricks of an old sanctuary; we want only to discover our identity and our role" (96).

Hasan goes further, calling for "changing our guiding patterns of thought and our language patterns, which have become a habit influencing our very thinking." The Arabs, he asserts, need this change most of all, "because our language is static to a great extent. The dictionaries we still use are those which were compiled many centuries ago; there is indeed not a single new dictionary that reflects one new vista or development in our thought" (96).

GOMAA AND FAWZI

The great debate about Egypt's cultural identity, which raged before and just after Nasser came to power and issued his call for Arab unity, tended to become gradually less topical and less important as the years passed. In the wake of the conclusion of a separate peace settlement with Israel, in 1980, however, the debate was renewed, though with far less heat. A symposium organized by Tel Aviv University on the subject "Self-Views in Historical Perspective in Egypt and Israel" included two Egyptian intellectuals, Hussein Fawzi and Ahmed M. Gomaa. Gomaa, scholar and author of *The Foundations of the League of Arab States,* titled his lecture "The Egyptian Personality—Between the Nile, the West, Islam and the Arabs," declaring that it was not his purpose "to indulge in great detail in an academic exposé of Egypt's self-view and the prospect of its historical legacy," and that he would "merely mention a few pertinent points." (Gomaa's essay is included in Shamir, *Self-Views in Historical Perspective in Egypt and Israel;* quotations are drawn from pages 33–36.)

Gomaa's first point concerned the impact of the environment on the Egyptian personality. "The Nile," he said, "has unquestionably been central in the evolution of a homogeneous society and political community, with central authority based on a well-established bureaucracy. In Egypt, the concept of nationhood was never questioned. Even during the long periods of foreign rule, Egypt retained its specificity of culture and life, absorbing foreign influences without being submerged by them and without losing its identity."

> This is reflected in several basic traits which can still be distinguished among the ordinary Egyptians, by whom I mean the peasants who form the majority of the population. Foremost among these is the inner serenity. The regularity of the Nile inundations, the rarity of natural disasters such as earthquakes and floods, gave life on the banks of the Nile a placid quality. Even when an exceptional summer flood took its toll of homes and lives, the reaction was one of acceptance. The Nile symbolized a deity, to be accorded veneration and annual offerings in thanks for its bounty. At the same time, it was a personified deity with which people found comfort in identifying themselves.

A second trait associated with the Nile as the dominant force, Gomaa added, was "respect for a central, dominating government." In fact, he said, respect for central authority is endemic to a society dependent for its survival on an irrigation system that requires an effective political authority to maintain and regulate it: "The Nile and the central authority were, in fact, two faces of the same coin. Both were viewed with respect and veneration bordering on worship. Hence, hard labor in building the pyramids or colossal temples was gladly undertaken as a sacred duty to the central authority. This is the imprint of the Pharaonic heritage on the Egyptian self-view, an attitude that has tended to discourage violent political and social upheaval such as we have seen in other societies."

A third trait is enormous patience, underlain by a sure belief in ultimate reward and accompanied by endurance and self-discipline in the face of difficulties: "These are sometimes transcended by recourse to fatalism and religion, at other times by simply laughing the difficulties off. Either response is one of escapism, a tendency not to face unpleasant realities." Two more traits that developed as a result of this lifestyle are "flexibility, the ability to adapt to changing conditions and circumstances; and superficiality, the tendency not to investigate the depths of unpleasant realities or developments."

The second point taken up by Gomaa was the variety of Egyptian responses to the impact of modernity: "The opening to the West first came with the Napoleonic invasion, and was extended under Muhammad ʿAli, the founder of modern Egypt. There followed a scientific and cultural revival."

> But contact with the West also bred antagonism and bitterness, which intensified after the occupation by Britain. The response was Islamic fundamentalism, which has acquired growing political and social significance. Another response was the secular trend which had its origin in the 1920s and 1930s. In fact, there was a dialogue and a dispute between three basic trends. The first, Westernized, called for a secular civilization. It claimed that Egypt, a Mediterranean country, is a continuation of Europe and must draw on European culture and technology. The second trend was Pharaonism. It called for abandoning or putting less emphasis on both the Islamic heritage and the West, and giving more emphasis to the Pharaonic past. In other words, it gloried in the Egyptian past and in an Egyptian nationhood separate and distinct from all foreign influences.

What developed during the 1940s and 1950s was more or less a synthesis of these three trends, Gomaa remarked:

Retaining the Pharaonic past and its heritage as background, the Egyptians drew increasingly from modern, secular, European concepts. Thus, Egypt's legal system, the structure of its government and its parliamentary system were all based on European models. But in culture, the Arabic-Islamic impact was much stronger. Modern literary Arabic had developed in Egypt, and it was in Egypt that the greater modern Arabic writers had emerged. . . . In the 1940s, one variant of this synthesis skewed towards Nazism and Fascism. It gave rise to similar, extremely nationalist ideologies which drew upon religion or exploited religion for their own ends. Another development in the 1940s was the rise of militant religious trends—such as the Muslim Brethren.

The third point that Gomaa was careful to stress was what he termed "the Arab commitment of Egypt." There is no point in trying to minimize this impact, he said: "It is no simple matter for any political system in Egypt . . . to contend with the pressures of Arabism in Egypt. We in Egypt are Arabs. . . . It is not important whether we are 'purely' Arab or not 'purely' Arab, what is important is whether we view ourselves as Arabs or not Arabs. The self-view is what matters."

It is true that, historically, Egyptians cannot be regarded as "purely" Arab. We have a Pharaonic past, and the Copts in Egypt claim to be the direct descendants of that Pharaonic era. The Muslims themselves are of the same descent, and they only partly intermarried with the Arab invaders. What matters now is that after several centuries of Arabization, after Egypt became the seat of the most prominent Arab-Islamic university in the world of Islam, namely al-Azhar, after Egypt housed the most prominent writers in the Arabic language—Egypt now has an Arab self-view. . . . This is not only a matter of sentiments or perceptions. It is also a matter of self-interest of the first degree. We now have one and a half million Egyptians working in the Arab countries . . . [who] support at least three more million living in Egypt. . . . In addition there are about one quarter of a million Egyptians married to Arabs all over the Arab world, either Egyptian men having Arab wives or Egyptian women married to Arabs. These facts put extreme pressure on any politician, no matter what stand he takes.

In sharp contrast to Gomaa's conclusions, Hussein Fawzi (1900–1988), one of the most prominent members of the older generation of Egyptian intellectuals, stressed Egypt's distinctive personality, asserting that the

Egyptian people had "succeeded in maintaining [their] identity despite conquest and occupation." (Fawzi's essay, "Egypt's Place in the World— Past and Present," is included in Shamir, *Self-Views in Historical Perspective in Egypt and Israel;* quotations are drawn from pages 59–61.) Egypt's contribution to world civilization has been threefold—"three histories, and I have lived them all. They are all part of me."

First, the Pharaonic times. Besides being a great civilization in its own right, it also influenced the Greeks. The Greek philosophers came to ancient Egypt, they visited the temples, they talked with the priests. And through its impact on Greek civilization (and on Rome, and on Christianity, both of which also had some contact with it), Ancient Egypt influenced indirectly the development of European civilization.

Second, Egypt's Christian period. Little is known about the Church of Egypt in its early days, but it proved that it had its own personality. The Coptic Church is one of the most ancient churches in Christianity; Alexandria is much older than Byzantium. The Copts, that is the Egyptians, never accepted the new-fangled ideas of the Byzantines. Monasticism, in all its forms, was begotten in the Egyptian deserts. The Coptic monks traveled as far as Ireland, and the Irish recognize the Coptic origins of many of their laws and establishments. The hermits of Thebayid and other places had a great impact on the Graeco-Roman world. Much evidence of these developments remains to this day.

Third, Islam in Egypt. Mention of al-Azhar is sufficient to prove that Egypt contributed to Islam just as it contributed to Christianity.

All these are historical facts, Fawzi added: "Egyptians cannot forget what they were in Pharaonic times, in Christian times, and in Islam. In each of these periods Egypt was an entity." The people succeeded in maintaining their identity despite conquest and occupation:

Throughout the ages, its rhythm of life has always proceeded undisturbed. The Egyptian people [have] continued to till the soil and to plant, to build and to craft, molding [their] unique civilization and weaving the long threads of Egyptian history into the fabric of a strong society. Egypt's landscape is resplendent with monuments to this continuity of history, this perseverance. The Egyptian people [have] built pyramids, temples, churches, and mosques; engineering works, from irrigation basins to dams to the Suez Canal; palaces, monuments, and centers of learning. Together they bear witness to the endurance, the dedication, the unity of the Egyptian people.

Fawzi concluded:

This unity is in no small measure an expression of the people's intimate contact with its land. Only by combined effort could they control the waters on which Egypt's civilization depends, the waters of the Nile. Egyptian civilization, the triumph of a people united against the adversity of nature, has been a source of inspiration to the nations with which it came into contact. Many of the achievements of the Egyptian people, particularly in medicine and engineering, in building, architecture, and art, in the organization of government and society, left their mark on world cultural history. No less important was Egyptian concern for the spiritual dimension, beyond temporal life. In all these fields, Egyptian civilization has continually manifested its world significance and uniqueness.

As we have seen elsewhere in this chapter, statements of the way Egyptians conceive of their identity and their image often come in response to accusations leveled at them by fellow Arabs and having mostly to do with Egypt's Arabness. One such accusation came in the early 1990s, when President Anwar el-Sadat decided to change his country's name from the United Arab Republic to the Arab Republic of Egypt. In response, Rif'at al-Assad, a prominent Syrian Ba'th Party functionary who also happened to be Syrian president Hafiz al-Assad's brother, addressed an open letter to Sadat, objecting to the change and lamenting that whereas Egypt had preserved its Arab name until Sadat's assumption of the presidency, things had now taken a different turn, owing to the new regime's "particularism and Egyptianization."

One instructive answer to this open letter came from the Egyptian writer and publicist Foumil Labib, who, in an article in the Cairo weekly *Al-Musawwar,* stressed the following points (quoted in Nissim Rejwan, "Egypt's Stake in the Peace Process," *Jerusalem Post,* November 18, 1991):

- Talk about Egypt's change of name marks a return to an old Ba'th Party allegation concerning "Pharaonism" (*fir'awniyya*)—a charge that had created a "complex" in President Nasser, who consequently decided to delete the name "Egypt" and replace it with "Arab." "We," Labib adds, "have now cured ourselves of that complex. We do not disown our Egyptian-ness because we don't intend to disown our distant past and its glories, of which we feel quite proud."

- Nasser had surrendered Egypt's name in pursuance of pan-Arab leadership. Sadat, in contrast, "does not seek leadership; what he wishes to accomplish is to liberate Arab lands and to ensure the well-being of the Egyptians."

- The man who revived Egypt's name also happens to be the man who decided to fight and who attained the victory of October 1973: "Who knows? Perhaps the name 'Egypt' has some magic for the soldiers fighting at the front." After all, Egypt has a unifying influence on its citizens—in contrast to the general run of Arab countries, which are torn by narrow communal and denominational conflicts.

- Egypt has always been open to proposals for Arab unity and Arab unification, but she does not want unity to be a mere slogan. One of the factors that led to the collapse of the tripartite union between Egypt, Syria, and Libya in recent history was "Syria's insistence on gaining certain economic privileges that tended to impoverish her partners." In this connection, Assad is asked to remember a saying of Syrian coinage: "Libya pays, Egypt leads, and Syria gets the trophy."

ELEVEN

THE WEST'S INROADS

In November 1956, shortly after the Suez crisis, the American writer Dwight Macdonald (1906–1982) asked Taha Hussein in Cairo what he thought of the Hungarian revolt. Hussein, the gray eminence of Egyptian letters and one of the chief disseminators of Western culture in the Arabic-speaking world, had this to say in reply: "I am not informed of what has been happening in Hungary, because I have only seen the reports in the British and French press and they are not trustworthy" (as reported in *Encounter,* January 1957, 12–13).

Hussein's reply was a fair reflection of the attitude of the Egyptian and Arabic-speaking intelligentsia vis-à-vis a civilization with which they had the strongest of cultural and material ties, and which was in large measure responsible for the emergence and training of that very intelligentsia. Nor did this process of disillusionment and hostility start with the Suez conflict or even with the establishment of the State of Israel. The attitude of the Arabic-speaking world to the West had always been one of ambivalence—of admiration and an urge for emulation on the one hand, and of resentment and rejection on the other. But following World War II, the general mood began to be dominated by a variety of sharp sentiments, ranging from suspicion and hostility to soaring self-confidence; sometimes, indeed, there was discernible in their attitude a feeling of scorn, derogation, and downright superiority.

Several factors accounted for this growing hostility—the Palestine debacle, the feeling of frustration that followed the consistent failure of pan-Arab unity ventures, and so on. But there were many more deep-seated factors at work. Gustave von Grunebaum, an Orientalist, remarked that from the standpoint of the West, "the greater the success of Westernization, the greater the political resistance to the West, but all the greater, [is] the resistance to every feature of full Westernization, the political utility of which is not immediately discernible" (quoted in Rejwan, *Nasserist Ideology,* 127).

It may be useful to give at least one example of this ambivalence in its less extreme form, and from an earlier period, before turning to more recent manifestations of it. Ahmad Amin (1886–1954) was a prominent Egyptian Muslim author, educator, and man of letters. As far as the influences of the West were concerned, Amin was in no way hostile to them; in fact, as the editor in chief and leading light of the Authorship, Translation, and Publishing Committee as well as editor of the cultural weekly *Al-Thaqafa*, he was responsible for bringing to the reader of Arabic many of the philosophical, literary, and scientific products of Western culture. This did not seem to conflict with his traditionalism as a Muslim, nor did it impede his own work as a historian of the old school.

Until 1947, the year in which he visited London, Amin had not paid much attention to such topics as Westernization, East-West contrasts, or the comparative merits and demerits of these two civilizations. Following his visit, however, he wrote a book, *Al-Sharq wal-Gharb* (East and West; 1955), in which he set out to discuss these subjects. Here Amin, who in the past had taken a rather positive position on the influence upon Islam of Greek, Jewish, and Christian cultures, and thus sought to justify and encourage contemporary borrowings from Western civilization, suddenly announced that his whole attitude on the West had undergone a basic change, and that his visit in a Western country had led him "to doubt the soundness of the prevailing belief that, regarding civilization (*hadara*), the West was ahead of the East." Among the things that Amin found wanting in the West were its worship of power, its pride, the excessive freedom that it granted women, and the lack of balance between the material and the spiritual. Besides, the West was already in decline (Amin's criticisms of the West are summarized in Rejwan, *Nasserist Ideology,* 134–135).

Amin's revised ideas about the West and its culture were pursued five years later with an even greater bitterness and intensity of feeling in *Yawm al-Islam* (Islam's Day), a volume that concluded his seven-volume study of Islam's social and cultural history. Here the hostility is so overt that Amin accuses Christians in general of hating Muslims, a hatred that he says is evident in their support of the Jews tearing Palestine out of Arab hands. He also takes issue with Taha Hussein's assertion that the East does not differ so much from the West, and again makes a sharp distinction between the spirituality of the former and the materialism of the latter.

Amin's strictures illustrate fairly the prevalent Arab-Muslim attitude to Western cultural encroachment. This attitude was to grow in the intensity of its hostility, and it is safe to assume that had Amin lived to see the Suez crisis and its aftermath, he would have been more resentful of the West than his more Western-oriented contemporary Taha Hussein.

That the Westernized Muslim Arab's negative reaction to the West should have intensified seems, in retrospect, to be natural. For as the Arabs gained political independence, and as many of their young intellectuals came to know Europe more closely, they—paradoxically—started to learn more about themselves, and to appreciate more those cultural characteristics that, rather than revealing their affinities with the West, distinguished them and set them apart from it. Inevitably, too, the more thoughtful among them found that they were not entirely pleased with the results of their now century-old encounter with Europe. Rightly or wrongly, some of them started to see that Europe's "cultural invasion" of their way of life and habits of thought had in the end given them very little while virtually robbing them of their distinctive traditions, their true personality, and their authentic cultural identity. The most interesting feature of this consciousness has been that its most vocal exponents have been those who themselves were most affected by Westernization, and who have a fairly intimate knowledge of Europe and its ways.

The impact of the West on the Levant, and on the Arab world as a whole, brought the Arabs face to face with an assortment of practical problems related to their society, their culture, and the best way to meet the West's challenge without losing their uniqueness and intrinsic traits. In *The Future of Culture in Arab Society* (1953), Muhammad Kamel ʿAyyad, a leading Syrian writer and intellectual, tackles the problem of cultural borrowing, and reaches the conclusion that emulating Western methods and techniques is the Arabs' only alternative for meeting the challenge of living in the modern world.

ʿAyyad first invites us to consider the difference between that position and the Arabs' mindset in the periods when they borrowed from and assimilated foreign cultures:

> We are now weak, with most of our homeland under foreign occupation or influence, in sharp contrast to the situation of our ancestors, who were conquerors and rulers. Such a contrast has deep psychological consequences. . . . It naturally inclines us to cling to our own customs and traditions and fight shy of Western culture. . . . Unlike our ancestors, we face the world with a glorious past behind us and with a rich cultural heritage that, however, is old. This may be an incentive to awakening and progress, but it can also be a heavy burden, hindering us from moving freely and confidently into the future. (152)

The adoption of Western ways and methods is all but inevitable: "We cannot choose our ways of living to our own liking: they have to fit into a pattern quite literally imposed upon us. . . . The transformation of our life is manifest, not only in our adoption of new industrial techniques and inventions, but also in architecture, in the expansion of cities and the planning of them; in administration and government, commerce, education; and in the changes taking place in the status of the family, the position of women, and social relations generally" (152–153).

To be sure, there have been many attempts to borrow and adopt various aspects of Western civilization. Since the beginning of the twentieth century, the Arabs, well aware of the material strength of the West, have realized that they will never be able to resist Western imperialism until they adopt its ways. Thus the practice of borrowing from Western culture has continued uninterruptedly since about the middle of the century, but without clear plans or aims. "One need only examine the list of works translated into Arabic during this long period," ᶜAyyad writes, "to see what chaos has reigned in our cultural life. Not only is the number of translated works small; but they have also been chosen simply according to the translators' personal preferences, or because they were easiest to translate or were expected to have a good market." The Arabs consequently remained unaware of the greatest and most representative works of Western literature and of its essential and fundamental tendencies.

ᶜAyyad continues:

This cultural chaos is still more strikingly illustrated in the studies relating to our own cultural heritage, in which, strange to say, our encounter with the West has been the most important factor. For the Orientalists of the West were ahead of us in collecting the earliest Arabic manuscripts, editing the works of our ancestors with infinite care and scholarship, scrutinizing them with depth and discrimination, and in appreciating their merits; whereas our own efforts were, until very recently, limited to publishing the more trivial of them, plagiarizing the work of the Orientalists, and republishing it, mostly in distorted versions. And although this state of affairs has changed for the better in recent years, we still lag behind Western scholars in the study of these works, in showing their significance for the advance of world civilization, and in using them to illuminate our own history and civilization. (153)

A great and majestic role awaits the intellectuals and the educated classes—the elite—of Arab society, ᶜAyyad concludes. He enumerates four aspects of this crucial role:

- To revive the cultural heritage upon which our future culture must be built.

- To bear the heaviest burden of the new culture that we must assimilate if we are to fulfill the requirements of the age—especially of the modern scientific thinking that must become the predominant characteristic of our own culture. We will also have to study the main intellectual trends of the times and the forces that govern the development of modern societies.

- To achieve that unity between the mind, the sentiments, and the will that does not, however, rule out a variety of forms and a plurality of forms of expression. Variety is indispensable for the vitality, growth, and efflorescence of a culture—up to that limit beyond which variety becomes an impediment to harmony.

- To discharge fully its responsibilities to the public, maintain continuous contact with it, and take upon itself the enlightenment, guidance and orientation of the public mind. For men cannot grapple with the problems of their common life unless they are sustained by a comprehensive conception of the universe, a vision of the ends of life in keeping with their knowledge and in harmony with their sentiments and predispositions. In every age and every nation this has been, and will be, the supreme function of the cultured elite and the intellectuals— the dissemination of a universal guiding point of view. (165)

CONFRONTING THE "CULTURAL INVASION"

While ʿAyyad was calling for more borrowing of and adaptation to Western ways, other Arab intellectuals of his generation were enumerating the negative aspects of what they deemed the West's "cultural invasion" of their world. A good sample of this is a lecture delivered by Abdel Karim Ghallab, an academic from Morocco (reprinted in *Al-Adaab* [Beirut], May 1965). Unlike the more vociferous exponents of the "cultural invasion" theory, Ghallab took an approach considerably less sweeping, though by no means less damning. What he, for example, calls "the linguistic invasion" has resulted, according to him, in certain psychological "complexes" being manifested among Arab intellectuals and writers in the states of the Maghreb— Morocco, Algeria, and Tunisia. The foreign invader had discouraged the teaching of Arabic, substituting his own language instead. Arabic thus became discredited in the eyes of the educated, who were attracted by what seemed to them a far more powerful, useful, and expressive foreign tongue. This in turn resulted in the splitting of their personalities, living as they were in two worlds: culturally and linguistically in the West, physically in their own lands.

The effect of this on literary production and creativity was catastrophic, Ghallab argues. It led to the creation of two kinds of writers: those brought up on a foreign language and capable of writing and creating in it, but shying away from doing so because they lived among people speaking another national language, who probably could not appreciate their work; the others mastering the national language, Arabic, but suffering from narrow horizons and unable to draw on the rich literature of the world, since they did not know a foreign language adequately. In both cases, Ghallab asserts, the loss to Arab literature was considerable.

Another, probably more damaging aspect of Europe's cultural invasion was, according to Ghallab, the introduction by the imperialists of harmful social and intellectual values. Among these "destructive values" were communalism and racism, so that "society has been split up into Muslim, Christian, Jewish, Kabayli, Berber, and Kurdish—with the resulting disintegration of the cohesive society that would have been capable of creating a unified Arab thought based on one Arab nationality."

The creation of numerous "splinter" nationalities in the Arab world, and the resulting establishment of several sovereign entities, was thus an outcome of the influence of the West, which chose to transmit its own ideas of European nationalism into the Arab world, whose inclinations, according to Ghallab, are toward unity and solidarity. And the worst of it, we are told, is that the West, after transmitting these destructive ideas to the Arabs, has now deserted its own narrow view of nationalism and begun advocating European unity instead of the old slogans calling for "Germany for the Germans," "France for the French," etc.

The opinions expressed by Abdel Karim Ghallab—and by the Iraqi poet Nazik al-Malayka before him—are by no means universally accepted. For although no Arab intellectual would today advocate full and unquestioning Westernization, or would even say that the encroachments of Western culture on his own culture were an unmitigated blessing, there are many who would look for a solution somewhere between the two extremes of absolute rejection or acceptance. In this respect it is instructive to examine the reactions that al-Malayka's outspoken indictment of Western cultural influences provoked among Arab intellectuals. These reactions were on the whole neither too heated nor convincing—a fact that can be taken as an indication that her views were, generally speaking, not unpopular in these circles.

Yet as far as can be made out, there was not a single attempt to defend al-Malayka's views en bloc. The only available reactions to these views appeared in the Beirut cultural monthly *Al-Adaab*—which had published the text of al-Malayka's lecture as well as that of Ghallab in its March 1965 issue—and they all took issue with her views, though not, interestingly enough, with Ghallab's. These criticisms, submitted by three leading intellectuals of three different nationalities, dwelt on two main aspects of her attitude—namely, the idealization and romanticization of the Arabs' cultural and literary heritage, and the wholesale condemnation of Western literature, which she dismissed as totally irrelevant to the Arabs' specific experience (these three responses, by Idris, al-Zubaydi, and Safadi, are excerpted in Rejwan, *Nasserist Ideology*, 140–141).

First among al-Malayka's critics was the Lebanese writer Suhayl Idris, *Al-Adaab*'s founder and editor. He submits that the picture she paints of classical Arabic literature as being invariably great, moral, and creative has no basis in fact. According to Idris, too, al-Malayka's vision of Islamic society as an ideal one is also distorted, for the purity and goodness of the Islamic faith as such did not prevent its religious leaders at certain periods of Arab history from persecuting scientists and philosophers and suppressing free thought. Strangely, Idris avoids taking issue with al-Malayka's central thesis, namely, that Western culture is completely alien to the Arabs' tradition and temperament and worldview, and that the Arabs' adoption of Western cultural traits tended to destroy their specific personality and estrange them from their own selves and identities. In dealing with her strictures in this area, for instance, Idris merely makes a case for Western literature per se and submits that Arabic literature, being still in a formative stage, inevitably has to borrow from and even imitate other, maturer literatures. He justifies this view by arguing that since Europe itself in medieval times drew upon the riches of Arab civilization, it would not be "shameful" for the Arabs now to borrow and take from Europe.

This refusal to face al-Malayka's central thesis is significant in that it further emphasizes the deep ambivalence with which contemporary Arab intellectuals relate to the West. It is noticeable in the rejoinder to al-Malayka written by ʿAli al-Zubaydi, an Iraqi intellectual and professor of literature. Repeating the argument that the Arabs should refrain from idealizing and romanticizing their past and their heritage, which he says contain both good and bad, he makes the point that although Western imperialists were responsible for a number of the Arabs' present failings and misfortunes, "our responsibility is greater and our stocktaking should be fiercer with ourselves than with them; for, had we not ourselves failed our countries and our minds, the foreigner would have found access neither to our minds nor to our countries."

Al-Zubaydi also cites Nasser and other leaders of Arab nationalism to show that Arabism is progressive rather than regressive, positive rather than negative, and humanistic (*insaniyya*) rather than racial. He occasionally lapses into sheer polemic and makes a few highly rhetorical statements, such as that the Arabs should reject "reactionary ideas," that their culture and personality are strong enough to withstand Europe's influences, that in condemning Western literature one ought to distinguish between its good and its bad aspects, and that attention should be paid to the fact that the Arabs' fear of innovation is exploited by their enemies as proof of their stagnation and as a justification for foreign dominance. In fact, he makes no serious attempt to come to grips with al-Malayka's charges and reservations.

Little light on this subject, again, is shed by al-Malayka's third critic, the Syrian writer and novelist Muta‘ Safadi, though he does touch upon some of the specific points raised in her lecture. Accusing her of generalizations and inaccuracies, Safadi disagrees with the statement that Islam is basically different from Christianity because the former is organically linked to life—nay, is life itself—while the latter, with its doctrine of original sin and its otherworldly tendencies, is divorced from life. In this he too fails to convince, since he tends to overlook the crucial fact that unlike Christianity, which allows for the separation of church and state, Islam is both a religion and a worldly system, and in this significant respect at least it does differ essentially from Christianity.

Safadi's uncertainty about the whole issue becomes apparent when again he manages to avoid the real issue in replying to al-Malayka's charge that the Arabic language has been adversely influenced by translations from foreign languages and, even more importantly, by the borrowing of certain aspects of Latin grammar and syntax into a language that is structurally different from European tongues. All he has to say in justifying these innovations is that they make for greater variety of expression and are useful in literary forms such as the novel and poetry. Finally, Safadi keeps significantly silent about al-Malayka's argument that the whole temperament, personality, and spirit (*ma‘nawiyya*) of the Arab are different from those of the European, and that any attempt to graft the latter onto the former tends to lead to harmful results.

A VARIETY OF REACTIONS

The truth is that Arab-Muslim reactions to the impact of Western civilization have at no time been uniform. Since it started to make its presence felt in the Arab world, the West has met with three types of responses in the area. One has been uncompromisingly hostile and unreceptive; another was extremely hospitable—its proponents were willing to become uncritically Westernized; and the third lay somewhere between these two extremes. Advocates of the last type showed a willingness to learn from the West while remaining fully aware of the shortcomings of its culture and the advantages of their own culture and tradition.

By the mid-1950s, however, the first type of Arab reaction to the West had almost disappeared, apart from some scattered pockets of resistance represented by religious zealots who appeared only half convinced themselves. The enthusiasts, on the other hand, had equally dwindled in number, and it was scarcely possible to find one Arab thinker advocating full and unconditional Westernization. As for the preserve-the-good-aspects-of-both-cultures school of moderates, there were signs already that some of them were beginning to have doubts as to the practicability of their chosen course. At present, however, the trend seems to be moving in a distinctly anti-Western direction.

At first these reactions used to be rather unsophisticated, their war cries being such terms as "cultural tutelage," "cultural imperialism," and even "cultural enslavement." What is more significant, these cries came from conservative, older-generation Muslim intellectuals whose attitudes toward things non-Muslim were predictably hostile. Two examples of this kind of reaction can be given here, one from Egypt, the other from Iraq. The first comes from Anwar al-Jundi, author of a four-volume work called *Landmarks of Contemporary Arabic Literature* (up to 1940). The fourth and last of these volumes, *Contemporary Arab Thought in the Battles of Westernization and Cultural Mobilization,* offers a survey—in 648 pages—of "various attempts to impose cultural tutelage on Arab thought, beginning with those made by Turkish imperialism and ending with those of Western imperialism and Zionism" (Jundi's conclusions, along with those of Bazzaz, below, are quoted in Rejwan, *Nasserist Ideology,* 128–129).

However, Jundi's conclusion that all is well on the cultural front, and that the Arabs have emerged victorious from the intellectual battle forced upon them by Western rule, was not shared by all. ʿAbd al-Rahman al-Bazzaz, then director of the Arab League's Institute of Higher Arabic Studies, in Cairo, and later prime minister of Iraq, argues that Western imperialism has left behind it a sizable cultural legacy of which the Arabs must try to rid themselves. He grants that, with Algeria finally independent, the Arabs are well on their way to political independence, and that, everything being equal, they will sooner or later attain economic independence as well. What they would then need would be "cultural independence," since "no nation ought to consider itself completely independent unless its political and economic independence is accompanied by the lofty ideal of intellectual or spiritual independence."

Intellectual independence does not mean that the Arabs should avoid the West and discard everything western, Bazzaz writes; it is a call for self-realization, for a feeling of uniqueness, and for a desire to contribute to the human heritage on a basis of equality and true partnership, free from submission and tutelage. Right now the Arab world abounds with the bad effects of intellectual imperialism in fields such as language, literature, social habits, and standards of living: "In our everyday language, in the names we give things, . . . in our political and social outlook, and in every walk of life." Colloquial Arabic contains hundreds of Italian, Spanish, French, English, Turkish, Persian, Indian, and other terms, he complains.

One of the worst effects of intellectual imperialism in the Arab world today, Bazzaz argues, "is to acquiesce in calling our homeland 'the Near East' or 'the Middle East,'" which implies that Western Europe is the measure of all things, and that the Arab world is given only a relative status, since it is "East" only in relation to the Westerner. To the Arab, however, the appellation signifies "absolutely nothing." He also mentions, as a curiosity, Nehru's habit of calling the Arabs West Asians. The description, he submits, was geographically correct, but it too failed to give an adequate idea of the existence of one Arab nation: "We Arabs are one of those large nations that inhabit two great continents, and whose being extends from the East to the West. Therefore, any attempt to define us vis-à-vis one continent, or in relation to some imperialist Western countries, will fail, since it gives no adequate expression to our actual scope and status."

In the post-perestroika era, Bazzaz's strictures notwithstanding, Arab writers and publicists continued to define themselves and their people's situation in relation to others and to Western countries. In Egypt, two noted stalwarts of the Nasserist left, Muhammad Hasanein Haykal and Ahmad Bahaeddine, spoke of the completely changed fabric of relations between East and West and of the international scene generally—a change, Haykal lamented, taking place at a time when "the Arab world appears to be losing most of its assets: its wealth, its strategic value, its cultural weight, and, ultimately, its political leverage" (Haykal's and Bahaeddine's remarks are quoted in Nissim Rejwan, "The Arab World Is Losing Ground," *Jerusalem Post*, January 27, 1991). The Arab world and Egypt, Haykal warned, were in the process of moving from one historical era to another. "I fear," he added, "that until now we have been situated at the margin of history; but if we fail to put our perceptions of the times into focus, we will end up being outside history and not merely at its margins."

While basically concurring with this appraisal, Bahaeddine formulated his verdict in terms that sound somewhat less ominous. Referring to the likelihood that the Arabs will emulate what the Poles, Hungarians, Czechs, and other Eastern European countries had done by way of introducing democratic multiparty systems, he pointed out that the Arabs tended to view these societies as "primitive," and that this perception was quite erroneous, even though the political systems of these countries had been backward. He argued, however, that in their socioeconomic and cultural development, the Arabs still lagged behind Eastern European nations, and thus lacked the right background for making a similar change in their political systems.

But if some Arab thinkers saw the root of the evil in the lack of technological know-how and the absence of a democratic system of government, one Arab political scientist professed that a great deal could be accomplished by establishing an Arab institute for strategic studies and international affairs. In the course of a lengthy interview in the Beirut daily *Al-Nahar*, Professor Hisham Sharabi of Georgetown University asserted that the creation of such a research institute was a vital necessity. "We cannot," he protested, "reasonably continue to import information about our own countries from abroad, and thus acquire an understanding of ourselves only through the eyes of others. We have, both here in our Arab world and abroad, experts and specialists in all scientific pursuits, and we can establish the largest and greatest of institutes in the field of strategic studies and any other fields of study and research we need" (quoted in Nissim Rejwan, "Arab States Face Challenges from the West," *Jerusalem Post*, February 4, 1992).

Sharabi is aware, however, of a certain danger that seems to beset such establishments, and to avert such danger he pleads that experts and scholars taking part in such enterprises be allowed to contribute their share without having to become "officials or employees of the state." It is interesting to note that Sharabi takes the matter of the West, and of borrowing from it and emulating its ways and norms, completely for granted.

TWELVE

THE DIFFERENCE ISRAEL HAS MADE

In mid-May 1948 the regular armies of Transjordan, Egypt, Syria, Lebanon, and Iraq—as well as a Saudi Arabian formation fighting under Egyptian command—crossed international borders into what until then was Mandate Palestine. Their declared aim was to prevent the implementation of the United Nations Partition Plan for Palestine, passed on November 29, 1947. Their advance was checked, and ultimately the invading armies were driven back—and within just over a year armistice agreements were signed between Israel and Egypt, Lebanon, Jordan, and Syria, in that order.

For the Arabs, that defeat was nothing short of a "disaster" (*nakba*)—and they have, ever since, been brooding over the meaning, implications, and ramifications of the event. They have also searched for ways of undoing or at least mitigating the effects of their setback, almost always without success. Indeed, through one diplomatic-military blunder after another, they kept losing ground to Israel, and actually ended up strengthening it. Their frustration reached unprecedented dimensions with Israel's crushing victory over Egypt, Jordan, and Syria in June 1967, which for many Arabs signaled another and even greater nakba.

The question of what the precise effects of all these momentous events have been on the Arab world as a whole is one of those moot points that even the most exhaustive historical, sociological, or psychological research still leaves unresolved. To take a few examples from the purely political field—namely, the series of military coups d'état staged in a number of Arab countries during the years following "the disaster":

Would Husni el-Za'im have effected his putsch in March 1949—a coup that would be followed by two others before the year ended, Hinnawi's in August, Shishakli's in December—had the Syrian army and the political regime not suffered setbacks in the first Arab-Israeli war?

Would Colonel Gamal Abdel Nasser and his group of Free Officers have staged their revolt in July 1952 had it not been for the allegedly defective weapons, as well as other shortcomings of the regime, that they had discovered while serving on the front in 1948–1949?

Would Abdel Karim Qassim and his comrades have succeeded in toppling the Hashemite regime in Baghdad in 1958 had it not been for Nuri al Sa'id's behavior during the Suez crisis eighteen months earlier?

Again, would Noqrashy Pasha have been assassinated in Cairo in December 1948, King Abdullah shot to death by a Palestinian in the Mosque of Al-Aqsa in Jerusalem in July 1951, Glubb Pasha ousted by Hussein in February 1956, Yemen intervened in by Nasser in 1962, except for the chain of events that followed the Arab defeats in the late forties and fifties?

These questions—and there are many others in fields other than the political—are plainly unanswerable. Nevertheless, it would probably be safe to say that these and many other changes and upheavals were bound to take place in the Arab world sooner or later, Israel or no Israel. The argument, heard in foreign as well as Arab circles, that regional instability and turmoil, growing hostility to the West, the inroads that communism and the Soviet Union managed to make, even the use of Arab oil as a political weapon, were all wholly or largely the result of the creation of Israel is plainly an oversimplification.

This, however, is not tantamount to saying that Israel's creation—and the few decades of encounter between Zionism and Arab nationalism that preceded the event—did not affect the Arabs. It is enough to glance at only two areas where the establishment of Israel and the long aftermath of conflict and wars that followed have had far-reaching and tangible effects in the Arab world. I refer to the growth of the Arab-nationalist idea and the drive toward modernization and Westernization.

It is a truism of the social sciences that groups, and especially "struggle groups," are fed on conflict—so much so that they often reject approaches of tolerance and reconciliation from the other side, lest the close nature of their opposition be blurred and their unity and coherence threatened. A year or two after the Six-Day War, an Israeli paper published a report in which a thirteen-year-old lad from the Israeli Arab village of Umm el Fahm proclaimed himself to be a follower of the Fatah, the Palestinian guerrilla organization that eventually grew into the Palestine Liberation Organization. "The Jews," he was reported as saying, "live together in their own State. I want to live with Arabs in my own State."

On a larger and more meaningful scale, the influence of Jewish nationalism on Arab nationalism and the pan-Arab movement has been fairly evident. Quite early in the proceedings, the Palestine problem was turned into an all-Arab preoccupation. This development—which until the early 1970s proved extremely detrimental to the cause of the Palestinians themselves—was made possible by the efforts and blunders of all parties concerned. The Zionist leadership argued all along what in effect was the pan-Arab case in its purest and most dogmatic form—among other things by insisting that the Arabs of Palestine were part of "the great Arab Nation" and that Palestine itself was only a tiny strip of "the glorious Arab homeland." The British contributed their full share, first by inviting leaders from all the Arab countries to take part in the Round Table Conference in 1939, and then by the creation of the Arab League a few years later. The Palestinians made the blunder of pan-Arabizing their problem. And the Arab states, grouped in the new league, found they had little choice but to join one another in a military-political venture in 1948, though with motives so widely disparate that they had no chance whatsoever of success.

However, while the pan-Arabization of the Palestine problem brought the Arabs nothing but failure and defeat during the first twenty-five years of Israel's existence, it paradoxically began to yield fruit in the early 1970s. For one thing, with considerable chunks of Egyptian and Syrian territory occupied by Israel and the remaining (Jordanian) parts of Palestine coming under Israeli administration, the issue became an all-Arab one not only ideologically but physically as well. Moreover, the humiliation caused the Egyptians, Syrians, and Jordanians by the defeat of 1967 was felt by every Muslim-Arab "from the shores of the Atlantic to the Arab [Persian] Gulf," as Arabs like to describe the boundaries of their domain. The result was an unprecedented solidarity in the Arab ranks, embracing regimes as disparate as those of Saudi Arabia and Egypt, Kuwait and Algeria, Morocco and radical Syria, Libya, and all the rest. Even the warring Iraqi and Syrian factions of the Ba'th Party joined in arms.

The other sphere in which Israel's presence affected the Arab world—that of modernization and Westernization—is more difficult to assess. One argument—and there is no tested way of refuting it—says that Israel as a challenge to the Arab world has caused little if any acceleration in the modernization and technological progress in the Arab world, and that the performance of the Arab armies in the Yom Kippur War showed only that some of them had had technology brought down to their level rather than the other way round.

But although this remains sheer speculation, there can be no doubt about the incentive that Israel has given to this process. Ever since the 1948 nakba, Arab thinkers and intellectuals have been studying the causes of their condition and recommending ways for changing or improving it. The gist of their findings was that the Arabs, if they were to survive the Zionist danger and possibly rectify the damage that had already been done, had to change their whole approach to life. As Constantine Zureiq put it as far back as 1948:

- Machinery must be acquired and used on the widest possible scale—which, along with industrialization, would put an end to tribalism, feudalism, and other obstacles to "true nationalism."

- The state must be completely separated from the religious establishment—and sectarianism must be replaced by national unity.

- The mind must be organized and systematized through training in the empirical sciences.

- A spiritual revival must be effected. (quoted in Rejwan, *Arabs Face the Modern World,* 132–133)

In a sense, of course, Zureiq's was a cry in the wilderness. In sixty long years the Arabs have failed to attain any of the goals set out in his four points. Nevertheless, some considerable progress has been made—and though it remains a moot point, it would probably be true to say that the process was accelerated by the challenges that Israel constantly posed to the Arabs.

The road remains long and full of obstacles, however, and articulate Arabs realize this full well. The outcome of the Yom Kippur War, of October 1973, though depicted by Arab governments as a resounding victory, does not seem to have turned the heads of ordinary educated Arabs in quite the same way. Arab newspapers and periodicals came out with appraisals and reappraisals that—side by side with the rhetoric that continues to form an inseparable part of these publications—often gave sober and remarkably insightful estimates of the Arabs' positions and attitudes. Shortly after the war, an Egyptian university lecturer, Mahmoud ʿAwadh, wrote an article in which he wondered whether the Arabs had passed from "the age of political infantilism" (*Kul Shaiʿ* [Beirut], December 12, 1973). Unconvinced that they had, the writer demanded that in their dealings with a changing, dynamic world the Arabs look to something other than "mere oratorical rhetorics, high-sounding slogans, and inflammatory language."

What is more revealing, ʿAwadh demanded that his fellow Arabs "cease to live in a world of ghosts and spirits, in which we have all the right on our side and the rest of the world is totally in the wrong." He also pleaded for Arab leaders to stop depicting the world "as merely another version of Heaven and Hell, with its States being mere versions of Angels and Devils—

in which of course we comprise the angels and 'the others' are the devils." These evil spirits, he explained, were presented by Arab leaders now as imperialism, now as neocolonialism, now as Zionism, and now as Communism. In the end he appeals to the Arabs not to let future historians say of them: "These were people who knew what they didn't want, but never knew what they wanted!"

While it is difficult to gauge the difference that Israel has made, it is hard to believe that without the challenge of its presence in their midst the Arabs would have devoted so much effort to scrutinizing and evaluating the character of their society and their culture. Munif Razzaz, a leading member of the Ba'th Party in Syria, admits that the 1948 war between Israel and the Arab states "gave the Arab nationalist movement a tremendous impetus, as did the 1967 war later on" (Razzaz, "Arab Nationalism"; quotations are drawn from pages 360–361). Until then, he adds, "the colonialist challenge had all the ugly characteristics of any colonialist movement; but nobody could imagine that colonialism would last for ever." Zionism was different, however: "It had all the characteristics of an alien colonialist power, and, in addition, the will to stay for ever, with a racist, exclusively Jewish character, which was reluctant even to accept the presence of Arabs within its boundaries."

> Since then, the struggle against Zionism has become the first concern of Arab nationalism, replacing the struggle against the dying force of colonialism. The vicious character of Zionism came to be regarded as being far more important than any colonialism, and the struggle against it formed the practical fulcrum of the urge for Arab unity. The successive defeats of Arab regimes in their wars with Israel only succeeded in strengthening the Arabs' lack of faith in their own regimes and in augmenting their revolutionary fervour. The association of most of these rulers with the West, which created Israel and supported it through all these years, only deepened the anti-Western feeling of the masses, and increased their loss of faith in their traditional leaders.

In addition, Razzaz writes, Zionism supplied a continuous external challenge to the movement of Arab nationalism: "On the one hand this was useful in the sense that the movement was strengthened by such a challenge. On the other, it thwarted the 'positive' and 'creative' element of the movement and kept it being its 'negative' and 'reflex' character. And so, instead of a healthy growth of the Arab masses towards unity, freedom, socialism and neutralism, the whole movement was taken over and distorted by military groups which justified their existence by the imminent military menace of Zionism."

And so, as the "facts" emerged and the "illusions" were discarded, a revolt began. This revolt was inspired and directed almost exclusively by army officers who, being aware of the disasters they themselves had suffered, were convinced that the responsibility lay entirely with their governments, whose corruption, complacency, and inefficiency were brought out most acutely by their conduct in the Palestine conflict. These officers were mostly drawn from the ranks of the middle classes, and were thus close to the people and more conscious of their needs. They also knew more than the majority of their compatriots (not excluding their political leaders) about the exigencies of the modern world, and were more aware of the urgent need for reforms.

The first to rebel was a Syrian colonel. Husni el-Zaʿim was described as a picturesque and loyal military type, of mixed Turkish and Kurdish rather than Arab origin, who had received his military training on French lines. On March 30, 1949, without bloodshed, he unseated a government that he thought unworthy of its charge. El-Zaʿim at first proved popular with the Syrian masses, but being first and foremost a Syrian nationalist and patriot, he soon came into conflict with Arab nationalist groups inside Syria on the one hand, and with Baghdad—which was then contemplating the famous Fertile Crescent Plan—on the other.

El-Zaʿim's experience was significant in that he was the first Syrian ruler seriously to start exploiting inter-Arab discords and rivalries. Sensing danger from Baghdad, he declared a few months after seizing power that "Syria relied on the support of Egypt and Saudi Arabia and constituted with them the Cairo-Damascus-Riyadh triangle." Just over five weeks later, el-Zaʿim was murdered by a group of pro-Iraqi army officers, who thus staged the second Syrian coup d'état within six months.

A few months later, however, another army officer was to stage a third coup, and to stay for some years. Colonel Adib Shishakli was a better politician than el-Zaʿim. He held power for four years, managing to survive and weather many storms. He was the first military ruler of an Arab country who actually contributed something toward those reforms that have constituted the raison d'être of all military coups; by 1954, when he allowed himself to be forced out of office bloodlessly by another set of army officers, he had made a significant contribution to the development of Syria. He left power when conditions were favorable to an upsurge of leftist groups, and in September 1954 the elections held there gave the Arab Baʿth Socialist Party its first success.

THE NASSER PHENOMENON

The most significant, because the most durable, upheaval against the corruption and inefficiency of any Arab political regime took place in Egypt on July 23, 1952. Unlike the Syrian coups, the movement that swept away the Egyptian monarchy and instituted the Free Officers' rule was not the work of soldiers alone, though it eventually became controlled almost exclusively by the military. Having passed through the Palestine fiasco and thought over its lessons, these officers, drawn mostly from the lower middle class, reached the conclusion that the blame for their shameful defeat on the battlefields of the Holy Land lay not simply with their own high command, but also with the government, the monarchy, and the entire old political setup. After a few years of groping, and of dealing with foreign affairs, these officers managed to introduce a reform program that eventually won them considerable popular support.

Indeed, despite the fact that his part in later Arab and international developments tended to depict Gamal Abdel Nasser—who in 1953 became the head of the new Egypt—as mainly a political figure, a maneuverer and conspirator, this should not obscure his preoccupation with social reform. In his booklet entitled *The Philosophy of the Revolution,* Nasser goes so far as to write: "I dare say that the Revolution of July 23 was not the consequence of the war in Palestine, nor was it caused by those defective armaments which cost the lives of so many soldiers and officers, nor by the electoral crisis in the Officers' Club (which was the immediate cause of the movement). Those are but the factors that hastened its maturity" (Nasser's booklet and pronouncements are quoted in Rejwan, *Nasserist Ideology,* 111–113).

Here, of course, Nasser is trying to explain the deeper, largely social causes of the revolution, which the others seem not to have grasped. Nasser traced the commencement of this revolution, generally dated from the events of July, to a much more distant past:

Some people want to regard July 23, 1952, as the starting point of our revolution; but the truth is quite otherwise. July 23 was only the last phase of the revolution. Its beginnings were to be seen on July 11, 1882. On that day the peaceful city of Alexandria was subjected to bombardment by the British aggressors. The hateful occupation followed. Egypt revolted. The peasant soldier Ahmad 'Urabi sallied out at the head of a group of free officers and soldiers to repel the aggressors. But the revolution did not then attain its objectives. It was then new-born, and being only an infant, it had to bide its time, to grow up and attain its maturity before it could decide to take action. Thus, the first aim of the Revolution, from the first day of its life, has been to liberate Egypt.

In the same booklet, Nasser describes how he and his fellow Free Officers sought "a revolution springing from the hearts of the people, bearing out their hopes and sweeping forward into the future." In later years, in innumerable pronouncements, and finally in the famous Charter for National Action, Nasser continued to elaborate on this theory of social revolution, culminating his efforts in the proclamation of what now has come to be known as Arab socialism.

Barely fifteen years after Israel's war of independence, in 1948, and nearly eleven after the 1952 revolution in Egypt, the figure of Nasser became the most imposing and respected in the whole Arab world. But it was not as a social reformer and the founder of Arab socialism that he was so popular in the Arab mind; it was also, and mainly, as a man who symbolized not only the Arabs' defiance of European domination but also their first successful attempt to defeat it. The year 1956, which saw the failure of the Anglo-French and Israeli military expedition to Suez—a failure that, though the result of purely diplomatic considerations, was successfully depicted by Nasser as a renowned victory for himself and for the Arabs—made Nasser the first champion of Arab unity, and it is as such that he has since held his unique place in the Arab world.

But it was also as the self-appointed leader of a united Arab domain, extending from the Atlantic to the Persian Gulf, that Nasser faced his gravest difficulties. Following his successful bid to merge Syria with Egypt into one Arab Republic, proclaimed in February 1958, prospects initially appeared to be fairly bright for drawing more Arab countries into the union. But first in Lebanon and then in Iraq, these pan-Arab hopes of Nasser's foundered on the rocks of strong feelings of local patriotism, mutual jealousy, and age-old rivalries—and above all on the reluctance of the Arab "have" countries to share their resources with the "have-nots."

In this connection the Iraqi experience was especially bitter to the pan-Arabists of Egypt. After overthrowing the Hashemite regime in Baghdad, in July 1958, the Iraqis seemed quite favorably inclined toward Cairo, and one section of the revolutionaries—headed by Abdel Salam ᶜArif—was even in favor of an immediate merger with the United Arab Republic. Here, however, Iraqi nationalism proved stronger than Pan-Arabism, with the result that the new revolutionary regime in Baghdad was soon completely alienated from Cairo, a development that doomed to failure the Egypt-Syria union itself.

Soon after, another pattern of inter-Arab relations prevailed. On February 8, 1963, the anti-Cairo regime of Abdel Karim Qassim was overthrown by the combined forces of the Ba'th Party and other pan-Arab groups in Iraq. Exactly four weeks later, on March 8, the Ba'th staged another coup d'état in Damascus, thus toppling another anti-Cairo Arab regime. Since the Ba'th, like Nasser, believed in "liberty, Arab unity, and socialism," the stage was set for a link between Egypt, Iraq, and Syria—and negotiations were in fact started shortly afterward. As a result of those negotiations, a tripartite agreement was signed in Cairo on April 16, 1963, proclaiming the federation of the three Arab countries in a renewed United Arab Republic.

The federation agreement, which seemed to fulfill a long-cherished dream shared by all Arabs, was hailed as an event ushering in a new era in Arab history, one matched only by the period started by the great upsurge of Islam over thirteen centuries before; predictions were made about the imminent collapse of the "reactionary" monarchies in Saudi Arabia and Jordan. (In the latter, indeed, pro-Nasser and Ba'thist elements actually attempted a coup.) However, as the days went by, the projected federation appeared to be less cohesive and less real than it had been made to seem. Paradoxically, the Ba'th Party, a diehard pan-Arab group, started having doubts about Nasser's intentions, and a state of affairs emerged in which this Arab-nationalist group was fast turning itself into a bulwark against immediate and unconditional Arab union under Cairo's leadership.

Again it seemed, as with Syria during the merger and as with Iraq under Qassim, as if local nationalism, differences in social structure, cultural levels, and customs—and above all, perhaps, conflicting material interests—had gained the upper hand.

MODERATES VERSUS REJECTIONISTS

Throughout this period, the Arab attitude toward Israel and its ideology remained one of rejection, based largely on ignorance, though seasoned with pronouncements and declarations bordering dangerously on European-style anti-Semitism. In the aftermath of the Six-Day War, however, and amid the bouts of self-criticism and self-flagellation that swept Arab intellectual circles, there was hardly an accusation that was not leveled—rightly or wrongly—at contemporary Arab society and culture. Except for the most vicious sounding among them, these onslaughts were usually accepted with equanimity by Arab publics and governments alike. Yet right from the start a certain unwritten code governed all these efforts—namely, that no practical conclusions or proposals could follow from them as far as Israel's status and future in the Middle East were concerned. Cecil Hourani's celebrated call to the Arabs, shortly after the war, to recognize Israel and make peace with it on the best terms they could get was passed over in silence or dismissed as "defeatist" (Hourani, "The Moment of Truth," *Encounter,* November 1967).

By a remarkable coincidence, another of the Hourani brothers was to come under critical fire over the same issue. Professor George Hourani (1913–1984) taught philosophy in various American universities for over three decades, and was known for his careful scholarly English translation and interpretations of Ibn Rushd's *Kitab Fasl al-Maqal* (The Last Word, sometimes rendered as On the Harmony of Religion and Philosophy). A Lebanese Arab, he was also interested in Middle Eastern affairs and was president of the Middle East Studies Association (MESA) in 1968. Apparently speaking in all three of his capacities—as a philosopher, an Arab, and a student of the Middle East— Hourani chose for his MESA presidential address the subject "Palestine as a Problem of Ethics." The lecture in its original form attracted little attention; it was printed in the association's bulletin, and then reprinted, instructively enough, in *The Arab World,* an Arab League–financed publication in English. A few months later, a new Lebanese periodical, *Al-Qadaya al-Mu'asira* (Contemporary Affairs), printed an Arabic translation of the address in its first issue—and it was only then that Hourani's views became known to a wider circle of Arab readers.

In his lecture, Hourani offers a sort of ethical balance sheet between the Arab and the Jewish claims to set up a state of its own in Palestine. His conclusion is that the Arabs might do best "to accept the Jewish presence and the state of Israel in part of Palestine." Such an acceptance should, however, "be more than a mere bowing down to force majeure, or a temporary tactical withdrawal until the opportunity for reversing the situation arises." It could and should be a "moral decision." Like all moral decisions, "it is not to be made in a vacuum of complete freedom, but as the best thing to do in the circumstances, with all their constraints." Professor Hourani regrets that the Arabs "unwisely" rejected the Palestine Partition Plan of 1947, and points out that another attempt to drive the Jews into the sea would mean "a long and bitter struggle with more refugees, death and destruction on both sides."

As to the basis on which the Arabs would be ethically justified to accept the Jewish presence and state in part of Palestine, Hourani argues that the Jews came to that part of the world because of promises made to them, established themselves legally and through hard work, and became settled, so "much hardship would be inflicted if they were forced to emigrate to other countries, new or old, and many individuals would undergo undeserved suffering." Among the points he discusses is the basic Zionist argument that Jewish homelessness and the threats to Jewish national identity in the Diaspora necessitated their resettlement in their own national home. He points out, however, that "the weakness of this argument was that it did not establish the necessity of Palestine as the national home."

Despite these reservations, and despite the extremely cautious terms in which he formulates his theses, George Hourani's lecture provoked some scathing criticism from Arab-nationalist intellectual circles. The Beirut cultural monthly *Al-Adaab,* the leading organ of these circles, was the first to mount the attack. Suhayl Idris, a leading exponent of radical Arab nationalism, called Hourani's appeal "a suspect voice." Self-criticism, he said, was right and legitimate—though after the June debacle, some of it deteriorated into sheer masochism and self-flagellation. Occasionally, however, some voices are heard asking the Arabs "to accept the fait accompli and agree to surrender—now on grounds of morality, now allegedly to prevent misery and loss of life." Idris said he failed to understand the brand of ethics according to which demands are directed to the oppressed and the oppressors are absolved of responsibility.

George Hourani's was not the only "suspect voice" taken on by Idris. The same issue of *Al-Qadaya al-Mu'asira* that carried Hourani's article featured an interview with Charles Malik, a former foreign minister and chief UN delegate from Lebanon as well as a veteran philosophy professor. In this interview, Malik was reported to have expressed the forlorn hope that "the whole of the Middle East, namely, Turkey, Lebanon, Israel, Jordan, Egypt, and even Saudi Arabia and Iraq would become a neutral zone in the full sense of the word." The interviewer added here that Malik seems to believe, however tentatively, that there were prospects for peaceful coexistence with Israel. "The Arabs," he is quoted as explaining, "cannot attain self-determination separately from the Jews—and the Jews cannot do the same in isolation from the Arabs."

This too aroused Idris's wrath. At a time when the Arab nation, with all its peoples, its armed forces, and its commando units, was concentrating all its great potentialities in an effort to put an end to the injustice perpetrated against it through the creation of this state of Israel—a state that daily proved its expansionist aspirations and racist policies—at such a juncture voices calling on the Arabs to recognize Israel could be described only as "suspect voices."

Suspect or not suspect, the fact remains that voices such as George Hourani's and Charles Malik's—as well as those that never managed to reach the outside world—were usually quickly subdued. In the prevailing state of ideological polarization and increasing escalation on the battlefield, this was perhaps inevitable: bridges are the first to be blown up by combatants.

It is perhaps worth mentioning here that Hourani's argument proved unacceptable not just to the Arab-nationalist side. In a lengthy and well-argued article in *Midstream,* the Jewish monthly review published by the Theodor Herzl Foundation in New York, Ben Halpern, the well-known scholar and historian of Zionism, took issue with Hourani because the grounds he gives for a moral decision to accept Israel "are grudging and devoid of understanding"—adding that "if peace had to depend on Hourani's arguments we could give up all hope for it now" (Halpern, "A Problem of Ethics").

Beginning with the early 1990s, with the Arab world generally resigned to Israel's existence and with peace seemingly close at hand, Arab writers and political intellectuals started seriously to deal with the question of how best to cope with a post-peace-settlement Israel. The problem these writers envisioned involved not just the future shape of "the Zionist entity" and Israel's role in a postsettlement Middle East. Their main concern was how to decide which among a number of alternatives would be least detrimental to the Arabs. The answers to this and related questions can be grouped under two broad headings:

- The hardliners, including the former rejectionists, said the Arabs must now accept Israel as a fait accompli, but they had no obligation to agree to full-fledged normalization of relations with it. They argued that since Israel was far more advanced materially and technologically, normalization in the cultural and technological spheres would amount to "cultural invasion" as well as to Israeli economic and technological predominance.

- The moderates tended to accept, and even to favor, complete normalization of relations, on the ground that given their relatively small numbers and the variety of sociocultural groups they are composed of, the Israelis will eventually be integrated, even "absorbed," into their new habitat, as were Jews in Arab-Muslim domains from time immemorial. Some of these observers used the term "acculturation," arguing that in such a process Muslim Arabs will certainly have the upper hand. What, they asked, would a few million Jews be in an expanse containing 100 million Arabs and 90 million Muslims?

Neither of the two options noted above represented the official policy of any Arab country for any length of time. Even Egypt, the first Arab country to sign an official peace treaty with Israel, remained undecided, even though it obviously and openly tended to adopt a slightly moderated version of the hardliners' option, agreeing only to partial normalization of relations. There were, however, some dissenting voices even within the government. One of these was a proposal made by then-deputy prime minister Dr. Yousuf Wali, who in April 1993 asserted that the key to peace in the Middle East was an economic one and that the best way to achieve this was an "economic union." "We need to confront other such economic unions," he explained in an article in the Cairo daily *Al-Ahram,* adding that the proposed union would include Egypt, Israel, and North African and Gulf states (Wali's comments, along with those of Shukr, below, were reported in the *Jerusalem Post,* April 21, 1993).

Wali, long a key molder of policy, who also held the posts of minister of agriculture and secretary-general of the ruling National Democratic Party, explained that the market base of such a union (200 million people) would mean a better distribution of economic resources through complementary trade and production policies. "There is also a significant political dimension," he added, citing the "formulation of a political framework for peace in the Middle East" as the basis.

Wali's proposal did not pass unnoticed, however. Left-oriented opponents of the Mubarak regime sharply criticized the plan, describing it as merely "an echo of American-Israeli concepts." One of them, Abdul Ghaffar Shukr, writing in the opposition weekly *Al-Yasar,* asked, "Who is going to be the main beneficiary of the proposed Middle East Economic Union—Egypt and the Arab states or America and Israel?" The answer, wrote Shukr, was obvious—and the timing was obvious, too. Because of the Gulf War and the searing internal Arab feuds and divisions that the war had produced, the Arabs, he added, had never been in a weaker or sorrier position than their current one.

The weakening of the Arab world had exposed the Arabs to pressures from Washington, Shukr explained, citing as proof the replacement of Arab defense pacts by American-inspired security arrangements, as well as the idea of an economic union embracing all the countries of the region, including Israel and Turkey. Reiterating his claim that Wali had merely recycled Israeli plans, Shukr referred to Israeli statements and documents dating back to the 1960s. He also reminded his readers that Wali was one of the architects of the Egyptian-Israeli peace treaty, charging that, this time around, Wali wanted to play the same role in normalizing relations between Israel and the Arab world as a whole.

THIRTEEN

NEW LESSONS FOR OLD

Many hundreds of years ago the Romans reached the conclusion that the only thing one learns from experience is that one never learns from experience. Nevertheless, men kept drawing lessons from the experiences they happened to go through in frantic attempts to learn from them and thus avoid making the same sort of errors in their future dealings.

And Arabs have been no exception. Since the nakba that befell them in 1948, when their armies were defeated at the hands of "Zionist bands," they have kept relentlessly drawing lessons—hundreds of them—from that as well as subsequent experiences, but, like the rest of us, they never seemed to learn anything useful in consequence.

But they kept trying. The most recent collection of lessons that were to be learned pertained to the Persian Gulf crisis and the war in which Arab took up arms against fellow Arab—and the lessons industry soon thrived. You could pick up any Arabic newspaper or periodical those days and be struck by the number of commentators, academics, politicians, and leading military experts who volunteered to tell readers what, in their opinion, was the main moral of the latest trauma they were going through.

Because of the number and variety of these reactions, it would be best to group the proposed lessons under a few general subjects to which they pertained—political regimes, economic conditions, inter-Arab relations, the role of the intellectuals, education, sociocultural factors, and freedom of expression, among others.

"OFFICIAL THINKERS" AND "UNOFFICIAL THINKERS"

Among these problems, all of them already thoroughly thrashed out during the previous four decades, democracy now took—and continues to take—pride of place. A statement issued by the left-oriented Egyptian op-position group the Alignment Party sums up the position taken by practically every Arab writer and thinker who dealt with the subject throughout the crisis. "The absence of democracy in the Arab world," the statement said, "is the cause of all the troubles, since it deprives the Arab peoples from exercising control over their rulers and from actual participation in fateful decision-making, thus leaving the door open for individual adventures and the prevalence of tyrannical regimes" (reported along with Nassar's comments, below, in *Al-Ahali* [Cairo], September 13, 1991).

This position was reiterated by, among a great many others, the Association of Arab Lawyers and Jurists, which called upon Arab governments "to lift their custodianship from their peoples and grant them their rightful share in decision-making." The various human rights groups and other professional and academic associations followed suit, formulating their positions in virtually identical terms.

This general attitude has been elaborated by academics and specialists in almost every Arab country, the exceptions being those countries in which talk about democracy is not much tolerated—Saudi Arabia, Kuwait, and the other Gulf sheikhdoms and emirates. One of these academics is Naseef Nassar, a Lebanese scholar specializing in sociology and philosophy. According to Nassar, thinkers in the contemporary Arab world are of two kinds: "official thinkers and unofficial thinkers"—and it is only the latter who address public issues as free individuals, since the former are committed to the state and its ideology and act as servants of the interests of the ruling establishment.

Proceeding with this distinction, Nassar asserts that while independent Arab thinkers are prevented from playing a role in shaping public opinion, those who agree to serve the regime's interests have been able to influence events and help lead public opinion. Nassar then goes on to enumerate four factors that he says are to blame for this state of things:

- Current Arab regimes are either totalitarian or semitotalitarian, and they all seek to subjugate public opinion and place it under their sole leadership.

- The masses, which are usually the foundation for public opinion, are either illiterate or unable to relate freely to enlightened opinion.

- The prevalent sociopolitical culture continues to conceive of social, political, and cultural relations as being regulated by the twin authorities of secular rule and religious precepts, thus ruling out rational considerations and conscious solidarity as determinants of the common interest.

• Western capitalist powers exercise strong pressures, using highly effective means, to back traditionalist trends and dependence, leading to continued and deepening backwardness.

Nassar admits that these factors are not uniform in their impact and vary from country to country—"but the problem can be summed up in one short phrase, i.e., the absence of democracy." It is democracy, he asserts, and democracy alone "that can allow the independent thinker to address public opinion freely and out of a sense of responsibility and thus to play his due role of enlightening it and of helping effect change.

Turning to what he calls "subjective factors," Nassar puts some of the blame on the thinker and the intellectual, since they failed to be sufficiently aggressive and persistent. The more that Arab regimes insisted on manipulating public opinion, he writes, the less vocal the political intellectuals became—and this strange interaction between totalitarian tendencies and the lack of articulate and consistent response was largely to blame for the prevalent imbalance.

In conclusion, Nassar asserts that concepts and values such as liberty, democracy, and freedom of expression are, in the Arab world, still in need of much discussion and explanation if they are ever to become living realities for both the ruling elites and the masses. In failing to undertake this task of explanation and promotion, he suggests, Arab thinkers and political intellectuals have been the victims of a failure of nerve.

Self-criticism and soul-searching have been fairly regular features of Arab writings since the first Arab-Israeli war (1948–1949), which the Arabs perceived as a humiliating and inexplicable defeat. In the aftermath of the Kuwait crisis and the Gulf War, however, in which Arabs took up arms against Arabs and aided a foreign "neocolonialist" superpower in its attempt to destroy the military might of the one Arab country with a real potential for asserting the Arabs' honor and restoring their long-lost self-esteem, examples of such reappraisals and soul-searchings came out in numerous forms and numbers—articles, booklets, symposiums, lectures, and interviews.

One of the more outspoken Arab thinkers and writers to undertake the task has been the Moroccan teacher and scholar Muhammad ᶜAbed al-Jabiri (b. 1936), author of a number of books on Arab intellectual history and contemporary Arab culture. Speaking at a symposium titled "Vistas of the Arab Future," organized by the Arab Unity Study Center in Beirut, Jabiri delineated the three factors that he believed would determine the Arabs' future: the new world order taking shape now; the prospects of peace between the Arabs and Israel; and the legacy of the old world order and its bearings on individual Arab nation-states (Jabiri's comments were excerpted in Nissim Rejwan, "Arabs Assess Gulf War," *Jerusalem Post,* April 10, 1992).

On the new world order and its implications for the Arabs, Jabiri envisaged two possible developments as a result of the disappearance of the Soviet Union and recognition of the United States as the uncontested single world superpower. The West, he asserted, was likely to discard its old friends in the Arab area and the Third World, whom it had needed during the Cold War, and to try to establish self-supporting regional organizations to fend for their individual members. The West might also encourage the trend toward a democratic system of government, a more equitable distribution of Arab wealth, and an end to corruption and irrational behavior—all, obviously, coming "within the context of Western interests."

On the peace prospects between the Arabs and Israel, Jabiri believes that the current tendency in the Arab world "to put the Palestine question aside and turn to direct negotiations with Israel to bring an end to the conflict" will block the way to "the negative uses to which the problem was put in the past, so that it ceases to serve as a cover for all sorts of [other] problems and all sorts of conducts." This, Jabiri asserts, will compel those who previously exploited the Palestine problem in such ways to come out in the open and seek legitimacy elsewhere.

On the ascent of the individual Arab nation-state—as against the old pan-Arab perception of the future—Jabiri is unequivocal. "The concept of 'Arab Nationalism' is no longer a mobilized ideological slogan; it is now incapable of arousing the masses in favor of an ideological unity that owes its essence to the ideology of Arab nationalism," he asserts. The individual Arab state can no longer be rejected on ideological grounds," he explains. "It is no longer 'an artificial creation' and a result of inter-Arab divisions and fragmentation; it has to be viewed as a reality, and to be treated accordingly. The result is that the road to Arab unity must now pass through 'local patriotism.'" To attain such unity, he concludes, "democratic legitimacy" must be established in each Arab state.

PONDERING THE SIX-DAY WAR FIASCO

Among those in the Arab world who wrote to mark the twenty-fifth anniversary of the Six-Day War—and they were legion—there was a near consensus on at least one cardinal point: The *naksa* (setback) that the Arabs suffered in June 1967 changed the concepts they had held before the war and eventually led to a general acceptance of Israel as a fact of life in the region (the following section is adapted from Nissim Rejwan, "Accepting Israel as a Fact of Life," *Jerusalem Post,* June 12, 1992).

To be sure, the thesis took different forms and formulations. Some of the commentators—like the Egyptian economics professor Jamal Amin—attributed the change to the economic difficulties that the defeat caused Egypt, which Amin says, were worse than "the devastating economic crisis of the 1930s."

Others concentrated on the trauma brought by the war and its consequences, from which the Arabs have not yet recovered. Still others said that despite the disappointment and the despair, the war also proved—in the words of an editorial in the East Jerusalem daily *Al-Quds*—"that force and wars were no longer capable of imposing peace or attaining security." Twenty-five long years after its victory, the paper added, Israel had not gained the kind of peace and security it wanted the Arabs to accept.

But some dug rather deeper. The Lebanese poet Ghassan Matar, for one, recalled in an interview the lines he wrote immediately following the war. "I love you, Haziran (June)"—he sang—"for the resurrection of our dead. You have made of me, O mighty wound, a man!"

"This was how we responded to the naksa, as it was called then," Matar added. "We used to dream big dreams that defied despair and surrender, convinced that victory over our national enemy, Israel, was inevitable—till finally disillusionment dawned and with it a more objective reading of the situation."

What decided the issue for him, said Matar, was the discovery that the Yom Kippur War was "a political war, not a war of liberation"—and the last straw came when Egyptian president Sadat visited Jerusalem, a step that "carried clear indications of capitulation and an admission that our national rights had fallen into the hands of our enemy."

To cap it all, the 1982 war in Lebanon provided Matar proof positive that "there was not a single Arab cause that could bring the Arabs together in a unified front—neither now nor in the future."

Kamal Abul Majd, a former Egyptian minister of information and now a professor of public law at Cairo University, chose to see the bright side. "One of the most important consequences of the 1967 debacle," he said in a colloquium convened in Cairo to mark the occasion, "was that the peoples of the region started to clamor for a democratic system of government. Nasser himself responded to these demands when he announced on March 30, 1968, his willingness to introduce democracy and political pluralism; but he did not live to see this through. The process was completed by Sadat when the 1971 Constitution was ratified, instituting the multi-party system and the rule of law—a system that is still in effect."

In another symposium on the subject, also held in Cairo, ʿAlieddine Hilal, a professor of politics at Cairo University, thought one of the consequences of the war was the rise of the fundamentalists in Egypt and the demand that the Islamists be given an opportunity to run the affairs of government. He also said the 1967 naksa resulted in Egypt's changing the order of its priorities: instead of the destruction of Israel, its top priority became recovering territory occupied by Israel.

Various appraisals touched on the effects the defeat produced in various nonpolitical spheres, with one scholar—Nadeem Nʿeima, professor of literature at the American University of Beirut—going so far as to say that as a result of the 1967 setback, "our literature became journalistic to a certain extent, an ephemeral consumer literature—and so has our literary criticism!"

An even more damning appraisal of the situation came from another Beirut scholar, Mahmoud Sweid, director of the Institute of Palestine Studies. According to Sweid, "It is the Arab intelligentsia which bears the main part of the responsibility for what the Arab peoples have come to," since "the majority of Arab intellectuals joined forces with rulers and monarchs and continue to conspire with them against their own peoples"—as was the case in the Gulf War, when these intellectuals "acted in such an abysmal manner that the [Arab] nation will continue to suffer from it for a long time to come."

The irony here is that Sweid's rhetoric is precisely of the kind that many in the Arab world blamed for the Arabs' debacle of June 1967. To give one example: A few weeks after that debacle, Nizar Qabbani, a leading light in modern Arabic poetry, published an angry elegy that opened with these lines:

> My friend, mourn for the language of the past and the old books,
> The discourse punctured like battered shoes,
> The verse of profanity, slander, aspersion . . .
> I mourn, I mourn
> The thought that finally brought defeat.

In the course of this somber poem, which attracted a great deal of criticism and disapproval at the time, Qabbani also wrote: "No wonder we lost the war / We entered it / With the oratorical art of the Orient / And the innocuous sonnets of ʿAntar / We entered it with the logic of the drum and the lute."

Less emotional though equally emphatic were the works produced by a number of leading Arab intellectuals attempting to fathom the causes of the Arabs' inability to confront Israel. In the previous chapter we summarized briefly some of the answers offered by Constantine Zureiq. In his book *The Arab Mind* (1983), the Jewish anthropologist and ethnographer Raphael Patai (1910–1996) surveys the views of other Arab intellectuals. One of them, Salaheddine al-Munajjid, in a book entitled *Aʿmidat al-Nakba* (Pillars of the Disaster), offers a somewhat different prognosis from Zureiq's. In a chapter entitled "Our Scientific Backwardness," he writes that the Jews who came to Palestine from Europe

> had acquired a comprehensive specialization in all branches of knowledge, and especially in the experimental sciences: mathematics, biology, and the like. . . . We can count hundreds of Jewish scientists in the natural sciences, e.g., in chemistry, and the atom, while we still lag behind scientifically and technically. We have not mastered the experimental sciences, do not excel in them, and cannot name in them even five scientists of our own. Also the [Jews'] religious belief—which drives them hysterically towards progress, study, power and superiority—is lacking among us, and especially so since some of our thinkers and educated people want to remove religion and blot it out from our lives. (quoted in Patai, *The Arab Mind*, 262–263)

"These Jews," adds al-Munajjid, "have methodical minds which pass judgment with planning and schedules, and calculate the numbers, time and measure of everything; while we have confused minds, which incline to improvisation, are subject to emotions, and are impelled toward recklessness and extremism." Other advantages the Jews have and the Arabs lack:

- The Jews' planning extends into all areas and "aims at improvement, completion and expansion."

- The Jews adhere to reality, study it in an objective, scientific manner, and act to adapt themselves to reality or to adapt reality to themselves.

- The Jews maintain research centers, they value scholars, and they encourage those centers and those scholars to pursue pure research.

- The Jews, their wealthy, and their financial institutions in the world donate millions for research in Israel.

166

- The Jews derive benefits from all the scientific talents that can be found among them or which belong to them, whatever their kind or country or orientation.

- Israel, because of its efforts in science, is advancing with giant steps towards self-sufficiency and has begun to export its products—even those of a military kind—to Africa and Asia.

"All these things render Israel scientifically superior to us," al-Munajjid concludes. "Our age is an age of science. He who masters science is in a position to rule and in a position to impose his will. It is not possible that we should triumph in ignorance. It is not possible that we should advance in backwardness. It is not possible that we should prevail with delusions, nor with speeches, songs and talk" (quoted in Patai, *The Arab Mind*, 263–264).

The works produced by Arab writers, intellectuals, and men of letters enumerating the lessons their readers should learn from the defeat of their armies and the failure of their leaderships throughout the years of Israel's existence are numerous. In one of these, Abdel Rahman al-Bazzaz, an Iraqi law professor who became prime minister under the Ba'th regime, summarizes the lessons to be drawn as follows:

1. One Arab country alone can never be strong enough to defeat Israel; hence the Arabs must unite.

2. Despite formal agreements among the Arab countries, they often take opposing and even conflicting actions.

3. The Arabs must establish a united information and propaganda apparatus.

4. There is a lack of planning and preparatory study in our actions; most of our acts are characterized by emotionalism, immediate reaction, and a lack of thorough calculation of ultimate consequences.

5. As states, we act, in general and in most cases, out of both love and hate. Our hatred is so exaggerated that we burn all bridges to friendship or to peace.

6. We are inclined to place on others the responsibility for our mistakes. This is a psychic blemish in us, which develops in us from infancy.

7. We must recognize that Israel in itself represents a threat to us, and not only as a bastion for the imperialist powers.

8. We must effect a mobilization of our forces in a manner similar to
that of Israel. We must make sure that our army commanders will
be equal in their value to the commanders of our enemies, who are
clever, educated, and aware of the meaning of modern wars. . . . The
main problem is that of raising of the level of the Arab individual . . .
so that we shall at least approximate the level of the enemy. (quoted
in Patai, *The Arab Mind,* 265)

These reflections and appraisals, and the lessons drawn from them, were
written in the late 1960s. Three long decades after, with an overall peaceful
settlement of the Arab-Israeli conflict still in the offing, a different kind of
question began to be asked. In the preceding chapter, reference was made
to two alternative perceptions of the postpeace era, Israel's future status,
and the role it is supposed to play in it. A third perception of Israel's status
in a postsettlement Middle East, voiced by a much smaller and so far rather
less vocal group, envisages Israel's future in terms of "state versus community." It is this third choice that will be addressed here briefly.

In a closely argued article titled "The Future of Israel: State or Community?" (*Al-Ahram* [Cairo], May 12, 1993) Diyaa Rashwan, a research fellow at *Al-Ahram*'s Center for Political and Strategic Studies, dwells at some
length on the pros and cons of these two alternatives from the Arabs' point
of view—something along the line of which is best, or least bad, for the
Arabs: Israel's continuing to exist as an independent sovereign entity, or its
declining into an ethnic minority, one of many that make up the Middle
Eastern communal-cultural mosaic?

For those Israelis who have always thought that the kind of metamor-
phosis that could reduce the sovereign state of Israel to an ethnic-religious
minority must be the fond dream of every Arab, Rashwan has quite a surprise. After weighing the options at some length, he reaches the conclusion
that, everything being equal, it would be best for the Arabs if, instead of
disintegrating into an ethnic minority, Israel should go on being the separate independent state it now is. (It is worth noting here that, for reasons
not easy to fathom, Rashwan uses the word *jaliya*—literally "dispersion,"
"diaspora"—instead of an Arabic equivalent of "community," adopting the
terminology used by Israel for Jewish communities abroad. Interestingly
enough, jaliya and the Hebrew *galut*—"dispersion"—have the same root.)

Rashwan's main concern is that even if Israel should cease to exist as a
sovereign state, its Jews—who will then become the second-largest Jewish
community after American Jewry—will go on wielding the same dispro-
portionate influence on the societies in the midst of which they live. Since

the Arab states and their societies are less capable of resisting such influences and incursions than, say, the United States, France, and the former Soviet Union, the overall impact that the large Jewish community in Palestine will make on the fortunes of the Arab area as a whole is bound to be far greater. Israel's persistent drive for dominance of land and resources, Rashwan explains, is liable to turn into an even graver danger of dominating the Arabs' political and economic destinies and determining the general sociocultural processes of the whole area in ways favorable to local as well as world Jewries. One example cited by the writer of how tremendous an influence such a Jewish group can wield is the way in which the Jewish lobby managed to make Washington use the Soviets' need for wheat supplies to pressure Moscow into permitting Jews to emigrate.

Another major cause for concern is that considering how frail and divided among themselves some Arab societies are—especially east of Suez—there is a real danger of a coincidence of interests between the Jewish community and the various ethnic, cultural, and religious groups that make up these societies now. In an obvious reference to such minority groups as the Maronites of the Levant; the Kurds of Iraq, Turkey, Syria, and Iran; and the Shiᶜite Muslims of southern Iraq, Rashwan speaks of the possibility that the Jews' rich experience in this field may result in dangerous alliances between them and the various ethnic and religious groups of the Arab region.

In conclusion, Rashwan is careful to emphasize that the fears he expresses about the Israeli Jews' becoming an ethnic minority "do not spring from a so-called conspiracy theory that perceives in every Jew a hidden plot aimed at inflicting harm on an Arab." Rather, he writes, it is part of a strategic and historical assessment of the future that every nation is obliged to make for its own well-being.

FOURTEEN

THE INTELLECTUALS

Intellectuals have always been a subject of controversy in the Arab world, and the intellectual's role in society and politics remains a point at issue among the educated classes there. The Gulf crisis, precipitated by the invasion of Kuwait by Iraqi forces in August 1989, served only to intensify the debate, as some academics and writers took sides in favor of this party or that.

In Egypt, especially, intellectuals came under heavy fire—and from all directions. Groups and circles opposed to Iraq's move assaulted those who showed sympathy or even leniency toward Baghdad, while they in turn tried to defend their stand as best they could, considering they were swimming against the stream and against their country's stand.

More instructive were the sharp exchanges between the intellectuals themselves. Mutual recriminations and accusations were thrown around, and people on both sides brandished Julien Benda's famous work on "the treason of the intellectuals" as proof and justification for their particular stands. Things came to such a pass, indeed, that a respected Egyptian historian found it fit to start an article he wrote on the failure of the Arab left with a disclaimer: he announced that he had never worked for or been associated with any Kuwaiti institution—academic, governmental, or journalistic—the implication being that in opposing Baghdad's seizure of the emirate, he had no ax to grind.

"PART OF THE ARAB PREDICAMENT"

The subject was also tackled in calmer and more academic ways. "Defined in any way one chooses, the Arab intellectual is part of the Arab predicament," says Sa'deddine Ibrahim, a professor of sociology at the American University of Cairo and an active and outspoken Egyptian intellectual.

"As intellectuals," Ibrahim added in an interview published in the Cairo weekly *Rose el-Yousuf*, "we may have erred sometimes, perhaps most of the time. Perchance we lacked courage and thus betrayed our people, being their vanguard and consciences; perhaps we failed in our analyses and our perceptions of our present condition, allowing this to blur our vision and paralyze us; it may be too that we have traded our integrity for a livelihood, freedom for social justice, independence for material growth, traditionalism for modernity . . . Perhaps, perhaps." On the tricky subject of relations between the intellectual and the powers that be, Ibrahim was far more wary. Writing in the learned, Cairo-based Arabic quarterly *Al-Fikr al-ʿArabi* in August 1991, he wondered what an intellectual ought to do when he disagrees with what the regime asks him to do. His answer: "Let him excuse himself, politely and without undue fuss in the media."

In furnishing such an easy way out, however, Ibrahim seemed to be strangely unaware of the assumption implicit therein, namely, a ruler can expect an intellectual to do his will only if the latter has been safely "establishmentized." This, in fact, was the thrust of the argument made by Mahmoud Amin al-ʿAlim, an Egyptian intellectual of the left, in an article in the same issue of the quarterly. "The majority of Arab intellectuals today," al-ʿAlim writes, "have, consciously or subconsciously, become court poets, apologists for monarchs, and tools for justifying, guiding, and helping pass policies and measures imposed by the present Arab regimes and give them a false air of legitimacy."

Not that Ibrahim was not aware of all this; he was only much more careful. "As a rule," he told his *Rose el-Yousuf* interviewer, "government does not heed what intellectuals say—which is part of the former's problem, rather than the latter's." The intellectuals, he added, were not called upon "to draw an Arab strategy for the future." What they ought to do is just "to visualize situations in the far future"—visions that would become blueprints and strategies. Viewing them in this way, the Egyptian academic found that Arab intellectuals had done their bit—witness the multitude of future blueprints and strategies they had proposed since the late 1960s in the economic, educational, technological, and military spheres. The trouble, however, was that "while intellectuals generate ideas, the rulers generate venom." A great gap thus yawned between thinker and political authority, and Ibrahim said he himself was trying to contribute toward bridging that gap by organizing the prestigious Arab Thought Forum.

The Arab Thought Forum, an all-Arab think tank set up and financed by Jordan and acting, since 1981, under the auspices of Jordan's Prince Hassan, holds frequent conferences to discuss current topics of concern to the

Arab world. According to Ibrahim, the forum aims to test some of the ideas of its participants, who usually include equal numbers of men of ideas and people with the authority to make decisions. He cited the case of Prince Hassan himself, who, besides being the originator of the idea, is a man of authority as well.

Dealing with the same subject, another Egyptian academic, Fuad Zakariyya, remarked in an interview with Agence France-Presse on the extent of what he calls the "thought control" exercised by governments, especially in the Arab world. Zakariyya, a professor of philosophy at Ein Shams University who worked at the University of Kuwait for some years, said this hegemony over the minds of ordinary men was an outcome of the exclusive control that governments exercised over the education apparatus and the information media, adding that what the Arab regimes wanted to see was an obedient citizen incapable of debating their policies or identifying the basic flaws in the system under which he or she lived. In this state of affairs, Zakariyya added, the responsibility of the intellectuals was indeed a major one. The problem, however, was that governments possessed the power to encourage and help disseminate the ideas of certain intellectuals while suppressing those of certain others, so that the latter's voices and the impact of their ideas became marginal at best, heeded only by a tiny minority of people who held the same kind of convictions anyway.

Meanwhile dozens, thousands perhaps, of Arab men and women who could be branded intellectuals live and work in foreign lands, especially in the West. Fifty-one of these, many of them Paris-based, issued a manifesto, reprinted in the August 1991 issue of *Al-Fikr al-ʿArabi,* in which they appealed to fellow intellectuals to rally around eleven "cultural guidelines" designed to help the Arabs face the momentous changes the 1990s were bound to bring. One of these guidelines called for "absolute and unconditional support for every Arab intellectual subjected to persecution, harassment or coercion because of opinions he expresses or things he writes."

A growing generation of Western-educated, culturally Western-oriented Arab men and women, observing the huge gap which yawns between their conceptions and aspirations and the grim realities of their peoples' actual condition, pose questions about how to set out to resolve the many age-old contradictions they note in their societies. How does an educated, open-minded citizen of one of the countries of the Arab East give expression to his views? The answer is simple: If our hypothetical intellectual is equipped with a keen eye, an independent mind, and a searching, critical outlook, the chances are good that he simply cannot do it! This is doubly regrettable:

there is a great abundance of things to criticize and reevaluate in the Arab East, and there does not seem to be a lack of minds ready and able to take on the task.

As expected, the period following the Six-Day War produced great ferment among intellectuals, though considering the heaviness of the blow and the sheer depth of the shock, the awakening took some time to come. Many of these intellectuals would no doubt agree that it was high time, too. After all, during the two decades preceding the 1967 defeat so much utter nonsense was presented as almost revealed truth, so many hasty political experiments failed, and so much damage and suffering was inflicted that almost everybody was clamoring for a reappraisal. That no Arab thinker dared to proclaim that the king was naked was due solely to the suffocating and terror-stricken mental climate prevailing in Arab countries.

The few exceptions to this rule are mainly the small but steadily growing number of Arab scholars and teachers who, after taking refuge behind the safe walls of a British, American, French, or German university, or enjoying the safety of an American passport, have been trying to look objectively and critically at what has been going on in their native area. Hisham Sharabi (1927–2005) was one such scholar. A native of Lebanon, he was an American citizen and a professor of history and government at Georgetown University. One of his books, *Nationalism and Revolution in the Arab World* (1966), is a short critical appraisal of Arab political thinking in the 1960s. Although he did it rather subtly, what he managed to do in this short book was something that no Arab writer on politics could dare to do in his own country—namely, uncover the shallow and shockingly muddled character of much that passes as Arab-nationalist thinking and Arab revolutionary ideology. Right at the start he makes it clear, for instance, that though the Arab nationalists conceive of the Arab world as a single homogeneous whole and of the Arab people as a single nation bound by the common ties of language, religion, and history, "in reality . . . there is more diversity and differentiation in the Arab world than there is perhaps in other comparable regions of the world" (quotations from this book in the following paragraphs are drawn from pages 12–13, 96, and 99). He also explains that the Arab world has not constituted a single political entity since the brief period of Islam's expansion and consolidation into a Muslim empire during the seventh and eighth centuries.

Pursuing this theme further, Sharabi points out that the end of colonial domination in the Arab world, instead of bringing about a rapid movement of Arab unification, seemed instead rather to strengthen the tendency of each state to protect its own independence and resist submersion in a larger

Arab whole: "At no time in the past was the feeling of Arab brotherhood so strong or the feeling of Arab nationalism so warmly proclaimed; yet at no time in the past was the gulf between hope and fulfillment so vast and the realization of Arab unity so remote." The far-reaching progress attained in transportation and the mass media have indeed changed the situation somewhat, yet the rural world to which the majority of Arabs belong has hardly changed in any fundamental sense: "To this day the common man in Egypt still refers to the Arab countries to the east of Egypt as *barr al-sham* (geographical Syria), and one can safely assume that to the peasant of central Iraq or to the Moroccan villager of the Middle Atlas, Arab nationalism and Arab unity are terms which he has probably heard but which have little meaning."

In his last chapter—"The Language of Politics"—Sharabi, aware of the major part played by Arabic in Arab political life, offers a short glossary of a fairly representative cross-section of the current political vocabulary in the Arab world. The terms include such magic words as Arab nationalism, fatherland, Arabism ('Uruba, "a quasi-mystical term denoting the essence of being an Arab"), sovereignty, honor, traitor, people, and revolution.

But to go back to our original question concerning the crisis of the Arab intellectual. Sharabi dealt with this problem in a lecture delivered at a roundtable conference convened in 1960 by the Institute of Ethnic Studies at Georgetown University, Washington, D.C. In this brief lecture, Sharabi rightly pointed out that a strict empirical approach to the political and intellectual attitudes of the younger Arab generation would have to treat of such topics as Arab nationalism, communism, neutralism, and attitudes toward the West and Israel; it would have to analyze Arab literature, too, and enumerate specific problems that Arab intellectuals face or ignore. And so on. Sharabi warned that he intended to do nothing of the kind. Instead, he would limit his discussion to the political and intellectual crisis in which the younger Arab generation found itself. Reduced to its simplest components, Sharabi defined this crisis as "the opposition between efficacy as a principle of action and rationality as a principle of legal accommodation—between power as it becomes progressively more concentrated and personalized, and freedom as it gradually loses its political and constitutional foundations." Seen in this light, the crisis had "little to do with the form of government or, more precisely, with democracy as a formal principle of political organization." Rather, it had to do with the fate of the original goals and aspirations of the Arab revolution (the text of Sharabi's lecture is incorporated into his article "Political and Intellectual Attitudes of the Young Arab Generation," 59–61).

EXILE WITHIN EXILE

A most instructive and penetrating analysis of the plight of the Arab intellectual in the late 1990s was given by an Iraqi scholar living and working in Amsterdam. In a paper aptly titled "The Exile Within: Arab Culture in a Dismal Age" (*Arab Studies Journal,* Spring 1997, 4–17), Isam al-Khafaji goes to the root of the problem, tracing the phenomenon of the émigré Arab intellectual and professional—what in the Arab world is known as "the emigration of talents"—back to what happened in the various economic developments taking place in Arab societies, focusing his attention particularly on the subject of urbanization and the phenomenon of waves of migrants moving from provincial towns and villages to the few big cities in their countries. Indeed, he argues that Arab regimes became the product of these waves of migration, which have "asserted and perpetuated the dominance of cultural norms of the provincial towns in which the leaders of these regimes originated." Cairo and Alexandria in Egypt, Aleppo and Damascus in Syria, and Baghdad and Basra in Iraq—all these were, by the 1960s, "disintegrating in the face of [this influx to] new capital cities," while prosperous Beirut was allowed another decade before suffering a similar fate.

"With the passing of years," al-Khafaji relates, "with the creeping despair, came the St. Helena years. Those militant intellectuals, artists, and novelists who had been alienated from the brutal reality of the regime reigning in their countries, who had fought for modernity and against the legacy of backwardness, who had portrayed the misery of their people with Fellini's eye before going into exile, now began to paint and write about the sunny alleys and the delicious smell of mothers' baked bread in the earth oven, these same ovens and alleys that had been seen as rotten and primitive before leaving" (9).

> Intellectuals who had been associated with the Left and had attacked the ruling juntas in the Arab world for their conservative and reactionary stances were now reappraising, even revising, recent history, with a tender eye to the past that was "butchered by revolutions." An Iraqi journalist . . . spent several years, and a great deal of his meager personal income, searching secondhand bookshops to compile *The Book of Iraq,* a collection of hundreds of photographs taken from old newspapers and magazines. Other, less modest journalists and political activists turned into sociologists to write about the "civil society" of the 1940s and 1950s that the military juntas and revolutions had supposedly suppressed. (10)

This obsession with documenting the events of recent history introduced new techniques into Arab novels written after the 1970s: "As people were being confronted every day with horrifying news about the Lebanese civil war, Israeli massacres of Palestinian civilians, the abuses visited upon the regimes' suspected opponents, the scandals of super-rich Arabs, it became unnecessary for a novelist to employ stylistic exaggeration. It sufficed to insert long paragraphs from daily newspapers in a novel to convey the required shock effects to the reader."

Somewhere between Fellini's critical realism and romantic nostalgia, one should place the short-lived experimentation with Kafkaesque forms, an existentialist approach toward a harsh reality. This genre of writing was glimpsed in the late 1960s and early 1970s, when disillusionment with the revolutionary experience had not yet given way to a complete abandonment of rationalism and modernism: "Facing an incomprehensible world where supposedly revolutionary regimes were butchering secular, leftist, and democratic elements, many of these [writers] felt compelled to abandon a rational, realistic approach. But to depart from the rational, in this context, was to remind us—in the words of Claude Levi-Strauss—that 'beyond the rational there exists a more important and valid category, that of the meaningful, which is the highest mode of being of the rational'" (10).

The Arab intellectual or artist coming to the West in the 1990s was faced with a totally different reality. Otherness as an expression of collective identity was met with suspicion, the "clash of civilizations" mentality that in turn breeds otherness. The atmosphere of economic depression, coupled with post-Soviet triumphalism, helped create an image of the Algerian or the Pakistani ("them") that imposed conformity on the native Europeans ("us"): "As in soap operas, such images give the audience the comfortable feeling of seeing evil, not within themselves, but in another category neatly separated from good people" (12).

So what determines the form in which a writer or an artist expresses his/her alienation from reality? Is it his/her forced displacement in space? Is it his/her urban upbringing and world view which makes him/her incapable of adapting to more popular forms of culture that, because of their simplicity and vulgarism, can help to influence and educate wider sections of society despite marginalizing the previously existing sophisticated forms? From these questions follow another: why is the general audience more responsive and sensitive to the nostalgia for bygone days (even if they are not exiles) while they are less responsive to that other form of alienation, of the spatially resident writer or artist who mourns the death of city culture, be it Alexandria, Bombay, Aleppo, Baghdad, Basra, Damascus, Beirut, Casablanca, or even the cosmopolitan Berlin before 1933? (12)

"So who lives in exile now?" asks al-Khafaji.

The hundreds of Arab and Middle East intellectuals, writers, and artists in Europe and the West? Or those hundreds of thousands still there, in their geographic birthplace, which they no longer recognize because of the drastic and radical changes that have occurred there in the past three or four decades? Or perhaps it is the city, the urban space that has left. We are all at a standstill. It is the cosmopolitan, the transient city that is fleeing into exile. The Bombay of Salman Rushdie, the Shanghai of Steven Spielberg's *Empire of the Sun,* the Alexandria of Lawrence Durrell and Yousuf Chahine, the Beirut of Elias Khoury, who ends his *Mujammaʿ al-Asrar* (The Complex of Secrets) by describing Hanna:

"Ibrahim tried to explain to his old friend that he wanted to know the whereabouts of his family, the people who migrated in the nineteenth century to South America and lived with the mosquitoes, in the lagoons and with fear. They tasted humiliation that penetrates deep into the bones in order to build those houses with the red tiled roofs in the Mount of Lebanon. But they were aliens. 'All of us are aliens,' said Hanna. 'Here or there, what is the difference? A human being is always alien.' Hanna is alone. . . . A stranger in a strange city listening to his memories." (15)

But it is not only living in exile that has led to the tragic fate of the intellectuals: "In the first place, it was their total alienation from the existing structures that made it impossible for them to compromise with the positions and visions prevailing in their respective homelands. Their critiques of the norms being forced on their peoples by totalitarian regimes increasingly fell on deaf ears. Opposition to these regimes existed, but those new opposition groups were the cultural products of the regimes themselves." Thus, even when distinguishing themselves from these regimes, and even when developing a discourse for confronting these regimes, such opposition groups could not view the world differently. "It is this paradox," al-Khafaji concludes, "that makes the general public and audience more receptive to those figures that compromised with the ancien regime, which emerged into opposition only during these regimes' *quart d'heure* [fifteen minutes], than to those who opposed them from the beginning, and whose views and visions had already been radically different from the prevailing ones. The roots of this dilemma are to be found in the same process which I have tried to describe and analyze, namely, in the rise of radically new social groups that were alien and even hostile to the cosmopolitan cultures" (16–17).

PLAYING BOTH PRIEST AND SHEIKH

Sadiq Jalal al-ʿAzm (b. 1934), a native of Syria, is professor emeritus of modern European philosophy at the University of Damascus. In an interview published in the *Arab Studies Quarterly* (Summer 1997, 113–126), he was asked whether he agreed with the Syrian poet Adonis's contention that the intellectual's authority allows him to play a special role in the struggle against those Arab regimes that monopolize intellectual production. Al-ʿAzm had this to say:

> The role of the Arab intellectual changes from time to time. Generally speaking, I feel that the intellectual must distance himself from the state, even if it were a democratic state, since to do otherwise would diminish his credibility. Most productive Arab intellectuals have experienced problems with their governments at one time or another, and some have suffered the penalty of exile. The intellectual in our countries has a certain role which must be played with caution vis-à-vis the state, for otherwise he would lose his credibility and transform himself into an opportunist, a hanger-on, or a seeker of personal fame. . . . The term "intelligentsia" . . . was invented in Russia and spread to other countries[,] acquiring the sense of the dignity of learning and of knowledge. This acquired meaning of the term "intelligentsia" explains the problem of Arab intellectuals who aspire to attain the authority of the priest or shaykh. The most famous of our intellectuals seek disciples, not students. Instead of sharpening their critical faculties, Arab intellectuals resort to teaching their disciples how to be critical of their (the intellectuals') personal enemies and how to celebrate their teachers' genius. Thus, any discussion of the intellectual's freedom and his authority leads only to unpleasant argumentation.

As to the state's monopoly over culture, this is indeed one of the most serious problems confronting Arab societies today. In the past, intellectuals were in the habit of escaping being caught in this trap by manipulating the built-in competition between Arab governments. For a while, Lebanon was an open station for escaping the pressure of official Arab governmental control over culture. The Palestinian resistance movement was also able to protect intellectuals fleeing their own regimes and provide them with an opportunity to work within its institutions. Actually, the state's monopoly over culture did not succeed totally. Had there been one Arab state, this situation would have been far worse. (125)

In the years that followed, the position of intellectuals, writers, and academics not only did not improve, but in most cases it became even worse. This was especially true in the case of those who were generally critical of the powers that be, their running of the state's affairs, and their treatment of ethnic, sectarian, and communal minorities. One of the recent examples of this has been the arrest and trial of Sa'deddine Ibrahim, professor of sociology at the American University in Cairo and chairman of the board of the Ibn Khaldun Center for Development Studies in Cairo. In June 2000, Ibrahim, together with a number of his colleagues, was arrested and the center was shut down. The allegations against Ibrahim claimed that he had received foreign funding without the permission of the authorities and that he had used these funds to disseminate false information damaging to Egypt's national interest. It was also alleged that the Ibn Khaldun Center had committed financial and other improprieties, and it was even hinted that Ibrahim had been involved in espionage.

Three weeks after his arrest, Ibrahim submitted a statement to the State Security Prosecutors in which he said his arrest was really about "matters still unspoken," and then went on to speak about them. Extracts from the statement follow:

> This is not a case about Egyptians receiving foreign funding from abroad, for our government is the largest recipient of grants, gifts, aid and loans from abroad. . . . This case is not about discovering a group of thieves or embezzlers, whether of the European Union's money or that of any other donor organization. . . . Those who prepared this case and tried to implicate the Center should redirect their efforts to the serious crooks in this country. . . . Even if some young people betrayed the Ibn Khaldun Center, they are the deformed offspring of major swindlers who operate freely on Egyptian soil. . . . This case is not about giving national secrets to foreign bodies, though that is the broken record that Egyptian security forces never tire of playing. (*Al-Ahram,* June 7, 2001)

As for those "matters still unspoken," Ibrahim listed them in this order:

- The work of the Ibn Khaldun Center to ensure the integrity of elections and reduce the possibilities of fraud.

- The status and treatment of the Copts of Egypt, an issue that the center had addressed for the past five years.

- Women's participation in public life. The center helped in the founding of the Egyptian Organization for Women's Voting Rights at a time when the percentage of women participating in politics was decreasing in Egypt, although it was rising everywhere else in the world.

Ibrahim was not alone in criticizing the government's conduct in the case against the Ibn Khaldun Center. Mohammad el-Sayed Saʻid, deputy director of the Al-Ahram Center for Political and Strategic Studies, declared himself "confused and bewildered" by the measures taken against Ibrahim. "It was the government, after all," he wrote in an article in the same issue of *Al-Ahram,* "that initiated the open-door policy, and that policy calls for free interaction between private actors at the domestic level and the outside world. . . . Why should it not come as a total surprise to public opinion, then, when Ibn Khaldun Center, precisely by acting in conformity with the letter and spirit of these agreements, is convicted of criminal behavior? Here are paradoxes within paradoxes."

Where was the country heading, Saʻid asked? And he answered in part: "No one seems able to propose a creditable view of the future that could generate consensus. Intellectuals and politicians alike seem disoriented and confused as to the direction Egyptian society will or should take."

Postscript: Ibrahim was sentenced to seven years in prison on July 29, 2002; six codefendants received sentences ranging from two to five years; twenty-one defendants received one-year suspended sentences. On December 3, 2002, Egypt's Court of Cassation overturned the verdicts against all twenty-eight defendants in the Ibn Khaldun Center matter. Information on the trial is available at the Web site of Human Rights Watch: http://hrw.org/campaigns/egypt/.

Referring to Ibrahim's case and those of intellectuals who were similarly harassed elsewhere in the Muslim world, Akbar S. Ahmad wrote that the reality was that scholars there are "silenced, persecuted and chased out of their homes" (Ahmad, *Postmodernism and Islam;* quotations from this work are drawn from pages 31–32). The implications for society were enormous, he added. Instead of scholars "advising, guiding, and criticizing the rulers of the day, we have the sycophants and the secret services. The wisdom, compassion, and learning of the former risk the danger of being replaced by the paranoia and neurosis of the latter. . . . With those scholars silenced who can provide objectivity within the Islamic tradition and resilience in times of change, other kinds of religious scholars—like the Taliban—working in a different tradition interpret Islam narrowly. Islam for them has become a tool of repression." Here Ahmad cites a Muslim professor living in the United States, who told him in a private conversation, "The Muslim scholar is either caught between ignorant Muslims threatening him with *Jahannam* (hell) or the corrupt rulers threatening him with jail."

In some cases, however, intellectuals—Egyptian as well as Arab—come under fierce criticism from a writer associated with the Al-Ahram Center. Writing in *Al-Ahram* on April 10, 2004, Hassan Abu Taleb accuses Arab intellectuals of "a certain degree of political hypocrisy," calling them "those who used to call for reform without really meaning it." Some of these intellectuals, he explains, "want to exclude fellow political activists from public work," and some "want to keep Islamists barred from public work, thus depriving them of a legal conduit for serving their countries, leaving them to the mercy of detention and imprisonment."

Some intellectuals, Taleb charges, "believe that democracy should be confined to those sharing the same vision—a view that negates the very meaning of democracy." Other intellectuals, Taleb adds, "believe that secularism excludes religion from life, [whereas] religion is a driving force in the lives of Arabs and Muslims." Secularism, therefore, "should focus on regulating the role of religion, not denying it."

Accusing Arab political elites of the absence of genuine political rivalries, Taleb asserts that the alleged inability of Arab societies to experience democracy is "just an excuse the elites are making in order to stay in power, in order to pursue the same futile policies." What goes for these political elites and their desire to monopolize power, he adds, "goes also for some Arab intellectuals, [who] not only reiterate the same premises of the ruling classes but also provide the latter with theoretical and intellectual explanations." Some intellectuals believe, Taleb adds, "that the continuation of the status quo is their ticket to popularity."

PORTRAITS IN A MIRROR

Three Fictional Versions

For the concluding part of *Arabs in the Mirror,* I have chosen three representative short stories that provide a glimpse of a self-image—Iraqi, Syrian, and Palestinian. The stories are translated by the author.

THE HYENAS INVADE OUR TOWN

Shaker Khusbak is one of Iraq's leading short-story writers. "The Hyenas Invade Our Town" is taken from his collection The Cowards and the Beasts. *Khusbak is known for his leftist sympathies, so we can assume that his story is a parable on the repressions and the reported wholesale elimination of communists following the Baʿth anti-Qassim coup in Baghdad in November 1963.*

Peaceful and happy was our town, and its love filled our hearts. We were so fond of it that, we often gasped with awe while walking through its pine-shaded streets. What a lovely town! What a glorious river! The river descends from the top of the mountain, stormy and angry; but as soon as it reaches our town it starts streaming gently, as if it were resting on the bosom of a loving mother.

Our town was at its loveliest just before sunset. Then, when the date trees swam in rays of golden light, flocks of girls with their bright faces, embarrassed smiles, and black robes went out into the street. That was the only time of day when we could feast our eyes on the sight of them, so we used to crowd the town with our presence, group after group of young men strolling the street—except for Haji el-Salih, who was always to be seen walking alone. The fleeting looks that we exchanged with our girls were the only food of our love. For the girls of our town are conservative, and they refused to let our love go beyond those fleeting looks. Whenever our eyes caught theirs, they started whispering to one another, and though we did not hear those whispers, we were elated because we knew they were about us.

When the call for evening prayer resounded in every corner of our town, the roads and alleyways filled with young boys hastening back home and longing to have their supper after having finished with their games. Each quarter has its favorite game: the boys of the Old Alley played an old popular game, but those of the New Street preferred football, which they played every day of the week.

Our womenfolk, too, start at this hour to retire to their homes, having spent the afternoon chattering across the lanes and alleyways with their neighbors. They talked about everything—vegetable prices and the wedding of Mulla ᶜAbbud's son and hens that do not lay eggs and cheap-priced cottons—even about the reasons for my failure to wed despite my eligibility. So they rise, taking their weaving tools with them, calling their children, exchanging greetings, and entering their homes. Except for Hajja Um Mahdi, who always remained at the door when she noticed my coming, followed me with loving eyes until I reached the entrance of my home, and then gasped eagerly: "May you be guarded by Solomon's Walls!" Then she too entered her home, shutting the door behind her. Um Mahdi is a friend of my grandmother. She often held me on her lap when I was a baby, and I as often wet myself there, so she had to go to the river to purify her clothes before prayer.

When the sun set and darkness descended, the bazaars of our town became deserted, its shops closed, and life started stirring in the coffeehouses. On both banks of the river these coffeehouses were filled with the men of our town, shouting loudly and incessantly while playing their dominoes and other games. Only Fattah's coffeehouse was relatively quiet. It was the place where the Commoners engaged in discussions about their daily problems. They did not earn their livelihoods with ease, these people, but they constantly thanked Allah for his bounty. They had tasted happiness ever since they had been freed from the domination of the Senators and allowed to start earning their livings in freedom and security. They were happy with their lot, and they believed that they were members of one family, our peaceful and happy town extending its motherly care to them.

In Sham's coffeehouse, on the other hand, the shouts of young people debating politics became steadily louder. They vied with each other in expressing their loyalty to the Commoners and their determination to defend them to the last drop of their blood. But their shouts turned into whispers when they finished with politics and began exchanging news and views about affairs of the heart. They constantly pondered such questions as whether Laila actually returned Mahmoud's smile, whether Hana exchanged looks with Khalil, or whether Zahra really loved Salem.

All this was before the Hyenas invaded our town. The Hyenas began shouting terrible threats at our town after the Commoners raised their heads and got rid of the Senators' domineering. We giggled loudly whenever we heard these threats. We were confident we would wipe them out as soon as they dared storm our town. Each of us used to assure the other that they would never enter our town except over his dead body.

One morning the streets of our town were filled with the whistling sounds of shots, and the noise and hubbub reached the very skies. Hearts sank and faces grew somber and the frightened whisper was heard abroad: "The Hyenas have broken into our town!" A few went out into the streets to challenge the invaders, but they were felled by the bullets—and very soon everyone had taken refuge in his home, shut his doors, and let the Hyenas take control of our town. The Senators went merrily out into the streets, embraced the Hyenas, and shook their hands, but the latter's wanton bullets soon drove them back into their homes, frightened and shocked.

A somber silence fell on our town. Its alleyways became devoid of children and their happy noises; the streets were empty of strolling young men and women; and the coffeehouses no longer catered to their jolly patrons. The Hyenas were all around our town. They took up their positions at the entrances of alleys, in each street corner, and in the middle of each square. And they mounted their machine guns and directed them toward our hearts.

The people of our town told each other: "Why should we bother about the Hyenas? We will be secure if we refrain from doing them harm." So the following day they went to their bazaars, their offices, and their schools, pretending that nothing had happened and that the Hyenas had not invaded our town! Indeed, our people might have reached the conclusion that the Hyenas were not so beastly after all if it had not been for that incident involving Jasim Hamzawi. Jasim was hurrying to his shop one morning, staring at the ground, as was his wont. He was followed by his father, who walked much slower. Suddenly one of the Hyenas shouted: "Halt!" But Jasim Hamzawi did not halt, for he was not used to stopping when he walked, and he had no interest in anyone. Whereupon a spate of bullets were fired at him and he fell, struggling in a pool of blood. His father hastened to him, crying: "My son is innocent, O good people! He's innocent!" Jasim Hamzawi gasped with pain like a wounded bird, then died. His father carried the body and roamed the streets of the town, wailing, "My son is innocent, O good people! My son is innocent!" Finally, one of the Hyenas intercepted him and shouted: "Stop wailing if you want to save your skin! Your son didn't halt when he was told to do so. The same fate will befall all those who contemplate escape!"

Whereupon the people of our town told one another: "The Hyenas don't like crisp walk. We will avoid their harm by complying with their wishes." The following day our people started walking slowly in the streets, in the bazaars, and in the squares. It was indeed a funny sight, but we had lost the power to laugh. Our people looked as though they were loitering when in reality they were hurrying to do urgent business. Still, the Hyenas did not like it, and started barking in our faces: "Why don't you walk normally, you cowards!" And they fell upon some of us with the butts of their guns. Yet no one dared hurry his gait, lest he forfeit his life by doing so.

After a short while, the people of our town finally realized that the Hyenas were indeed beastly and that we would never be out of reach of their harm, even if we proclaimed our obedience to them. For one morning cars carrying loudspeakers drove through the streets and announced that the Hyenas had discovered a plot against them and that they were going to arrest all those suspected of being plotters and detain them in the house on the hill.

The Hyenas had turned the house on the hill, which was situated at one end of the town, into their headquarters. The house used to be the home of the hill's sentry, and had always provoked our curiosity when we were young and played in the huge park lying at the foot of the hill. It had a garden whose trees were ever full of strange and exotic birds with awe-inspiring colors and wonderful singing. We used to fancy that the inhabitants of the house on the hill were able to catch any number of those birds by merely putting their hands out its windows and taking them. Admiration for the house was by no means confined to the children. The grown-ups, too, were filled with wonder whenever they caught sight of it standing there at the peak of the hill, huge eucalyptus trees guarding it with their loving shade. The sentry used to love his house and feel great pride in it, and we were very fond of him and of his beautiful house. But that house had become a source of fear and terror ever since the Hyenas turned it into their headquarters. No one ever again contemplated getting near it.

As soon as the Hyenas invaded our town, workers climbed the hill every morning and labored there till evening. A few weeks afterward an ugly edifice with black walls and iron windows rose on the hill, adjoining the lovely house. These high narrow windows were like devilish eyes staring at our faces from the top of the hill. The huge bronze nails that dotted its huge black doors seemed to be monstrous jaws ready to cut our bodies to pieces. The builders related that in the new building they dug deep cellars where the water reached a man's ankles, that they hit huge nails into the walls, and that they fixed into the ceilings hooks from which dangled thick rough ropes.

Then our people started disappearing into the house on the hill, one after another. We never managed to know what took place inside that building, since those who entered it never came out. The Hyenas came out and went into the building with great noise and pep, mounting their machine guns, which were ever directed at our hearts. Frightening, whispered rumors started spreading about that building and the things that took place inside it.

Then everything began to be clear when the story of Kh'deir the son of Abbas the Baker spread through our town. The Hyenas had detained Kh'deir in the building on the hill, and all the appeals and beseechings of his father did not succeed in saving him. It was told that Abbas the Baker kept watch near the building day in and day out until the Hyenas grew tired of him. One night the town woke to resounding cries emanating from the house of Abbas the Baker. Hurrying to him, frightened, they saw Abbas embracing the dead body of his son Kh'deir and wailing frantically.

The people of our town could not make up their minds: Had Abbas the Baker gone mad, or was he unafraid of the Hyenas? For he took to cornering the townspeople one by one and telling them in a loud voice what had happened to his son in that building on the hill. He swore that Kh'deir's back was marked with rows of dark blue marks, and that his chest was full of deep wounds. He assured them that his son's arms and ankles bore obvious signs of thick rough ropes, that one of his ears was cut, and that both of his eyes were corked. And after finishing his tale he used to shout at them: "Do you now know what's going on? They torture our sons to death! Don't you care about it?" Whereupon his listeners used to whisper in his ears, making sure first that no Hyena was around: "Please, O Abu Kh'deir, don't raise your voice, lest the Hyenas hear!" But Abbas the Baker would get still angrier and shout at the top of his lungs: "You don't understand! They torture our sons to death! Don't you care about it?"

But our people grew still more frightened, and began avoiding Abbas the Baker whenever they saw him from afar, lest he repeat the story of what happened to his son Kh'deir in the building on the hill. Some started saying to each other: "Abbas the Baker is out of his mind!" But others said, "No, Abbas the Baker did not lose his senses; it's we who have lost our dignity."

Abbas the Baker then realized that our people did not want to listen to his tale. He decided to let them be, and spent the whole day walking the streets, shabbily dressed and audibly repeating to himself the story of what had happened to his son Kh'deir inside the building on the hill. Our people saw him and were filled with pity. Some said: "Abbas the Baker is no longer sane." But others shamefully murmured to themselves: "Nay, Abbas the Baker is saner than us all."

One morning the people of our town woke up to find there was no trace of Abbas the Baker. They asked one another worriedly, but there was no answer. Some said: "The Hyenas got impatient with Abbas the Baker and threw him into the river." Others said: "Abbas the Baker deserted this downtrodden town."

However that may be, Abbas the Baker was the warning bell for the people of our town about what was taking place inside that building on the hill.

A CARNATION FOR THE TIRED ASPHALT

Zakariyya Tamer (b. 1931) is a fiction writer living in Damascus. "A Carnation for the Tired Asphalt" first appeared in the Beirut literary review Al-Adaab in 1959. Its publication provoked a stormy controversy in Arab literary circles, and some accused the writer of "decadence." His stories are generally considered among the most outstanding works of Syrian literature.

A girl lay on her bed, yawning in the face of the youthful day, and listened with shut eyes to the singing coming from the neighbor's radio. A woman was singing, her voice a green city over which a soft sun floats, a blue sky, sparrows looking for an endless spring, echoes of sweet-ringing bells tolling across very sorrowful plains. The voice rose, heavy with ecstasy, longing, and innocence, wrapped up in music like feverish brown birds flying over a yellow field. The singing filled the girl's soul with a wave of awed strange pleasure under which hid a sorrow whose black roses might bloom at any moment. Her body, relaxed over the sheets, was as mature as old wine that had forgotten its birthday. It was a body without a man, a sea whose brown waves had gone to sleep and whose burning sorrow had begun to rise in silent, submissive wailing, a sea longing for the noise of boats and the rhythmic beating of oars held in the arms of faceless sailors, their bodies covered with a layer of rough hair and damp with unearthly scents.

Suddenly her mother's face sprang up in her imagination, and she could hear her sharp voice repeating as usual: "All men worship a woman slavishly when they scent her odor, but they will desert her in disgust the minute their desire is extinguished."

She remembered what an old neighbor woman once told her about a woman who had been kidnapped by seven men and could not escape their hold before several nights had passed. The vague glint emanating from the woman's eyes while relating the story made the girl inclined to believe that the kidnapped woman had been none other than the old neighbor in her youth.

She reported soundlessly: "Seven men and only one woman . . . Seven men!" And she imagined that the seven men had broken into her room. They were all around her, their hands hungrily touching her flesh. They were audibly panting, an animal smell issuing from them, sweat mixed with spring rains.

"She will be more beautiful when she is naked," said one of the men.

Immediately, fingers reached for her gown and tore it up. She did not feel any shame, but was overwhelmed by a flood of sweetness mixed with longing for some hot cruelty.

"So I'm naked now, and seven men are around my bed," she murmured to herself.

Said the first man: "Her face is a dove's chest. She's more beautiful than my mother."

Said the second man: "How beautiful she is! I have not come near a woman since I was born."

Said the third man: "Her flesh is smooth, brown, warm."

Said the fourth man: "I am tired, the softness of her breasts terrifies me."

Said the fifth man: "Her mouth is a trembling carnation."

Said the sixth man: "I shall perish if I don't fall like rain over scent's lost forest."

The seventh man shouted, imploring in despair: "Oh my god!"

And the girl whispered, trembling: "Oh, Oh."

Her mother's voice came from outside the room, calling her persistently, and the seven men disappeared. "I should be happy if mother died," she told herself, opening her eyes.

At that minute the midday sun was nailed over a road whose asphalt was treaded by men with downcast heads, heavily following a coffin. In the past it had been a tree that sparrows loved and under whose shade the tired found a refuge. Now it was a big wooden box in which lay cold and yellow flesh. He himself, only one day before, had been a man with his home, his tomorrow, his dreams, and his smiles.

"I'm tired."

"Is the grave far?"

"What shall we do after we bury the dead man?"

"I'm hungry. We'll eat."

In the graveyard the gravedigger had everything ready. He stood waiting, hiding a mischievous smile behind a mask of sorrow whose darkness deepened as the funeral procession drew nearer.

The coffin was put down on the ground near a deep ditch. Hands raised its lid, grasped the bundle, and lifted the body, wrapped in a piece of white cloth tied at the feet and head. A woman wailed. A man cried, soundlessly. *Go away, gladness! Shut your eyes, children! Death, where art thou? If I were to lay hands on you, I would slaughter you a thousand times in one quick passing moment.* The night of the ditch swallowed the body. The lid was covered with a large stone. A heap of earth was thrown over it. And after a few minutes everyone dispersed, and the graveyard was empty. There was only a raven, which, after settling for a minute on top of a tree, flew across the blue sky, clapping its black wings.

Two young men stopped near the graveyard. "I was extremely uncomfortable at the sight of the dead man's body," said the one with the tall lean figure that resembled a dry tree. "I too felt ill at ease—as if it were my own body that was being buried," replied the second, who was short and fat and whose eyes hid behind his dark glasses. "Yet death is a comfortable refuge for men who have grown old."

"We too shall grow old. We will never preserve our youth."

"Why do you speak like that?"

"I hate daytime. The naked light, the hubbub, the cruel sun, the crowdedness—all this makes me think continuously of death. I feel as if I could put my head to the asphalt so that it could be crushed under the wheels of a speeding car. Perhaps at the minute I heard the bones of my skull cracking I would say: Take my blood, O my city—a scarlet clover for your tired bosom."

"You talk like a madman," said the fat young man, laughing.

"We are all madmen. Dostoevsky was a madman. Sartre is an idiot who does not like the sun. Rimbaud was an ill-behaved child. Tchaikovsky a sad frog. Lorca a black nightingale. Kafka a stone cockroach. James Mason a drum."

"We are all torn-up drums that have lost even their empty voices. What's the use of standing in the sun? Let's walk."

A small girl standing behind the bars of a window facing the road smiled at the two young men. "When will you come back, Mommy! You're late, Mommy!" She was singing in an innocent, playful, sing-song voice.

"Allah is great, Allah is great," came the sweet voice of the muezzin from the dome of an old mosque.

"Come, let's pray," said the lean young man to his companion.

"Why pray? Perhaps even God hates us."

An old man, crossing the street with slow strides, murmurs, "What's the use of all the world's gold after I die?"

A young man in a movie house takes courage and nervously touches the arm of the girl in the next seat.

A laborer with a tired face yawns, murmuring to himself while chewing a big mouthful: "Every day my forehead cracks for your sake, O loaf of bread, O my great shame!"

Huddled on the ground in a narrow alley, a young man with blond hair, his curls dangling innocently over his pale forehead, was pressing his palms to the blood spurting from two deep wounds lying side by side on his chest.

"Oh, I'll die. Why did I have to accost his sister?" He turned round with a jerk: a ring of jostling human bodies and faces and wide, wide-open mouths and eyes.

"Who stabbed him?"

"We don't know."

"I saw a tall man running away."

"His blood is flowing profusely."

"Call the police and the ambulance!"

A woman with a well-formed body stands staring in horror at the blond youth, who is groaning painfully, writhing on the ground. A young man, taking advantage of the general commotion, stands behind the woman, his body glued to her flesh. The woman remains fixed in her place for a few minutes before she separates herself from him in a sudden movement, walking away with hasty steps. She had remembered her work: there was a baby lying in the darkness of his mother's womb, awaiting her hands. The time had come for his eyes to see the sun of this world, for him to become a creature with a name, a father, brothers, a home, a quarter, a city, and a small bed. He will grow up year by year.

"One coffee," a waiter shouts through the noise of the large coffeehouse, his voice lazily gaining momentum. *Waiter, bring a glass of cold water! The black stones are yours. Throw the dice; I shall win. I asked her: what would you lose by giving me a kiss? She replied innocently: and what would you lose if I don't give you a kiss? The car went out of order. The ass is still the boss. Down with my father! Long live our neighbor's wife! Fie, we shall all die!*

A grim-faced man steps into the cafe, sits behind one of the tables, and tells himself as he puffs his cigarette: "It's no use resisting. I'll commit suicide. My love deserted me and became a petty whore. I'm sad. She used to love the innocently smiling children, but she left me and became a petty whore. How beautiful she is. My pillow loves her hair. And her mouth, that ripe cherry orchard, always injected into my blood something old, born under an antique sun. Her eyes two innocent doves whose wings were broken the minute my love lay down on her back on the floor of my courtyard, under the branches of the lemon tree.

"I'm afraid," she had whispered in a trembling voice. "Don't torture me," I said. "I shall cry like a child whose mother is crucified before his very eyes."

My love then smiled with a drunken pleasure, as though her veins were filled with wine, while my hands forgot their old misery and dipped into a world of flesh that was later to become the property of many men. *You cheerless man! Have you laughed? My face is of decayed wood, skyless. Do the dead laugh? The cross of my city is a coffee shop and a street.*

What is your wish, you cheerless man who has more life than a virgin field? To sleep for a hundred years.

PALESTINIAN

Born in Jaffa, Palestine, Samira ʿAzzam (1927–1967) worked as a journalist and radio broadcaster. She lived in Lebanon from 1948 until her death. Her stories revolve mostly around Palestinians' experiences in exile, and she was deeply involved in Palestinian cultural life. "Palestinian" was first published in 1963 in the Beirut monthly Al-Adaab.

"Give me your identity," he said hesitantly, the words hurting his drying throat. "I shall just look at it and return it to you."

His neighbor did not seem to understand. "I mean your card," he urged, extending his hand with a trace of impatience. "Your identity card . . ."

The nervous hand still extended, the other took out a worn wallet, picked out the card, and handed it to him. But before he stepped out of the place, his neighbor's voice came from behind him: "And what do you want to do with my identity card, Palestinian?"

Had the neighbor heard the curse that he murmured in reply, he would no doubt have snatched the card back from his fingers. But he hastened to his shop, stood behind the soiled counter, opened the card, then thrust his hand into his pocket and took out his own new card. It was green and shiny, its cedar tree bearing healthy, unbent branches—a brand-new card that he had received just two weeks before. His picture appeared on one side of it, and every one of its three folds bore the round stamp of the Registration Department of the Ministry of Interior, and there was a fourth stamp on the back of the third fold. Four round, suggestive stamps whose vicious circles no suspicion could penetrate, and bearing the signatures of the Director and the Superintendent. Embracing each other, interlocked, the signatures had crooked, folded, fortified lines from which no name could be fathomed—just like the signatures of all those who held Fate in their hands.

The neighbor's card did not differ from his in anything except in its old, weathered look and the specifications of name, age, residence, birthplace, and date of birth. It was also different in that it bore signs of rough treatment and too much handling by soiled careless fingers that did not know how to deal kindly with that which came as a birthright, costing its owner no effort or anxiety or doubts or money. It was a card that was not the outcome of an infuriating, hateful, piercing feeling—in this quarter where he lived and where he had opened a grocery shop over ten years ago, during which time he sold his wares for cash, on credit, or for nothing when he was cheated—of not having managed to earn for himself a proper name or appellation.

For in this corner where his shop is situated—a shop in no way different from most other shops—he was no more than "Palestinian." It was as "Palestinian" that he was called, defined, cursed when needed. Like that Armenian cobbler whom he had known in his boyhood, and who had spent thirty years of his miserable life trying to patch up the quarter's shoes. No one cared, no one ever needed even to know whether he was called Hajop, as an Armenian's name could well be, or Sarkis or Artan. "Armenian" was his full name. Thus he lived and thus he died, his name cutting him off from both the living and the dead. The appellation probably had the added effect on him of complete stagnation, for the foreign accent never left his speech, and his interest in his surroundings never rose above the level of people's feet!

The two identity cards before him, his finger shifted between them, and the specifications danced before his eyes. A customer comes in, but he dismisses him with a sign of his hand, and he goes away angry and bewildered, not understanding why the man does not want to sell. Meanwhile the newspaper falls to the floor and he picks it up; the headline, printed in red over the pictures of the gang's members, horrifies him. But what is the use of reading the story for the fifth or the hundredth time? He will never know more than he already knows, and the man's picture alone spoke proof—the lean face more than half covered by spectacles, the baldness that starts right above the spectacles but that does not indicate a satanic brain. As for the rest, he knew only one of them, who had introduced him to that other.

Yes, he had worn a blue suit when he had entered the shop to buy a box of matches costing one franc. He had removed cigarettes from his pocket, taken one, and offered him another, which he declined. He had smoked half the cigarette while standing on the threshold, his face to the street. Then he had turned back and started loitering, like a man who wants to be drawn into a conversation, any conversation. But he had finally decided to broach the subject openly. He had heard—and he did not say how or from whom—that he wanted to be naturalized as a Lebanese. If that were his wish, there was only one way. And the price—yes, there was a price—two thousand pounds. A bit more, indeed, than what people used to pay. But the authorities' attitude was becoming increasingly firm. Besides, the Palestinians had left no stone unturned in their search for family names whose roots extend to Palestine—so much so that those lawyers who had gotten rich from the naturalization industry were beginning to be let down by the science of genealogy.

Two thousand? Too much! Or are you perchance going to link my branch to the trunk of a cedar tree that Solomon omitted to root out when he built himself a temple in Jerusalem?

Too much. Years ago, indeed, he had refused to pay a quarter of this sum to dig out some forefather in some good-hearted Lebanese village, or to invent a new life history for his grandfather Abu Salih, who, as far as he knew, had been born and had died in the village of Rama. Not that he had wanted to disown Abu Salih publicly. He just wanted his permission to rectify an accident of geography, to free himself from the term "Palestinian," a term that tied him to a herd from which all signs of individuality had been obliterated, a term that they used in pity when he refused to be an object of pity, or in anger when there was no ground for anger, or threateningly whenever his rivals among the small shop owners wanted to give vent to their hatred. The term that they have knit into the rumors and gossip through which they sought to interpret events to their heart's content, rumors that enmeshed him like thin but multiplying threads—a cloud of anxiety that made him feel that he, his shop, his four children, and his wife were but playthings for the interpreters of past events, and that his only guarantee against a possible transfer into permanent refugee status was to become naturalized.

This inner urge to naturalization used to weaken when the threads of rumor became looser and when his fears died down in the hub of daily living. It used to become stronger whenever something happened to shake his tottering existence—for instance, when his son left school but could not find work for more than two weeks: the law was quite unequivocal about it, and work in government offices and firms was forbidden to those who were not citizens. In the end, the young man had had to fly to one of those deserts where people get together like brothers in misfortune, and whose hardship knew no discrimination despite differences of nationality.

The urge became stronger and stronger whenever he decided to make a trip, for one reason or another, to his relatives who were scattered here and there, when he had to wait at the door of some office for a week in order to obtain a pass. When his father, who had lived in his brother's house in Amman, died, he cabled his relatives: "Delay him for a week. Otherwise bury him!" It was the most miserable joke to which the man at the telegram counter had ever listened laughingly.

Two thousand? Too much! The negotiator knits his eyebrows and takes out another cigarette. "You will never get a card for less. I believe you have tried, haven't you?"

Yes, he had tried. His case was kept pending for three years between the promises and excuses of the lawyer, who finally gave up everything except half the costs that he had received in advance . . .

"But will it be guaranteed?"

"You won't pay before you hold it in your hand; we get nothing in advance." The man's features relaxed, and the shade of a smile appeared on his face. Then he withdrew, his voice remaining resonant in the shop, fresh, soft and sweet. "Think it over, think it over; I shall pass by in a few days."

He did not think it over long, but tried to make his wife do some of the thinking. "Two thousand?" she asked, horrified. "Man! Is it a Minister's card? Others got it for three hundred or six hundred or even for free."

"Two thousand," he retorted, not overly convinced of what he was saying but fearful of letting the opportunity slip in this first round, "because we once thought three hundred was too much. One day we may have to pay ten thousand. Do you want your son to spend his life in an inferno with a temperature of fifty centigrade in summer in a land that knows no winter?"

"Do what you like!" she said, touched in her most sensitive chord. "If it is two thousand, then let it be two thousand. May God's blessing stay away from that money. That is if you can find it."

"I will find it if I have to empty half of my window. I shall display that card there, so that people will perhaps know that we have a name!"

It is an attribute of lying that it is decisive in its truthfulness. It was three weeks or four and everything was finished—with lightning speed. He did not meet that man who calls himself "professor" more than once. He had jotted down all the details on a piece of paper: the name, the names of wife and children, places of birth, ages. He had said that he would take care of everything, including documents and certificates, and that all he needed was photographs—and the two thousand, of course. The money was not all for himself. Expenses were various, and the parties were even more numerous.

The parties were indeed numerous. Five photographs printed on the paper of five counterfeiters—a gang with all the qualifications, its head a professor and the members no less proficient. And they had, as the paper said, many occupations. One of them confessed they had forged tens of cards. He was not the only fool; it took many fools to enable justice to take its course. *O my grandfather, Abu Salih, you have failed me. Why did you not choose to live twice, once tending an olive grove in Rama and once growing a vineyard at the foot of some Lebanese hill?*

Tear, tear up the newspaper and thrust your finger into the eyes of this "professor," through his dark glasses. But what use would it be to tear up the paper? You will never obliterate the reality of the fraud or undo the fact that you paid two thousand in return for a piece of cardboard and that you acted in concert with counterfeiters and . . .

How did he fail to realize it? He felt a fire eating through him. Is it not possible that these men have revealed the names of their customers? How stupid! Does he still have any doubts that this is going to be the ultimate result? Otherwise, how are the authorities to collect the forged cards? Tricked, or guilty of complicity? When he paid two thousand, which ate up half of his window, he was tricked. But by the time the truth is put down in the investigation papers, he will have consumed himself to the marrow of his bones, and the tale of his foolishness shall be smoke in his neighbors' cigarettes.

Tear it up, tear it up! It is beginning to eat into your flesh. Why do you put it back in your inside pocket? For all the two thousand that it cost, it is not worth more than this newspaper, for which you paid only a quarter. Tear it up. Your window will be full one day, and your existence will remain empty until you fill it with something other than fraud and the work of counterfeiters.

Tear it up! Or do you perhaps want more proof? The press does trade in lies sometimes, but it does not depict these lies as photographs of five men of whom you know two and will have the pleasure of meeting the rest when you are confronted with them.

Are you too cowardly to tear it up even while it rests between your fingers? Oh tear it up, tear it up, for it is worth no more than the paper on which it is printed. But no, leave it in your inside pocket. Leave it, because tearing it up will hide nothing, obliterate nothing.

He sat down, then stood up. He again sat down and stood up, pacing the shop like a blind bull. He turned to face the street. His confusion might be relieved by the rhythm of life outside, content with its lot, dreaming in nothingness. The petrol station emptying its fuel into the bellies of big shining cars. The fruit seller wiping the dust off his apples and trying to make them as red as possible. The butcher thrusting his knife into the flesh of the dangling carcass. And the barber working away on the surrendered head, a head that does not exude anxiety, like his own.

Going back into the shop, he turns to the torn newspaper, collects the pieces, makes them into a ball, and throws it away. Then he turns his face again to the street, only to see that eternal basket dangling by a rope from the balcony of the second floor, just above the shop. The basket was foolishly dancing under the balcony, and the voice of the neighbor issued from above, asking for something. She is always asking for some item, remembering her shopping lists only by installments . . .

But this time he does not hear her. Let her shout as much as she likes. He will not sell anybody anything. But the voice does not despair and the basket does not give up. The woman extends her voice across the street, like a bridge, reaching for the boy in the garage opposite and shouting in her drawn-out accent: "Where are you, boy? Tell the Palestinian to put a bottle of cola in the basket for me!"

Shaking behind the counter, the Palestinian felt the woman's voice pierce his jacket and reach his inside pocket, reducing the card to shreds, tiny shreds crowding his pocket, without strength or freshness!

SELECT BIBLIOGRAPHY

BOOKS AND ARTICLES

Abbott, Nabia. *'Aisha: The Beloved of Mohammed*. Chicago: Univ. of Chicago Press, 1942; London: Al-Saqi Books, 1985.

Ahmad, Akbar S. *Postmodernism and Islam: Predicament and Promise*. London: Routledge, 1992.

Adams, Michael, ed. *The Middle East: A Handbook*. London: Anthony Blond, 1971.

Ajami, Fouad. *The Arab Predicament: Arab Political Thought and Practice Since 1967*. Cambridge: Cambridge Univ. Press, 1981.

———. *Dream Palace of the Arabs: A Generation's Odyssey*. New York: Pantheon, 1999.

———. "The End of Pan-Arabism." *Foreign Affairs* 57, no. 2 (Winter 1978–1979): 355–373.

Ammianus Marcellinus. *The Roman History of Ammianus Marcellinus*. Translated by C. D. Yonge. London: Bell and Sons, 1911.

'Anan, Muhammad Abdullah. *Ibn Khaldun: His Life and Intellectual Legacy*. In Arabic. Cairo, n.d.

Anderson, Jon W. "Conspiracy Theories, Premature Entextualization, and Popular Political Analysis." *Arab Studies Journal* 4, no. 1 (Spring 1996): 96–102.

Arkoun, Muhammed. *Rethinking Islam: Common Questions, Uncommon Answers*. Boulder, Colo.: Westview, 1994.

'Awad, Louis. *Al-Funun wal-Junun fi Auropa* [The Arts and Lunacy in Europe]. Cairo, 1970.

'Awis, Sayyid. *Remarks about Culture: Some Facts concerning Egypt's Culture*. In Arabic. Cairo, [1970] 1978.

'Ayyad, Muhammad Kamel. *The Future of Culture in Arab Society*. In Arabic. Cairo: Arab League, Cultural Department, 1953.

'Azm, Sadiq Jalal al-. "An Interview with Sadik al-'Azm." By Ghada Talhami. *Arab Studies Quarterly* 19, no. 3 (Summer 1997): 113–126.

———. *Naqd al-Fikr al-Dini* [The Critique of Religious Thought]. Beirut: Dar al-Tali'ah, 1969.

———. *Al-Naqd al-Thati ba'd al-Hazima* [Self-Criticism after the Defeat]. Beirut: Dar al-Tali'ah, 1978.

Azmeh, Aziz al-. *Islam and Modernities*. London: Verso, 1993.

'Azzawi, Fadil al-. *Al-Adaab* (Beirut), January 1970.

Bayham, Muhammad Jamil. *Al-'Uruba wal-Shu'ubiyyat al-Haditha* [Arabism and the New Shu'ubiyyas]. Cairo, n.d.

Beinin, Joel, and Joe Stork, eds. *Political Islam: Essays from Middle East Report*. Berkeley and Los Angeles: Univ. of California Press, 1997.

Boutros-Ghali, Boutros, Mahmoud Kheiri 'Isa, and 'Abdel Malik 'Oda. *Al-Qawmiyya al-'Arabiyya wa Simat al-Mujtama' al-'Arabi* [Arab Nationalism and the Characteristics of Arab Society]. Cairo, 1960.

Cleveland, Willam F. *The Making of an Arab Nationalist: Ottomanism and Arabism in the Life and Thought of Sati' al-Husri*. Princeton, N.J.: Princeton Univ. Press, 1971.

Daniel, N. A. *Islam and the West: The Making of an Image*. Edinburgh: Edinburgh Univ. Press, 1958.

Dawn, C. Ernest. "The Origins of Arab Nationalism." In Khalidi, Anderson, Muslih, and Simon, *The Origins of Arab Nationalism*.

Douri, 'Abdel 'Aziz al-. *Al-Judhur al-Taarikhiyya lil-Shu'ubiyya* [The Historical Roots of Shu'ubiyya]. Beirut, 1962.

Esposito, John L. *Islam: The Straight Path*. New York: Oxford Univ. Press, 1988.

Fawzi, Hussein. "Egypt's Place in the World—Past and Present." In Shamir, *Self-Views in Historical Perspective in Egypt and Israel*.

———. *Sindbad Misri* [An Egyptian Sindbad]. Cairo, 1961.

Frye, Richard N., ed. *Islam and the West: Proceedings of the Harvard Summer School Conference on the Middle East*. The Hague: Mouton, 1956.

Gabrieli, Francesco. *Muhammad and the Conquests of Islam*. Translated by Virginia Luling and Rosamund Linell. London: Weidenfeld & Nicolson, 1968.

Gibb, H. A. R. *The Arabs*. London: Oxford Univ. Press, 1940.

———. "Social Change in the Near East." In *The Near East: Problems and Prospects*, edited by Philip W. Ireland. Chicago: Univ. of Chicago Press, 1942.

Goitein, Shlomo Dov. "*'Arabi 'al 'Arabim: Birrur Hadash 'al De 'otav shel Ibn Khaldun 'al ha-'Am ha-'Arabi*" [An Arab on Arabs: Fresh Light on Ibn Khaldun's Views on the Arab People]. *Ha-Mizrah ha-Hadash* 1, 118–119.

Gomaa, Ahmed M. "The Egyptian Personality—Between the Nile, the West, Islam and the Arabs." In Shamir, *Self-Views in Historical Perspective in Egypt and Israel*, 33–36.

Grunebaum, G. E. von. *Islam: Essays in the Nature and Growth of a Cultural Tradition*. London: Routledge and Kegan Paul, 1955.

Halliday, Fred. "'Orientalism' and Its Critics." *British Journal of Middle Eastern Studies* 20, no. 2 (1993): 145–163.

Halpern, Ben. "A Problem of Ethics." *Midstream*, August–September 1969.

Hamady, Sania M. *Temperament and Character of the Arabs*. New York: Twayne, 1960.

Hamdan, Jamal. *Shakhsiyyat Misr: Dirasa fi 'Abqariyyat al-Makan* [Egypt's Personality: A Study of the Genius of Place]. Cairo: Alam al-Kutub, 1967.

Hanna, George. *Ma'na al-Qawmiyya al-'Arabiyya* [The Meaning of Arab Nationalism]. Beirut, 1959.

Hijab, Nadia. *Womanpower: The Arab Debate on Women at Work*. Cambridge and New York: Cambridge Univ. Press, 1988.

Himadeh, Sa'id B. "Social Awakening and Economic Development in the Middle East." In Laqueur, *The Middle East in Transition*, 52–60.

Hitti, Philip. *History of the Arabs*. 10th ed. London: Macmillan, 1970.

Hourani, Cecil. "The Moment of Truth: Towards a Middle East Dialogue." *Encounter* 29, no. 5 (November 1967).

Hourani, George. "Palestine as a Problem of Ethics." *Middle East Studies Association Bulletin* 3, no. 1 (February 15, 1969): 15–25.

Husaini, Ishaq Musa al-. *Azmat al-'Aql al-'Arabi* [The Crisis of the Arab Mind]. Beirut, 1954.

———. *The Moslem Brethren: The Greatest of Modern Islamic Movements*. Beirut, 1955.

Husri, Sati' al-. *Al'Uruba Awwalan* [Arabism First and Foremost]. Beirut: Dar al-'Ilm li al-Malayin, 1955.

Hussein, Taha. *Falsafat Ibn Khaldun al-Ijtima'iyya* [Ibn Khaldun's Social Philosophy]. Cairo, n.d.

———. *Mustaqbal al-Thaqafa fi Misr*. Cairo, 1938. Translated by Sidney Glazer as *The Future of Culture in Egypt* (Washington, D.C.: American Council of Learned Societies, 1954).

Ibn Khaldun. *The Muqaddimah: An Introduction to History*. Translated by Franz Rosenthal. 3 vols. London: Routledge and Kegan Paul, 1958.

Ibrahim, Sa'd al-Din, ed. *Egypt's Arabism and the Debate of the Seventies*. In Arabic. Cairo, 1978.

Ireland, Philip W., ed. *The Near East: Problems and Prospects*. Chicago: Univ. of Chicago Press, 1942.

Issawi, Charles. *The Economic History of the Middle East, 1800–1914: A Book of Readings*. Chicago: Univ. of Chicago Press, 1966.

Keddie, Nikki R. *Sayyid Jamal al-Din al-Afghani: A Political Biography*. Berkeley and Los Angeles: Univ. of California Press, 1972.

Keddie, Nikki R., and Beth Baron, eds. *Women in Middle Eastern History: Shifting Boundaries in Sex and Gender*. New Haven and London: Yale Univ. Press, 1991.

———. *Democracy and Arab Political Culture*. London: Frank Cass, 1994.

Kedourie, Elie. *Nationalism*. Rev. ed. London: Hutchinson, 1961.

Kerekes, Tibor, ed. *The Arab Middle East and Muslim Africa*. London: Thames and Hudson, 1961.

Khafaji, Isam al-. "The Exile Within: Arab Culture in a Dismal Age." *Arab Studies Journal* 5 (Spring 1997): 4–17.

Khalidi, Rashid. "Ottomanism and Arabism in Syria Before 1914: A Reassessment." In Khalidi, Anderson, Muhammad, and Simon, *The Origins of Arab Nationalism*, 50–69.

Khalidi, Rashid, Lisa Anderson, Muhammad Muslih, and Reeva S. Simon, eds. *The Origins of Arab Nationalism*. New York: Columbia Univ. Press, 1991.

Khalidi, Walid. "Political Trends in the Fertile Crescent." In Laqueur, *The Middle East in Transition*, 121–128.

Khalifa, Muhammad. *Hawla el-Mas'ala al-Ijtima'iyya* [On the Social Question]. Cairo, 1974.

Khuri, Colette. *Ayyam Ma'ahu* [Days with Him]. Beirut, [1959] 1987.

Lane, Edward William. *An Account of the Manners and Customs of the Modern Egyptians, Written in Egypt during the Years 1833–1835*. London: Charles Knight, 1835. Reprint, London: Dent, 1908.

Laqueur, Walter Z., ed. *The Middle East in Transition: Studies in Contemporary History*. London: Routledge and Kegan Paul, 1958.

Laroui, Abdallah. *The Crisis of the Arab Intellectual: Traditionalism or Historicism?* Translated by Diarmid Cammell. Berkeley and Los Angeles: Univ. of California Press, 1976. Originally published as *La crise des intellectuels Arabes* (Paris: Maspero, 1974).

Lewis, Bernard. *The Arabs in History*. Revised ed. New York: Harper & Row, 1967.

———. *The Middle East: 2000 Years of History from the Rise of Christianity to the Present Day*. London: Weidenfeld & Nicolson, 1995.

Mernissi, Fatima. *Beyond the Veil: Male-Female Dynamics in a Modern Muslim Society*. London: Al-Saqi Books, 1975.

Muslih, Muhammad. "The Rise of Local Nationalism in the Arab East." In Khalidi, Anderson, Muhammad, and Simon, *The Origins of Arab Nationalism*, 189–203.

Nuseibeh, Hazim Zaki. *The Ideas of Arab Nationalism*. Ithaca, N.Y.: Cornell Univ. Press, 1956.

Othman, Norani, ed. *Shari'a Law and the Modern Nation-State: A Malaysian Symposium*. Kuala Lumpur: SIS Forum Berhad, 1994.

Patai, Raphael. *The Arab Mind*. New York: Charles Scribner's Sons, 1983.

Partner, Peter. *A Short Political Guide to the Arab World*. London: Pall Mall Press, 1960.

Qasim, Anis al-. *Ma'na al-Hurriyya fi al-'Aalam al-'Arabi* [The Meaning of Freedom in the Arab World]. Beirut, 1964.

Razzaz, Munif. "Arab Nationalism." In Adams, *The Middle East: A Handbook*.

Rejwan, Nissim. "Arab Conspiracy Theories." *Midstream*, February–March 1994.

———. *Arabs Face the Modern World: Religious, Cultural, and Political Responses to the West*. Gainesville: Univ. Press of Florida, 1998.

———. "Arab Women's Long Road to Liberation." *Midstream*, October 1988, 15–16.

———. "Arab Youths and their Discontents." *Midstream*, February–March 1992.

———. "Egypt's Search for a New Self-Image." *Midstream*, June–July 1974, 58–62.

———. *The Many Faces of Islam: Perspectives on a Resurgent Civilization.* Gainesville: Univ. Press of Florida, 2000.

———. *Nasserist Ideology: Its Exponents and Critics.* New York: Wiley, 1974.

———. "Why Arabs Can't Unite." *Midstream* 37, no. 6 (1961): 19–22.

———. "A Wild Goose Chase: To Cope, Must Islam 'Westernize'?" In *Islam and the West: Critical Perspectives on Modernity,* edited by Michael J. Thompson. Lanham, Md., and Oxford: Rowman and Littlefield, 2003.

Safran, Nadav. *Egypt in Search of Political Community: An Analysis of the Intellectual and Political Evolution of Egypt, 1804–1952.* Cambridge, Mass.: Harvard Univ. Press, 1961.

Said, Edward W. *Orientalism.* New York: Pantheon, 1978.

Salem, Eli. "Form and Substance: A Critical Examination of the Arabic Language." *Middle East Forum* 34, no.1 (1958).

Shamir, Shimon, ed. *Self-Views in Historical Perspective in Egypt and Israel.* Tel Aviv: Tel Aviv Univ. Press, 1981.

Sharabi, Hisham. *Introduction to the Study of Arab Societies.* In Arabic. Beirut, 1975.

———. *Nationalism and Revolution in the Arab World (the Middle East and North Africa.* Princeton, N.J.: Van Nostrand, 1966.

———. "Political and Intellectual Attitudes of the Young Arab Generation." In Kerekes, *The Arab Middle East and Muslim Africa.*

Touqan, Qadri Hafiz. *Maqam al-'Aql 'ind al-'Arab* [The Place of Reason in the Arab World]. Beirut, 1964.

———. *Wa'y al-Mustaqbal* [Consciousness of the Future]. Beirut 1953.

Tucker, Judith E. *Women in Nineteenth-Century Egypt.* Cambridge: Cambridge Univ. Press, 1985.

Tweini, Ghassan. *The Logic of Force: The Philosophy of the Coup d'État in the Arab World.* In Arabic. Beirut, [1954] 1966.

Vatikiotis, P. J. *Islam and the State.* London: Croom Helm 1987.

Wahbi, Muhammad. *The Crisis of Arab Civilization.* In Arabic. Beirut, 1956.

Ziadeh, Nicola. *Ayyami* (*My Days*). Beirut and London, 1992.

Zureiq, Constantine. *In the Battle of Civilization.* In Arabic. Beirut, 1964.

NEWSPAPERS AND PERIODICALS

Arabic Dailies

Ahram, Al-
Akhbar, Al-
Hayat, Al-
Quds, Al-
Sharq al-Awsat, Al-

Arabic Periodicals

Adaab, Al-
Ahali, Al-
ʿArabi, Al-
Fikr al-ʿArabi, Al-
Hilal, Al-
Katib al-Hilal, Al-
Kul Shaiʾ
Musawwar, Al-
Rose el-Yousuf
Sabah el-Khair
Sayyad, Al-
Usbuʿ al-ʿArabi, Al-
Wasat, Al-
Watan al-ʿArabi, Al-

Other Periodicals

Arab Studies Journal
Arab Studies Quarterly
British Journal of Middle Eastern Studies
Foreign Affairs
International Journal of Near East Studies
Jerusalem Post
Jerusalem Quarterly
Jerusalem Report
Jewish Observer and Middle East Review
Middle East Forum
Middle East Journal
Ha-Mizrah ha-Hadash (The New East; in Hebrew)

INDEX